D1252128

# Scenes from Provincial Stages:

## Essays in Honour of Kathleen Barker

Edited by
Richard Foulkes

THE SOCIETY FOR THEATRE RESEARCH

First published 1994
by The Society for Theatre Research,
c/o The Theatre Museum, 1E Tavistock Street,
Covent Garden, London WC2E 7PA



ISBN 085430 0554

Printed by Woolnough Bookbinding
Church Street, Irthlingborough, Northants.
Typeset by EMS Photosetters, Thorpe Bay, Essex

# Contents

# Illustrations

Grateful acknowledgement is made to the institutions and individuals indicated for permission to reproduce illustrations.

# Contributors

ROY AVERY was educated at Queen Elizabeth's Hospital, Bristol and Magdalen College, Oxford. He was successively headmaster of Harrow County Boys' School and Bristol Grammar School. He is a former president of the Bristol branch of the Historical Association.

J. S. BRATTON is Professor of Theatre and Cultural History at Royal Holloway College, University of London. Her publications include *The Victorian Popular Ballad* and *Acts of Supremacy: the British Empire and Stage 1790–1930*. She is a committee member of the Society for Theatre Research.

SHIRLEY BROWN is a Bristol-based freelance writer and broadcaster specialising in theatre. She is theatre editor of the Bristol/Bath listings magazine *Venue* and has provided programme notes for most Bristol Old Vic productions at the Theatre Royal since 1987.

CAROL J. CARLISLE is Professor Emerita of English, University of South Carolina. She is the author of *Shakespeare from the Greenroom: Actors' Criticisms of Four Major Tragedies* and has contributed to several collections of essays and to various journals.

FRANCES DANN lectures in the School of Cultural Studies at Sheffield Hallam University. She is Joint Honorary Secretary of the Society for Theatre Research.

TRACY C. DAVIS is Associate Professor in Theatre and English at Northwestern University. She has written numerous articles on Victorian Theatre and is co-editor of Routledge's Gender in Performance Series, for which she wrote *Actresses as Working Women*.

DEREK FORBES studied drama at the University of Bristol. His career included posts as County Drama Organiser, drama lecturer and head of department at Middlesex Polytechnic. He was Joint Honorary Secretary of the Society for Theatre Research 1981–90.

RICHARD FOULKES was appointed to the University Centre, Northampton in 1973. His publications include *The Shakespeare Tercentenary of 1864* and *The Calverts – Actors of Some Importance* both published by the Society for Theatre Research of which he is a committee member.

ARNOLD HARE was a member of the academic staff of the University of Bristol for thirty-six years, becoming Reader in Theatre History, and is the author of *Theatre Royal Bath – the Orchard Street Calendar* and *George Frederick Cooke – The Actor and the Man* (Society for Theatre Research).

GAYLE T. HARRIS works in the Library of Congress in Washington D.C.. She is a member of the American Society for Theatre Research. Her research interests include the Bateman family and international copyright laws.

JOSEPHINE HARROP is the author of *Victorian Portable Theatres*, published by the Society of Theatre Research under the editorship of Kathleen Barker. Dr Harrop was a contributor to *British Theatre in the 1890s*.

MARK A. HOWELL has taught at schools and universities in England and the United States and now teaches drama at Cheam High School, Surrey. He has contributed several articles on eighteenth-century theatre to *Theatre Notebook*.

CHRISTOPHER ROBINSON is Keeper of the Theatre Collection at the University of Bristol. His previous experience included writing television plays and documentaries. He has published a history of the Bristol Hippodrome.

SYBIL ROSENFELD was founding joint editor of *Theatre Notebook* and one of the founders of the Society for Theatre Research, of which she was Honorary Secretary for over twenty years. Her numerous publications span over fifty years. *Temples of Thespis* was published by the Society for Theatre Research.

GEORGE SPEAIGHT was for many years General Editor of Publications for the Society for Theatre Research and is himself the author of books on toy theatre, puppet theatre, circus, clowns and *Collecting Theatre Memorabilia*. He has presented toy theatre performances in the United Kingdom and overseas.

M. GLEN WILSON is Professor Emeritus, Macalester College, St. Paul, Minnesota. He has published more than a dozen articles on Charles Kean and his biography of Kean is now a completed manuscript.

# Dedication

Following Kathleen Barker's untimely death in August 1991 her friends in the Society for Theatre Research, initially individually and then collectively, turned their minds to what form of tribute the Society should pay to one of its most distinguished and dedicated members. Of the alternatives considered the idea of a collection of essays found most favour. It was felt that Kathleen would approve a project which advanced new work, especially on provincial theatre to which she had contributed so much herself.

I was privileged to be invited to edit the volume. The range of its contents reflect Kathleen's interests in terms of place, period and genre; its contributors encompass senior scholars and younger ones, all of whom were beneficiaries of Kathleen's encouragement and knowledge. The inclusion of contributions by American scholars reflects the fact that Kathleen was known and respected on that continent (and indeed others) as well as in Britain. We, the contributors to this book, are only the representatives of the wider theatre history community, which wished to see an appropriate memorial to Kathleen. Particular mention should be made of George Rowell, by adoption a fellow-Bristolian, who, as chairman of the Society at the time when the decision to publish this volume was taken, gave it his full support and to its editor the benefit of his wise counsel throughout.

Richard Foulkes

Kathleen Barker, photographed with the editor, at the University Centre, Northampton in 1978.

# Part 1
## *In Appreciation*

# Kathleen Barker 1925–91
# Personal Recollections

ROY AVERY

I FIRST met Kathleen, or, as I always knew her, "Katie", in the sunlit Great Hall of Bristol Grammar School in the summer of 1941. Wartime Bristol was experiencing severe disruptions. In order to make up for the lack of social and cultural life within our schools (caused by the blackouts, air-raids and staff shortages) and to serve the wider community, we helped to found the Bristol Youth Group. This consisted eventually of some 250 fifth- and sixth-form boys and girls. We launched major sports, drama, music, and debating sections which were active throughout the holidays as well as the terms, giving enjoyment to all the participants and assistance or entertainment to hard-pressed Bristolians. The headteachers gave their full cooperation to our extraordinary venture, including the use of their school premises and playing fields.

Katie became the secretary and I was her chairman. Teenagers, oblivious of the size of the tasks ahead and very confident, we had a very successful partnership. Her gifts as a meticulous and enthusiastic administrator were already impressive. She was never afraid to stand up for her principles, nor to criticize me if she felt that I was lacking the necessary sense of responsibility at times. We sped energetically all over the city and suburbs, "negotiating", as we thought, with individual heads, local authority officers, business people, clergy, caretakers, visiting Americans, anyone at all who could help us. Short, vivacious, heavily bespectacled, Katie was a veritable dynamo attached to a bicycle. Her determination, shining through those horn-rimmed spectacles, was irresistible, and her drive ensured that the BYG flourished.

One Saturday afternoon in 1942 we went together with a crowd of sixth-form friends to the war-scarred Theatre Royal. There we heard Derek MacCulloch, "Uncle Mac" of the BBC Children's Hour, make a powerful appeal to our generation to help to save the theatre from extinction by auction for conversion into a warehouse. We made our pledge of loyalty there and then. The rest is history, Katie's "History". On Tuesday 11 May 1943 she was an ecstatic young member of the audience on the opening night of *She Stoops to Conquer*. Sybil Thorndike, playing Mrs Hardcastle, came out front to deliver Herbert Farjeon's charming prologue, though it was, as Katie noted characteristically, in places "historically inaccurate".

In July 1943, helped by an enthusiastic teacher, we arranged a memorable conference at a local girls' school on the Beveridge Report, that dangerously radical herald of a more comprehensive Welfare State, another of Katie's great concerns. The Report, which we all hailed, was not to usher in Utopia for the workshy but would ensure that never again would so many families be living below the poverty line.

Katie's idealism, her passionate interests in theatre and politics then were firmly rooted in her family background. An only child, she was born in Bristol on 15 December 1925 – in St Matthews Road, Cotham, to which she was to return at the end of her life. She lived in a council house in Sea Mills for some years until she moved at the age of six to a comfortable, modest three-bedroomed house in the pleasant suburb of Henleaze. This was the family's home.

Her parents were devoted to her. Her father, Rennie, was a largely self-taught engineer who was an instructor in technical subjects before becoming a primary schoolteacher. He was a life-long supporter of the Labour Party, and edited the *Bristol Labour Weekly* in the heady days of the Left Book Club and an aspiring Fabian Society in the 1930s and 1940s. His dominant passion was Shakespeare. He was a founder-member and a leader of the Bristol Shakespeare Society. It was not surprising that Katie's friends and their parents were convinced that at the age of eleven she had read all Shakespeare's plays, knew much of them by heart, and could also converse readily on Dekker and Webster. I remember vividly my wonder and Rennie Barker's excitement on my first visit to their home. He took me upstairs to display his beautiful model of the Globe. The sense of awe was like the revelation of the Holy Grail. He shared his knowledge with a missionary spirit, as a lecturer in adult education often based at the Folk House by the Central Library.

Katie's mother, after whom she was named Deborah, was born in Italy. Katie's grandmother was governess to an Italian family and married the valet of an Italian duke. Mrs Rossi was a powerful influence on her family. Self-styled "The Dragon", she had a formidable and vigorous personality, disciplined and very caring. It was Mrs Rossi who ensured that her granddaughter was a regular attender at church and Sunday School, usually Anglican, though Katie was to be confirmed in the Methodist church on Easter Sunday 1941. From her mother, who was a secretary at the thriving Bristol Aircraft Company, she inherited her secretarial skills and many interests including gardening, and tennis for which she represented her school. Indulgent, cheerful, very hospitable, Mrs Barker supported her family's scholarly, almost eccentric enthusiasms and gave Katie a loving, stable home. From them Katie also inherited her great stamina.

Resilience was needed in her early days at school where her intellectual precocity and her lack of height, which made her look even younger that she was, brought very mixed reactions from ragging to reverence. During a bad patch her father insisted that boarding school was the solution. At bedtime the eight-year-old told her mother, "Daddy can make me take the exam, but he can't make me pass it!" She pressed her parents to send her to one of Bristol's leading schools, Colston's Girls, her mother's old school.

It was a happy decision. A wise headmistress, Miss Gladys Morgan, and her capable colleagues understood her. She had the company of lively and enquiring girls. "I was pretty clever," writes one, "but Katie B. was head and shoulders above us. Yet, like most brilliant people, she was very modest. That does not mean that she stood aside – indeed she had no hesitation (like Mr Dick) in 'putting us all to rights' when necessary, always courteously but implacably. To us she seemed to know Shakespeare by heart and was not afraid to state her interpretation of him, but never boastfully, always from conviction and correctly." Her precise and adult use of language became a school legend from the first day she arrived. "May I appropriate this chair, please?"

Katie was always a year ahead of her age-group yet inevitably top of her form. Her name became well known throughout the school, being constantly read out at assemblies for her examination successes. Though a vigorous tennis player, earning colours, her build and poor eyesight were disadvantages in other sports. Characteristically she doggedly swam her length of the pool to gain a point for her house. The school magazine was full of her work, ranging from an excellent juvenile parody of Francis Bacon, "Of Imitation", to a twelve-year-old's speculation on "Oddities", beginning "We are all odd; we differ only in degrees of oddness." Her last contribution showed a boisterous aspect, her wartime experiences of a sixth-form camp, potato-planting on a Somerset farm. "At the end of the day we reappeared stuck all over with thorns and streaked with soot."

There is little record of the future theatre historian's active participation in drama. At Infants' and Junior School she was eager to recite on stage and she later took her part in form plays. As Feste in *Twelfth Night* she is still remembered for yelling into the wings, "Will you come on!" when a hapless girl missed her cue. I seem to remember her shivering on the school stage in a yellow cycling cape as a survivor in *The Admirable Crichton*. Her "awesome intellect" (as one friend describes it) was more effectively employed in coaching fellow-students in the sixth form, especially in Latin or helping them to interpret the complex regulations for college admissions.

Her brilliant academic progress culminated in the award of an Exhibition in English to Lady Margaret Hall in March 1943. It was a vintage year for Colston's and she had school friends at St Hilda's, meeting fairly regularly for tea and coffee. They reminisced over school days and eked out their clothes rations by adapting their useful sixth-form dress of navy-blue skirts and white blouses. Her most memorable tutor, who was later to become Dame, was Helen Gardner. I used to meet Katie in the undergraduate queues for food at the popular "Cake Factory" in North Oxford. She came to tea with me at Magdalen and invited me to be her partner at the LMH ball at the end of Trinity Term 1944, shortly before I left to join the RAF. We were not the most natural of dancing partners but enjoyed the grand occasion, being introduced to the principal before whirling around enthusiastically to another quickstep.

On VE Day in Oxford Katie danced with abandon. "We were all together round a garden bonfire," writes her friend. "A certain M. H. Roberts who gained great fame later as Margaret Thatcher was there too! After Schools, greatly daring (don't forget this was 1946), we went up to Town and had a very decorous meal, but, my goodness, how bold we felt!" It is ironic to imagine Katie, whose council estate neighbours prophesied that she would become the Labour Party's first woman Prime Minister, dancing in the garden with Margaret Thatcher.

I remember discussing Katie's future with her. Career opportunities for women in austerity Britain so soon after the war were much more restricted than they were later to become. She was frank that she lacked the patience and devotion to be a teacher, much as she liked helping individual pupils. Without the First that so many had confidently prophesied, she searched around anxiously for fulfilling work, turning resourcefully to her secretarial and administrative skills after brief training and apprenticeship as a school secretary. She returned as soon as possible to Bristol as assistant personnel manager with the Electricity Board, and started a drama club there appropriately called "The Faraday Players". She then moved to a post in Edinburgh with an engineering firm, assiduously briefing herself on all the technical vocabulary required.

In a period of rapid change and uncertainty over her real profession, Katie readily accepted the invitation and challenge of her lifelong friend, Barbara Mogford, to join - part-time - the Women's Royal Auxiliary Air Force. "She thought it might be fun", said Barbara, and so she became a popular and somewhat unexpected member of Fighter Control Unit 3507. She learned her radar, attended her lectures, carried out all her duties and enjoyed camps. If not on duty at weekends she was to be seen hurtling around Bristol on her motor-scooter during her visits home.

In 1955 she became secretary to the head of the Appointments Board at Bristol University, where her colleagues remembered her affectionately as a "Super Secretary", extremely hardworking, uncomplaining and very loyal. "She typed away as if her machine would break." She was to return briefly to the university again as Leverhulme Fellow from 1968-69, when she also served as sub-warden of Badock Hall. In congenial surroundings she displayed her administrative gifts, her high academic standards, invaluable counselling of the women students and her brisk sense of humour.

Katie's varied experiences equipped her for the happy and successful culmination of her professional career with the University of London from 1961 to 1987, when she retired. She became a tower of strength at the Institute of Education, spanning a hectic period of rapid expansion and much controversial change. Derek Forbes, who was later to become Joint Honorary Secretary with her of the Society for Theatre Research, has many memories of her outstanding professional ability. He writes:

> From my position as departmental head in one of the London colleges, responsible in part for the training of teachers, I came into advantageous contact with Kathleen through her work as the Institute's Schools Liaison Officer. Arnold Cannon (at Trent Park College) has an abiding memory of her sterling work on the Schools' Rationalisation Scheme, whereby schools in the Greater London area and inner home counties were allotted to specific colleges for their students' classroom practice. Following this, a situation that had previously been a free-for-all scramble, made acrimonious by the frantic expansion of teacher-training in the 1960s, became smoothly and harmoniously effective. She was able to balance, and satisfy, the needs, preferences and rivalries of two-score or more colleges, hundreds of schools and innumerable subject departments.
>
> Such was her competence, judgement and fair but firm handling of meetings that she would be asked to chair or steer committees dealing with matters often quite remote from the work of her own office. She had the task of matching the Institute's many students with the right schools for their practices and the right tutors to supervise them. She would, when necessary, go out into the field herself, and, not having a car, travel considerable distances by public transport. Her ex-students remember Kathleen's supervision of their practice with appreciation, for, as well as being rigorous in the standards she expected, she was understanding and unfailingly helpful. "Rigorous", "meticulous", "fair but firm", "unfailingly helpful" – these are words that will crop up again and again in tributes to Kathleen. They are certainly words that her friends and colleagues in the Society for Theatre Research will apply to her.

She wrote two books about her beloved Bristol, a delightful survey of five centuries of entertainment, *Bristol at Play*, and her celebrated, definitive *Theatre Royal, Bristol, 1766–1966: Two Centuries of Stage History*, published after thirty years' dedicated research. Her further work on provincial theatre history led to her well-deserved doctorate from the University of Leicester.

Her generous editing of other scholars' work, the latest being Jo Harrop's *Victorian Portable Theatres*, and assistance with advice (as witnessed in recurrent authorial acknowledgments) were part of her zealous fostering of research. She was a prime mover in setting up the S.T.R.'s fund in 1987 for granting research awards, a very successful initiative which she generously supported in her will. One of the major awards first offered in 1993 is in her name.

All her preoccupations, together with the nursing of her widowed mother, never diminished Katie's zest for life and learning. She loved to lecture and did so on both sides of the Atlantic with great conviction and verve. Friends remember her divertissement about the music-hall performer, Harry Clifton, which she presented with musical illustrations. My special memory is her story of a night at the Theatre Royal, Bristol, at the end of the Napoleonic wars, when the audience all stood to sing "God Save the King" except for one man in the front stalls who remained obstinately seated, still wearing his hat. "A Radical! A Radical!" shouted the groundlings. With great gusto they seized their protesting victim, rushed him outside and threw him off the quayside into the polluted water only to discover later that he was an Austrian visitor, who could not speak a word of English.

Keeping a cool head in the maelstrom of British education, Katie used her leisure wisely, created a large number of friends and enjoyed many more conventional interests. Barbara Mogford describes some of them. "Katie was very skilled indeed at embroidery. Many of her friends have beautiful examples of her work in their homes, scarves, cushion-covers, table-cloths." She was, like her mother, an indefatigable gardener who could never bear to see a single weed growing. Visiting Barbara for weekends at her Dorset cottage, she "used to bring with her her old RAF walking shoes and spend hours weeding my garden. A pair of Wellington boots, size 4, is still in my boot-box. She could be demanding at times but she was always accepted by my local friends as a distinctive and fascinating character." An early admiration for the violin and the music of Bach was augmented in her later years by a particular delight in brass bands and Radio Two. She scorned television and never owned a set.

She had maintained a *pied à terre* in Bristol after the death of her parents, constantly returning to see the plays at her beloved Theatre Royal. On retirement she became the proud owner of a comfortable Victorian villa near St Matthew's Church, Cotham. She plunged into this latest experience of freedom with zest, reorganising all those filing cabinets and boxes, gardening energetically, championing the local conservation movement and helping to organise the street carnival in historic Kingsdown nearby, searching out likely sponsors with her beady eye and powerful letters.

She now had no surviving relatives in this country, but was able to resume and increase many friendships whilst still retaining her self-sufficiency and independence. She returned to her strong Methodist roots and was a very welcome, regular member of the Victoria Methodist church with its university chaplaincy. She is remembered happily as never missing a morning service, "a most estimable lady" who loved to sing Wesley's hymns, provided always that they had "the right tunes". In one of our last conversations we had a lively discussion of the good and bad features of local ecumenicalism. Despite her knowledgeable criticisms she was always an optimist, agreeing with Francis Bacon: "Religion, being the chief band of human society, it is a happy thing when itself is well contained within the true band of unity."

Former school friends like Pamela Phelps who visited Katie during the school's centenary celebrations in early 1991 found her "happy in her house, happy to be in Bristol, happy to talk Colston's – she even looked the same!" She was busy preparing her lectures for the University's Colston's Society symposium, an international conference on the Enlightenment. Her very sudden illness was a hammer blow. Angry at first at the inefficiency of a mistaken diagnosis, she rallied immediately, set to work to put her affairs in order and meet her greatest challenge. Time was very short. To visit Katie in hospital was to be cheered, moved and inspired by her "no nonsense" approach to life and death, and her abiding faith and courage.

The curtain falls but Katie lives on in the minds of all who knew her, a friend and true scholar of cheerful dedication and shining integrity.

Grateful acknowledgements to Katie's friends, neighbours and colleagues for all their help.

# Kathleen Barker and the Society for Theatre Research

DEREK FORBES

KATHLEEN BARKER was twenty-two when the Society for Theatre Research was founded in June 1948. Her association started early. A foretaste of her later devotion to the Society's administration was recorded at the time of the first A.G.M. in April 1949: "The committee wishes to express its gratitude to the many members who have offered their time and services in support of its work, and in particular to Mr George Devine and Miss Kathleen Barker for duplicating documents. . . ." (S.T.R. Bulletin no. 4). Next, Kathleen was prominent in the founding of the Bristol Group of the S.T.R., and was elected the group's Hon. Secretary in early 1950 (continuing until late 1952); one of the group's activities was a working party on the history of the Bristol Theatre Royal. Also in 1950 came Kathleen's first venture in *Theatre Notebook*, "The McCready Prompt Books at Bristol" written jointly with Joseph Macleod (*TN* IV.4). (A full list of her twenty-eight contributions to *Theatre Notebook* is appended.) Two years later, under the imperious editorial eye of Muriel St Clare Byrne, she was contributing her transcription of "A Bristol Theatre Royal Inventory" to *Studies in English Theatrical History in Memory of Gabrielle Enthoven, OBE* (1952), the Society's third Annual Publication.

When Kathleen's professional life brought her to London in 1961, she was elected at the first opportunity to the S.T.R. Committee (AGM of 1962), and then re-elected every four years until 1987. During the 1960s, she gave her first lecture to the Society, "The Terrys and Godwin in Bristol" (season of 1966–7), and took the chair for "The Story of Exeter's Theatre" by Margaret Toms (season of 1969–70). All the time she was quietly working away at her history of the Bristol Theatre Royal.

In 1970 Kathleen was elected Honorary Secretary of the S.T.R. – jointly with Jack Reading until 1981, then jointly with Derek Forbes, being re-elected annually until her retirement in 1987. She shouldered many tasks at different periods during her time in office. She handled correspondence, matters of committee steering, committee and AGM agenda and minuting, drafting of reports. She gave emergency help with the treasurership of *Theatre Notebook* and the S.T.R., and the administration of membership, at times of particular crisis. She contributed vigorously to the work of sub-committees. For the Publications Sub-Committee, for example, she undertook the sale and distribution of books from stock, and part-storage, and was in demand as an in-house editor of Annual Publications (and relished being described by one of her authors as "an editorial blend of the Brothers Cheeryble and Genghis Khan"). Helping generally with hospitality and representation, she seldom missed attending the Society's lectures. Those present who did not know her personally will surely remember her giving forthcoming announcements at S.T.R. meetings. With what Margaret Collins, Lectures Sub-Committee convenor, has aptly described as "generous enthusiasm", Kathleen provided numerous suggestions for speakers, as well as giving her own memorable lectures to the Society, and to the American Society for Theatre Research (where she had many contacts and some close friends). She was adept at fielding casual research enquiries. On many known occasions, and inevitably many more unrecorded, she was prepared to give researchers specialised help with their investigations. On at least one occasion this was understood, privately, to have extended to supporting the work of a young researcher from her own pocket.

In 1974 Kathleen took out life membership of the S.T.R., a mark of confidence which coincided with the Society's publication *hors série* of her *magnum opus*, *The Theatre Royal, Bristol, 1766–1966: Two Centuries of Stage History* (1974). "In those days," says Jack Reading, "such a book was too ambitious for the S.T.R.'s Annual Publication programme. With some difficulty I sold her the idea of trying the old custom of subscription publishing which, at first, she dismissed out of hand as being too amateurish and only agreed when I reminded her that it was in the best eighteenth-century tradition. The book then went forward with a sell-out before printing." A similar procedure was used for her subsequent book, *Bristol at Play: Five Centuries of Live Entertainment* (Moonraker Press, Bradford-on-Avon, 1976, in association with the Society for Theatre Research).

Coming into the 1980s, we find Kathleen lecturing to the Society on "Thomas Youdan, the Sheffield music hall pioneer" (season of 1979–80), organising a reception to honour Sybil Rosenfeld's eightieth birthday in 1983 and a one-day outing in 1986 to tour Matcham-designed theatres in Portsmouth and Southsea, and taking the chair in 1987 for John Tearle's lecture on "The Conways and the Tearles – a Theatrical Dynasty?" During this period she was working on the supplemental material to the Society's great bibliography, *English Theatrical Literature 1559–1900* (1970), latterly with John Cavanagh; she continued to do so after her retirement from the Hon. Secretaryship in 1987. She went back to live in Bristol, but continued to turn up at meetings in London. In December 1987, Kathleen herself entertained and informed the S.T.R., and the Music Hall Society of which she was also a keen member, with a lecture on "Harry Clifton – a rather Private Entertainer", a soirée with musical illustrations.

Kathleen's organisational work for the Society did not, gladly, end with her retirement from major executive office. During the previous year she had been instrumental in promoting the initial S.T.R. scheme for making grants for theatre research. When, in 1987, the Research Awards Sub-Committee was formed to activate the scheme, she accepted nomination as the founding Hon. Secretary. For the first four years of the awards (first granted in 1988) she administered and honed the procedure and serviced the operation. Appropriately, in January 1990 she took the chair for the Society's lecture on "Miss Bateman: the American Years" by Gayle Harris of the Library of Congress – the first recipient of a major research award of the S.T.R. for her work on Kate Bateman.

The last Annual Publication that Kathleen saw through the press was Josephine Harrop's *Victorian Portable Theatres* in conjunction with a reprint of "*Old Wild's*" (1989). The author's acknowledgment, typically, was to her as "the most supportive and helpful of editors". Then Kathleen commenced a task that was to be cut off by her last illness, the editing of Richard Foulkes's *The Calverts – Actors of Some Importance* (1992). Here Kathleen was appreciatively reciprocating for the author's earlier supervision of her doctoral dissertation.

In April 1991 she took the chair at short notice (following the death of George Nash) for Kalman Burnim's lecture on "The Jewish Presence in the London Theatres in the Eighteenth Century". This was Kathleen's last appearance at a function of the Society; she was already in pain. She died in August. In her will she left a proportion of her estate to the S.T.R. to enhance the research awards so dear to her heart; ultimately this amounted to over £48,000. Her obituary by George Rowell was printed in *Theatre Notebook* XLVI.1 of 1992, and later that year her last contribution to *Theatre Notebook* was published posthumously (XLVI.3). Also in 1992, an *ad hoc* research award in her memory was granted to Joseph Donohue to assist with his study of the Empire Theatre of Varieties and the licensing controversy of 1894. After the settlement of the estate, the Society was able to grant its new major award from her bequest for the first time in 1993, namely "The Kathleen Barker Award of the Society for Theatre Research". It went to Deborah Vlock-Keyes of Brandeis University for work on patter and the politics of eccentric speech in Victorian popular culture. The Kathleen Barker Award will be given annually. Thus will her life, distinction and power for good continue to be celebrated.

## Contributions to *Theatre Notebook*


**4**, 76–81 (co-author) "The McCready Prompt Books at Bristol"
**16**, 39–55 "Michael Edkins, Painter"
**18**, 58–60 "The Enthoven Purchase Fund – the First Ten Years"
**18**, 79–91 "The Theatre Proprietors' Story"
**22**, 27–43 "The Terrys and Godwin in Bristol"
**23**, 167–8 "George Cressall Ellis" (note)
**27**, 21–22 "John Hippisley's Earliest Farce"

| | |
|---|---|
| **29**, 81-84 | "An Early Seventeenth-Century Provincial Playhouse" (comment **37**, 14, 15, 20 nn. 1, 4) |
| **30**, 35 | "Charles Kean's tomb" (note) |
| **33**, 86-87 | "Children in Arms" (note) |
| **38**, 144 | "Royal Kent Theatre" (note) |
| **39**, 25-31, 68- 75, 140-9 | "Thirty Years of Struggle: Entertainment in Provincial Towns between 1840 and 1870" |
| **42**, 39-43 | "A Footnote to *Fratricide Punished*" |
| **42**, 79 | "Richmond, Surrey: index of performers at the Second Theatre Royal" (note) |
| **43**, 50-57 | "'Mr M' and the Bath Company: an Unfortunate Application" |
| **44**, 123-5 | "Death of Henry Irving's Mother" (note) |
| **45**, 84-93 | "Churches and Stages in Restoration and Eighteenth-Century Bristol" |
| **46**, 118-22 | "The Revival of Theatre outside London with special reference to the West Country (c. 1700-1788)" (a lecture printed posthumously). |
| | Reviews **20**, 84-85; **26**, 160-1; **28**, 141; **31/2**, 45-46; **40**, 47-48; **42**, 87-88 and 88-89; **43**, 45. |

## Kathleen Barker's Publications reviewed in *Theatre Notebook*

| | |
|---|---|
| **17**, 23-24 | *The Theatre Royal, Bristol: the First Seventy Years* |
| **21**, 48-49 | *The Theatre Royal, Bristol: Decline and Rebirth 1834-1943* |
| **28**, 143-4 | *Entertainment in the Nineties* |
| **32**, 96 | *Bristol at Play: Five Centuries of Live Entertainment* |
| **35**, 39 | *Early Music Hall in Bristol* |

[Compiled by Derek Forbes with help from Margaret Collins, Eileen Cottis, Tony Latham, Jack Reading, Sybil Rosenfeld, and Olive Youngs]

# The Kathleen Barker Archive in the University of Bristol Theatre Collection

CHRISTOPHER ROBINSON

THE archive material bequeathed by Kathleen Barker to the University of Bristol Theatre Collection is in itself an imposing memorial to a lifetime of meticulous research into her specialised subject of regional theatre and other forms of entertainment during the eighteenth and nineteenth centuries.

Basically the archive comprises eighty stout arch-files, each one containing between 600 and 800 quarto or A4 sheets, most of them double-sided, on which virtually everything that ever appeared in print, in newspapers and theatre journals, relating to provincial entertainment has been painstakingly reproduced, mainly by a manual typewriter. Only later in her life did Kathleen resort to photocopiers.

Her authoritative history of the Theatre Royal, Bristol, from 1766 to 1966, is related in 267 pages, but the reference material she assembled covering this period fills twenty-four files, or something in excess of 16,000 pages.

A Herculean labour of equally awesome proportions is represented by the ten files in which are reproduced the dates and cast-lists of every production staged at the Theatre Royal from its opening until the foundation of the Bristol Old Vic Company in 1946. These were transcribed, again on the manual typewriter, from original playbills held in the archives of the Bristol Record Office. They are of enormous benefit to the Theatre Collection which receives many requests for information on eighteenth and nineteenth-century plays and players in Bristol. These enquiries can now be dealt with immediately and directly, thus avoiding what could be for some people the inconvenience of a personal visit to the Record office.

In her short but informative and entertaining book *Bristol at Play*, published in 1975, Kathleen explored a wide spectrum of popular entertainment from the fifteenth century to 1975. Her research for this resulted in six hefty files labelled *Bristol at Play* covering an astonishing variety of entertainment from fairs, circuses, equestrian spectacles, travelling showmen, sword-swallowers and freaks, to music-hall, pantomimes, concerts and, of course, the "legitimate" theatre.

A further fifteen files are filled with the results of Kathleen's research into theatre and popular entertainment in Nottingham, Sheffield, Newcastle and Brighton in the nineteenth century. Once again the sheer scope and variety of the material and its impeccable collation is staggering. This enormous undertaking was justly rewarded by a Ph.D. in Victorian Studies at the University of Leicester in 1982 for her 432-page thesis, *Provincial Entertainment 1840–1870: The Performing Arts in Five Provincial Towns.*

Everybody who knew Kathleen will remember her keen, sharp, perceptive eyes. They missed nothing and certainly not when they scoured every page of every issue of the *Era* between 1840 and 1879. The result was some seven thousand pages accommodated in ten files and containing every reference in that paper to entertainment in the provinces.

By the time she launched into this massive project Kathleen had graduated to A4 paper and the photocopier, but a large proportion of the material, whether a four-line announcement or a substantial article covering two or three pages in typescript, was transcribed by her faithful and evidently robust typewriter.

There is enough material for a book in her file on Harry Clifton (1832–72), the music-hall artist famous as the composer of *Pretty Polly Perkins of Paddington Green* and "motto" songs such as *Paddle Your Own Canoe*, which became as popular in the drawing-room as they were in the halls.

A curiosity is the file on the lesser known but fascinating Harvey Teasdale, "the converted clown". Born in Sheffield in 1817 Teasdale was a minor theatrical manager, clown and skin performer on the northern circuits and occasional manager of a number of public houses in Sheffield. He appears to have been an unscrupulous rogue with a self-confessed "appetite for strong drink". He had a turbulent marriage which ended when his wife left him, together with their two daughters. Teasdale spent a good deal of time pursuing her through England and Ireland, convinced that she was "on the game" and was bringing their daughters in the same way.

The climax came in the summer of 1862 when he forced his way into a house in Sheffield where she was staying and made a typically botched attempt to kill her and then himself. For this he was sentenced to two years hard labour in Wakefield Prison.

During his confinement he experienced a spiritual conversion (which didn't stop him from repudiating his unfortunate wife's claims on him) and after his release he returned to Sheffield where he joined a group of temperance evangelicals known as the Hallelujah Band.

At a meeting in the local Temperance Hall he publicly ripped to pieces and burned his costumes, monkey suit and scripts, thus severing his connection with the stage and the iniquities of his past. In 1881 he published his autobiography, *The Life and Adventures of Harvey Teasdale, the Converted Clown and Man-Monkey.* It went into twenty editions and sold 40,000 copies, though only three are known to exist today.

Kathleen, in her inimitable way, tracked down one of these and a photocopy of it is in her file on Teasdale which provided the source for one of her lively lectures.

In one of them she said "... it is even more true of early Music Hall than of the Theatre that the provinces are *terra incognita* in historical consciousness ...", but no-one has done more than she in exploring and illuminating these shadowy areas. Her lecture on Teasdale is a typical illustration of her conviction that in any period of theatre research the minor figure is likely to be more significant than the major one.

Fortunately all of Kathleen's lectures are preserved in typescript. She began one of them by saying: "Hands up all those who knew anything about Thomas Youdan before they saw the title of tonight's talk." We can be sure that by the end of it her audience had not only learned virtually all there is to know about Thomas Youdan, but also experienced a vivid insight into the world in which he lived and worked.

Curiously, the archive contains files on only one individual nineteenth-century actor - the Norfolk-born Charles Dillon. Equally curious is the fact that there is no entry under his name in either *The Oxford Companion to the Theatre* or *The Cambridge Guide to Theatre*. Kathleen, however, accumulated enough material from newspapers, theatrical journals and other sources from all over Britain and abroad to fill no less than ten bulky files. She contributes a chapter on Dillon to *Shakespeare and the Victorian Stage*. Was she contemplating a biography of Dillon? I can remember her joy when the Theatre Collection acquired a tuppence-coloured print, complete with sequins, of Dillon as Richard III - a joy now explained.

Kathleen's bequest also includes her library which, unsurprisingly, contains a substantial amount of material relating to popular entertainment and regional theatre. This is doubly welcome as they are two areas which the Theatre Collection has been expanding over the last two or three years.

The archive has not yet been fully catalogued but has been sorted and shelved and is accessible for research. Any enquiries should be directed to the Keeper of the University of Bristol Theatre Collection, Department of Drama, Cantocks Close, Woodland Road, Bristol, BS1 1UP.

# Part 2
## *In Tribute*

# The "Regular Theatre" at Jacob's Well, Bristol 1729–65

MARK A. HOWELL

THE three main types of eighteenth-century provincial theatre buildings were known to contemporaries as Long Rooms, Regular Theatres and Theatres Royal. A survey of the known external dimensions of eighteenth-century theatres shows that Long Rooms and Regular Theatres were the most common. Theatres Royal were exceptional: only ten opened before 1788.[1] Long Rooms and Regular Theatres measured, on average 65ft 7.5ins long and 30ft wide, externally (Appendix 1). Theatres Royal measured 107ft 6ins by 54ft, externally (Appendix 2). So, when we speak of typical eighteenth-century theatres, we cannot justifiably picture the large Theatres Royal.[2]

The purpose of this essay is to diagrammatically reconstruct the theatre at Jacob's Well, Bristol, as a case-study Regular Theatre: the most common purpose-built provincial theatre buildings of the eighteenth century. I preface this reconstruction with a reminder from C. Walter Hodges that, in the business of proposing a diagrammatic reconstruction of a lost theatre, the "only certainty about it is that somewhere it is wrong".[3] This reconstruction is highly conjectural: the building, opened in 1729, was demolished in 1786.[4] Only one deed plan partly depicts its exterior walls. However, a reconstruction has long been necessary as a visual context for interpreting and discussing the theatre's surviving account books and production budgets, covering 1741–8.[5]

The term "Regular Theatre" derives from the wording of the 1788 Stage Licensing Act, but it was in use long before. An article in the 30 November 1747 issue of the *Bath Journal* used the phrase to describe respectable stage performances. Bath architect John Wood used it to describe the new theatre opened in Orchard Street in 1750.[6] The 1788 Act restored the rights of provincial local authorities to licence play performances for the first time since 1737. By implication the Act also legalised the construction of provincial theatre buildings not licensed by Parliament. The preamble to the Act clearly identifies the reasons for its introduction. It cites a demand for what it calls "constant and regular" provincial theatres built, like Jacob's Well, at the summer resorts for the middle and upper classes:

> Whereas it may be expedient to permit and suffer in towns of considerable resort theatrical representations for a limited time . . . it shall . . . be

lawful . . . for the justices of the peace of any county . . . to grant a licence to any person . . . for the performance of . . . plays.[7]

Before 1788 many provincial theatres probably evaded the 1737 ban partly by providing regular stage performances to respectable tourists in Long Rooms. Spa resorts, like those at Bath, Richmond, Yorkshire, and Truro often opened temporary theatres for short seasons as an added attraction. Local authorities understood that these theatres played to respectable audiences, and closed at the end of the season. One of the earliest purpose-built spa theatres was the theatre at Jacob's Well.

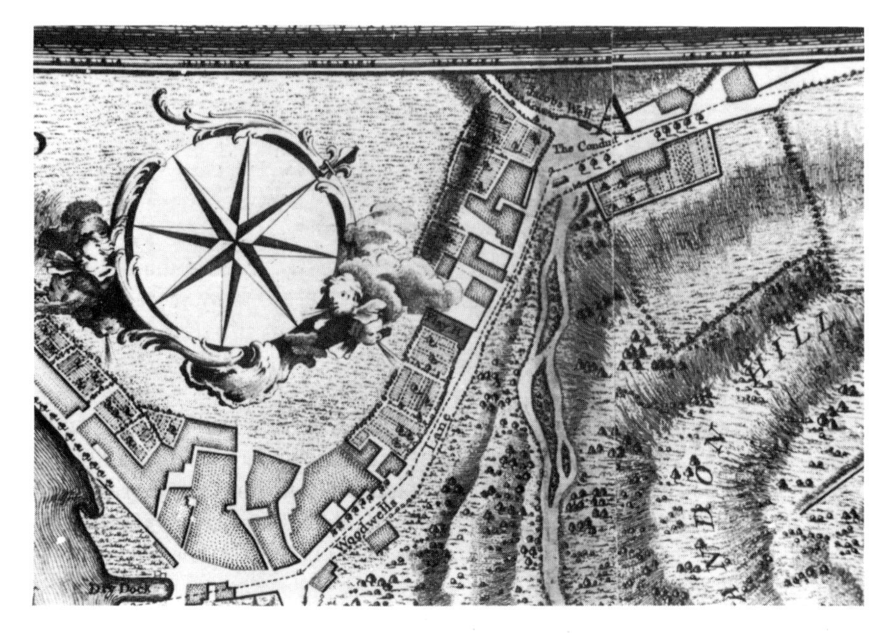


1. Map of Bristol, 1742, John Rocque. Detail showing Jacob's Well Theatre, labelled "Play H.".

We must remember the theatre at Jacob's Well was illegally built. Before 1737 theatres were licensed by local authorities. I know of no licence for Jacob's Well. Kathleen Barker proved the Bristol authorites held strict moral and religious objections to theatres. When Gay's *The Beggar's Opera* stormed Bristol with forty-three performances they restrained theatres as "public nuisances and nurseries of idleness and vice".[8] The public responded by rioting. A year later John Hippisley, the original Peachum, opened Jacob's Well. Like Hogarth's pictures, showing the respectable hand-in-hand with the illegal aspects of society, the theatre's site reflects both the respectable middle-class audience of hotwell tourists and the illegality of operating theatres in Bristol. The theatre fronted Woodwell's Lane, now Jacob's Wells Road, Clifton, two or three yards outside Bristol's county boundary (illustration 1). The fact that the theatre stood so far from Gloucester, the county town, certainly made it difficult for Bristol to close the theatre until 1737. Barker cited this as the main reason the theatre evaded closure.[9] After 1737, however, the legal situation changed. Parliament outlawed any theatre not licensed by Royal Patent. Barker accounts for the theatre's subsequent survival by dismissing the 1737 Act as ineffective with regard to "respectable established provincial companies", which the Jacob's Well players certainly were.

Jacob's Well opened for short seasons from June to September. Its actors therefore included respectable members of the Patent Theatre companies like John Hippisley himself. Bristol newspapers printed long lists of summer "Arrivals", including dukes, lords, knights and members of the royal family, all attracted to Clifton's own version of the London pleasure grounds. Clifton had its own hotwell and Vauxhall Gardens. The theatre was part of this middle class attraction. Both the gardens and the theatre closed in the 1760s.[10] So, the theatre's respectable status helped it survive the 1737 Act.

But other, more specific, reasons enabled it to develop. The respectable society of Merchant Venturers (henceforth referred to as the SMV) owned the site. The SMV was perhaps the most powerful and influential organisation in Bristol during the eighteenth century. It owned most of the Clifton property and developed the wells, baths, and promenades around the parish.[11]

The support of a justice of the peace also helped the theatre at Jacob's Well evade the law. Listed amongst seventeen theatre shareholders, paying £200 each in an "Abstract of Mr John Taylor's Declaration of Trust for the Proprietors of the Theatre at Jacob's Well", an indenture dated 5 February 1748, is John Brickdale, a justice of the peace for Somerset and Gloucester.[12] (His son, Mathew Brickdale, later MP for Bristol, supported the King Street Theatre's first bid for a Royal Patent nearly thirty years later in 1773.)[13] The indenture deals with the payment of John Taylor's £200 shareholder subscription to the theatre.

The development of Bristol theatre buildings, from the Long Room at the Clifton Hotwells (c. 1705), to the Regular Theatre at Jacob's Well (1729), to the Theatre Royal in King Street (1766), provides a model for the development of other eighteenth-century provincial theatres. The Stage Licencing Act meant that provincial theatre companies needed to establish first temporary, then permanent, and then Royal theatre buildings.

The first venue in Clifton used by the Jacob's Well company before the theatre at Jacob's Well opened was the Hotwells Long Room. No evidence survives describing the Hotwells Long Room at this time, though a 1797 Bristol guide book described it as ". . . built very early in the century, and . . . then one of the principal Rooms [*sic*] in the kingdom".[14] This Long Room was part of the

Glocester [*sic*] Hotel. It was known later in the century as the Barton Hotel and also the "old or upper room" (as distinct from the "new or lower rooms", built on the south side of Hotwells Road, on the shores of the river Avon).[15] The same source describes the room's dimensions as 90ft long by 35ft wide by 35ft high. No deeds or builders' contracts for this venue survive and very few extant Bristol newspapers cover the late 1720s. The Bath company gave regular performances at the Hotwells Long Room under actor-manager John Power in July and August 1705.[16] Newspaper entries dating from 1726 provide the only documentary evidence specifically identifying the Long Room's use as a theatre.[17] In the summer of 1728 John Hippisley acted there in *The Beggar's Opera* under John Gay's direction. *Farley's Bristol News* for 18 May 1728, reviewed the production:

> On Tuesday last the Bath company of comedians performed *The Beggar's Opera* in the Long Room near the Hotwell to an audience of 200 persons of the first rank with universal applause: And we hear that they are commanded to perform the same again on Tuesday next when Polly Peachum will play in the dresses presented to them by the nobility at Bath, which we think a plain proof of their merit . . . Mr Gay will be present at the performance.

The Long Room stood very near the site of the theatre at Jacob's Well and possibly provided a dimensional model for the theatre. In my conjectural diagrammatic reconstruction, the Jacob's Well Theatre measures 37ft externally. The Hotwells Long Room measured 35ft wide.[18]

The only contemporary public notification of the Jacob's Well opening exists in a small advertisement in a London Jacobite newspaper, *Fog's Weekly Journal* dated 28 June 1729:

> That they are building a very spacious theatre at Limekilns lying convenient for coaches as well for the rope walk leading to the hotwell.

John Rocque's 1742 map of Bristol proves this advertisement refers to the Jacob's Well Theatre. Rocque's map shows the theatre, marked "Play H[ouse]" in Woodwells Lane (now Jacob's Wells Road) the south end of which leads to the "Road from Hotwell" and "Rope Walk" (illustration 1). In his *Memoirs of the Bristol Stage* (1826), Richard Jenkins reproduced a similar advertisement from, he claimed, the *London Weekly Journal* of 28 June 1729. Jenkins' source differs from *Fog's* only in adding that *Love for Love* was the opening performance. The wording, however, is so similar to the extract from *Fog's Weekly Journal* as to make it likely that these were, in fact, the same announcement from the same newspaper. Jenkins possibly invented the section on *Love for Love* perhaps on the basis of other evidence now lost. I have been unable to discover any surviving edition of any newspaper known as the *London Weekly Journal* for the date quoted

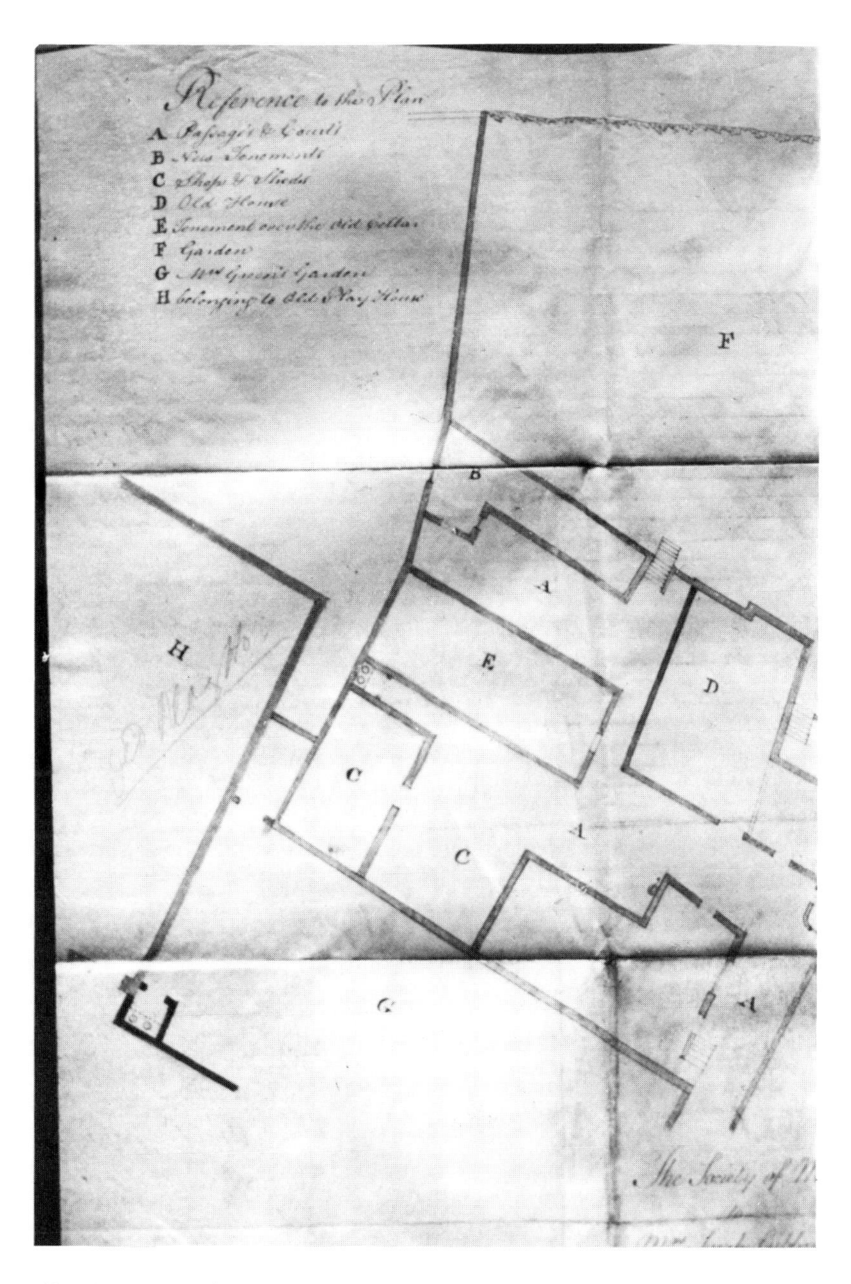


2. Deed plan showing part of exterior walls of theatre at Jacob's Well (H), 1786. Deed dated 25 May 1786 to Sarah and Jo Gibbons.

by Jenkins, beyond *Fog's* quoted here. The editions of the *Bristol News* covering the Jacob's Well seasons during the period 1728–39 are lost.[19]

Records amongst the SMV archives provide the source for diagrammatically reconstructing the site dimensions and the building plan here. A deed dated 2 June 1746 is the earliest record of an agreement between John Hippisley and the SMV.[20] Prior to 1746 Hippisley sub-let the site from one George Martin. This agreement existed between them from 1729 when Hippisley opened the theatre. The deed shows that Hippisley leased part of an old site known from 1703 as a piece of ground called

> the Margarettes and so granted to . . . Richard King and George Martin . . . (on which he the said John Hippisley hath erected and built a playhouse or theatre)[21]

In 1703, some twenty-six years before the theatre opened, "the Margarettes" consisted of a half acre plot leased to Richard King.[22] After his death this became two separate properties. In June 1723 George Martin leased one of these properties, measuring 43ft wide, north–south. Hippisley subsequently leased George Martin's part of "the Margarettes". It therefore follows that the theatre site measured 43ft wide, north–south. The site's east–west length is more difficult to determine because all the pre-1729 deeds omit the measurement, arbitrarily reciting the plot dimensions as:

> being about 43ft in front on or towards the said Lane there . . . and extending backwards about that length up to the hedge there

To find the site's length we need to refer to a nineteenth-century deed. A drawing on a deed dated 2 October 1817 leasing the property to Richard Williams shows the site plan "whereon formerly stood a messuage or tenement formerly used as a playhouse" (illustration 3).[23] Williams built a set of tenements called Cottage Place on the site in 1803. The plan's scale, whilst badly drawn, provides approximate measurements which confirm the site's 43ft width, including a 4–5ft wide passageway running along the southern boundary. Its length scales at 135ft.

The 1746 deed granted Hippisley a tavern along with the theatre site:

> the said John Hippisley is by divers good ways and means in the law become entitled to a messuage formerly a public house and called the Horse and Groom but now in his own possession (which messuage is the said messuage recited to be erected by the said Richard King).[24]

The deed implies that Hippisley closed the Horse and Groom and used it as his

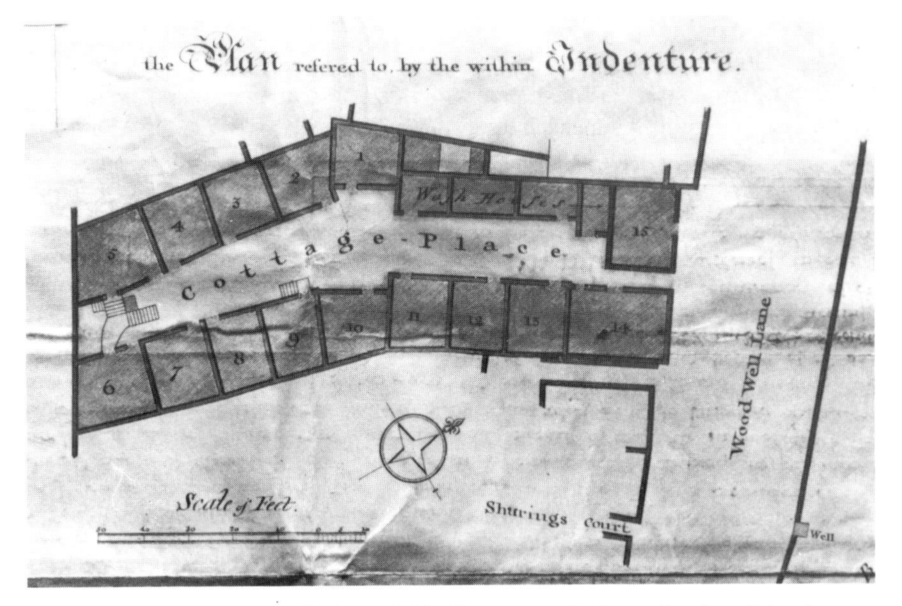


3. Plan of Cottage Place, Clifton, 1803. Tenements built on the site of the theatre at Jacob's Well.

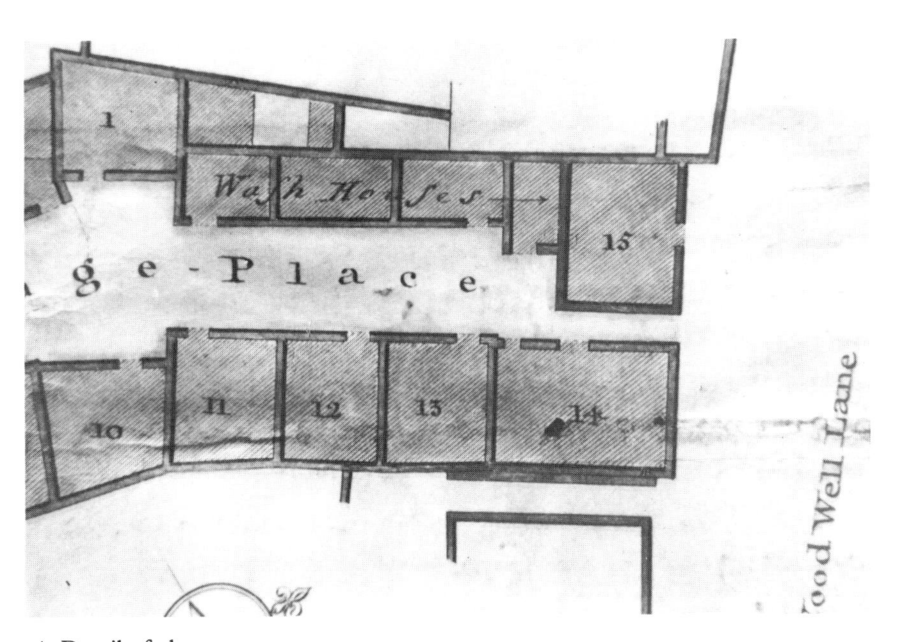


4. Detail of above.

home. Jane Green, Hippisley's daughter, leased the Horse and Groom and garden from the SMV as late as 1785.[25] The Horse and Groom can be seen in Rocque's plan as the first building north of the theatre, separated from it by a garden, and fronting Woodwells Lane (illustration 1). Rocque depicts a curious projection on the south side of the theatre, fronting Woodwell's Lane. Circumstantial evidence identifies this as a tavern which stood on this site c.1745. The same projection can be seen in J. J. de Wilstar's original 1746 survey for the SMV. This tavern can be seen in a nineteenth-century plan attached to a deed between Daniel Shewring and the SMV.[26] The plan shows the neighbouring site south of the theatre as it appeared in 1745 and labels this tavern "M - One Public house" (with a "Court" to its west side). It is likely therefore that, along with the old Horse and Groom separated from the theatre by a garden, a newer tavern stood immediately adjacent to its south wall. This fact may have given rise to a local folk tradition, still perpetuated in Bristol, describing Hippisley passing beer to his audiences through a hole in the theatre's wall. The nineteenth-century historian John Latimer, called this tavern the "Malt Shovel".[27]

Diagrammatic reconstructions usually rely, to a greater or lesser extent, on conjecture informed by eye-witness descriptions from a variety of sources such as legal documents, newspapers, diaries, memoirs and correspondence. No reliable picture of the Jacob's Well theatre interior survives. What may be an eighteenth-century picture became associated with the theatre in 1953. No evidence of any kind has ever confirmed this suggestion. Before his death L. G. Turner, a Bristol resident and theatre history enthusiast, claimed someone sent him the picture. The Victoria and Albert Museum carbon tested and dated the picture as eighteenth century, but there was no proof that it showed Jacob's Well. The original was lost when Turner died but the University of Bristol Theatre Collection retain a photograph.[28]

My reconstruction of the theatre's interior therefore rests on linking systems of geometry possibly used by eighteenth-century theatre-builders to the known dimensions of the theatre. On average the known exterior dimensions of eighteenth-century regular provincial theatres measure close to 65ft 9ins long and 30ft 10ins wide externally (Appendix 1). I assume the theatre at Jacob's Well had similar plan dimensions. If architects plotted the interiors of these Regular Theatres on a double square of 60ft by 30ft, these average dimensions would allow 5ft for box lobby space. A more specific comparison of these dimensions with the surviving Regular Theatre at Richmond, Yorkshire (1788) confirms their reliability. The theatre at Richmond, Yorkshire measures 67ft long externally and 28ft wide, with a lobby measuring 3ft 6ins at its narrowest and 6ft 6ins at its deepest. I hope to show that the theatre at Jacob's Well was an earlier example of this model.[29]

Two unpublished plans form the basis for the reconstruction: one shows the north side of the Jacob's Well Theatre walls in 1786 (illustration 2) and the other shows the Cottage Place tenements erected on its foundations in 1817 (illustration 4). These plans seem to suggest the theatre measured approximately 37ft wide and 62ft long externally, with a theatre cell (stage and auditorium) measuring 31ft wide internally. These dimensions suggest a theatre interior designed on a double-square or cube arrangement with average Regular Theatre dimensions. I hope the reconstruction will demonstrate that the building had 31ft high walls (derived from the 31ft internal width), from the pit passage floor to the roof eaves.

The first deed plan, dated 25 May 1786, shows the land just north of the theatre site, leased to Sarah and Jo Gibbons. The plan partly depicts the northern exterior walls of the theatre labelled in the key as "H - belonging to Old Playhouse" (illustration 2).[30] This plan unfortunately has no accompanying scale, making it difficult to take measurements of the theatre building. The external dimensions of the theatre can, however, be deduced by comparing its depiction in the 1786 deed with the 1817 site plan.[31] This comparison helps convince me the Cottage Place tenements were at least partly erected on the theatre's foundations. The last mention of the theatre survives amongst the same SMV records in a deed dated September 1803 to Samuel Powell, describing the theatre as "ruinous . . . premises . . . heretofore used as a playhouse". Cottage Place was built shortly thereafter.

Comparison of the north side of the theatre with the north side of Cottage Place indicates that the theatre's external dimensions may be measured from the latter. The external dimensions of the tenements numbered 11-15 form a regular rectangle set rather incongruously into the considerably more ad-hoc plan of numbers 1-10 Cottage Place. 1-10 Cottage Place may be a later addition to the former. The walls shown at right angles to the north wall of the theatre compare with the walls shown at right angles to the north wall of the "Wash Houses" in the 1817 plan. Number 1 Cottage Place seems to have been built abutting the theatre's west (or rear) wall.[32] The western corner of number 1 Cottage Place jutted between the two tenements labelled "B" and "E" in the 1786 deed plan. Furthermore, the dimensions of the 11-15 Cottage Place rectangle compare very favourably with the average external dimensions of eighteenth century Regular Theatres.

Accepting, for the moment, numbers 11-15 Cottage Place, with their accompanying wash houses, were built directly on the site of the theatre building, we may begin to deduce the latter's external dimensions from the external dimensions of the former. According to the unreliable scale, the plan of 11-15 Cottage Place forms a rectangle measuring roughly 40ft wide and a little under 64ft long externally; 37ft 6ins wide and 62ft long internally. The scale accompanying the original drawing is irregular, making it impossible to take anything but the roughest of measurements from the plan. However, a deed dated May 1802, showing a "Plan of Property at Jacob's Wells [sic] lately held for the life of George Drew Shewring" immediately adjacent to the south of the theatre site, is scaled more accurately.[33] It shows the southernmost walls of numbers

11-14 Cottage Place, which scale at 61ft long, externally. Assuming the walls of Cottage Place were built on the theatre wall's foundations, these deed plans enable us to conjecture the theatre measured between 61-64ft long and 37ft 6ins-40ft wide.

A document, simply entitled "Jacob's Well Theatre", provides a dimension which may confirm the theatre building's exterior width at 37ft.[34] The document, a transcript in the hand of the nineteenth-century Bristol theatre historian Richard Smith, is a mortgage agreement between John Hippisley and Roger Watts dated "1747 July 31". It recites a lease between George Martin and John Hippisley dated "1736 June 24". This is the only surviving record of any agreement between John Hippisley and George Martin. The SMV archives record no independent agreement between Hippisley and Martin and contain no record of this specific deed. Several mistakes contained in its text suggest that the document is a poor transcript. For example, it recites a deed dated "2nd June 1746" between Hippisley and the SMV. The original of this deed survives in the SMV archives and proves Smith omitted words in his transcript. For example, Smith's phrase "should so long live" replaces the original, more detailed, "shall happen so long to live". The transcript describes the theatre site as "in breadth in the front on or towards the east part thirty seven feet or thereabouts".

All the surviving deeds at the SMV archives, however, prove the theatre site measured 43ft wide. The latter figure is repeated in more than one original document, and may be taken as more accurate and reliable than Smith's transcript. There is reason to assume that Smith mistook the width of the theatre building for the site width. The wording of the paragraph containing the dimension reads:

> All that plot piece or parcel of void ground of him said Martin as the same was then measured alloted and bounded out situate and being in and fronting unto a road or highway leading from the City of Bristol towards Jacob's Well in the parish of Clifton in the County of Gloucester [ ] . . . containing in breadth in the front on or towards the East part thirty seven feet or thereabouts [ ] as the same were then bounded (be it more or less) and extending itself in depth or backwards on or towards the West part ranging along between the Bound Wall of a Garden . . . on or towards the north part and the Bound Wall of a tenement . . . on or towards the south part thereof.

The square brackets indicate the words I believe Smith omitted in his transcript. For example, the registered SMV lease dated 2 June 1746, describing the theatre site, includes, in brackets, the phrase "on which he, the said John Hippisley, hath erected and built a Playhouse or Theatre".[35] If Smith omitted such a phrase in his transcript in my first set of square brackets, the 37ft dimensions might well refer to the width of the theatre building. If my conjecture is correct, the second set of square brackets would then contain a reference to the plot of land on which the theatre was built measuring, as the SMV records prove it did, 43ft wide. It may be no coincidence that the interior width of the rectangle containing numbers 11-15 Cottage Place in the 1817 deed plan scales at 37ft 6ins wide, within 6ins of the 37ft dimension given by the lease-transcript.

It is worth summarising the conclusions reached thus far about the theatre's site and external dimensions. The site measured 135ft long and 43ft wide. In 1817, according to the Cottage Place plan, a passageway running along the south side of the site (within the site limits) measured 4-5ft wide. Comparing the theatre outline depicted in the 1786 deed plan with what seems to be the theatre outline depicted in the 1817 site plan suggests it measured between 61ft-64ft long and 37ft-40ft wide externally. The transcript lease gives "37ft" as a dimension for the theatre width. In the following I will describe one way eighteenth-century builders may have arrived at these dimensions for a theatre like Jacob's Well. This conjectural description rests on the assumption that theatre builders of the day employed *ad-quadratum* geometry in conjunction with the land surveyor's standard unit of measurement: the rod line.

When laying out the plan of the building on the site, the builder probably used either a 16ft 6ins long rod, or a 49ft 6ins long three-rod line. As architectural historians Eileen Harris and Nicholas Savage point out:

> Until quantity surveying became an independent profession in the early nineteenth century, the measuring of building works, upon which contracts and evaluations were made, was performed chiefly by builders.[36]

This method of measuring building works changed very little from those used (according to John Orrell) by the seventeenth century theatre builder Peter Street. In his 1738 "Table of English measures used in Lands and Buildings", William Salmon Jun. lists the 16½ft "Statute Pole or Perch", the same measuring tool used by Street in 1600.[37] The SMV's 1746 *Survey of the Manor of Clifton* properties, including the Jacob's Well theatre site, is measured in a scale of perches. We can imagine the builder of the Jacob's Well Theatre laying out the plot of the building on site in much the same way as John Orrell described Peter Street working on the site of the seventeenth-century Fortune Theatre.[38] It may be no coincidence, therefore, that the Jacob's Well site width of 43ft matches the 43ft stage width of the Elizabethan Fortune Theatre built by Peter Street in 1600.[39] As Orrell explains, builders regarded 43ft as the height, within 1½ins, of an equilateral triangle whose sides are 49ft 6ins or three rods long. Put another way, 43ft is related *ad-triangulum* to 49ft 6ins or the three-rod line.

To diagrammatically reconstruct the Jacob's Well theatre's plan at box level we need to work to two assumptions. First, that all the building's supporting walls measured 1ft 9ins wide, like those theatres at Penzance (1787), Richmond,

Yorkshire (1788) and Truro (1787); and second, that the architect employed *ad-quadratum* geometry and the three rod line to plan the theatre. The builder-architect may have begun, like a land-surveyor, laying out on the ground a 43ft (or 42ft 10ins, in precise *ad-quadratum* terms) wide square. This square plotted the theatre's site width. Describing a circle with sides tangential to the 43ft square enabled the architect to centrally plot the position of a smaller square measuring 30ft 3.75ins wide. The northern and southern sides of the 30ft 3.75ins square are 6ft 3.125ins from the northern and southern site boundaries.

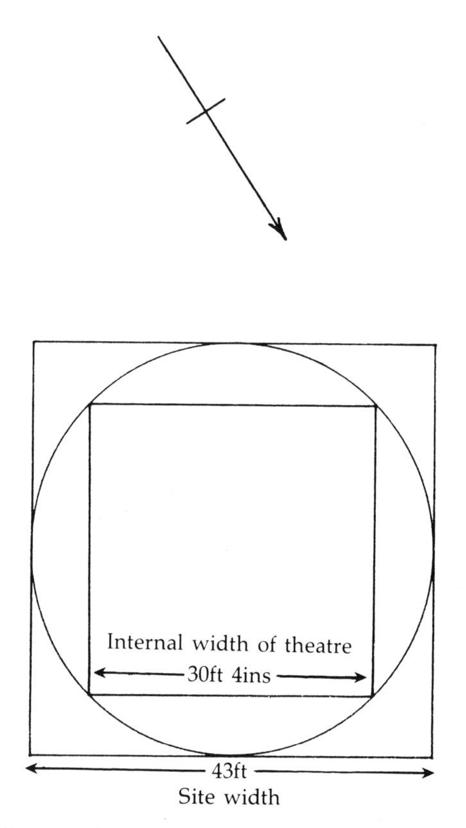


5. Jacob's Well Theatre. Geometry plotting width of site and theatre.

I conjecture that the theatre's stage and auditorium occupied the 30ft 3.75ins wide plot of land, situated centrally within the 43ft wide site. At Truro, Charles Ebdon employed a 30ft x 60ft double square as the basis for his design of a Long Room theatre. On the assumption that the Jacob's Well architect followed the same model, I have diagrammatically reconstructed the theatre's stage and auditorium on a double square pattern measuring 30ft 3.75ins by 60ft 7½ins. In the plan, the northern and southern sides of the 30ft 3.75ins wide square plot the centre lines of the walls surrounding the theatre's auditorium and stage.

The reconstruction enables us to measure the exterior dimensions of the building's plan more precisely. The plan accompanying the 1786 deed (illustration 2) proves the theatre's northern exterior wall stood on the northern site boundary. The south side of the 30ft 3.125ins square plots the central line of the theatre's south wall exactly 36ft 6.875ins from the northern site boundary. This dimension is within 5.125ins of the "37ft or thereabouts" measurement erroneously recorded as the site width in the undated lease-transcript quoted

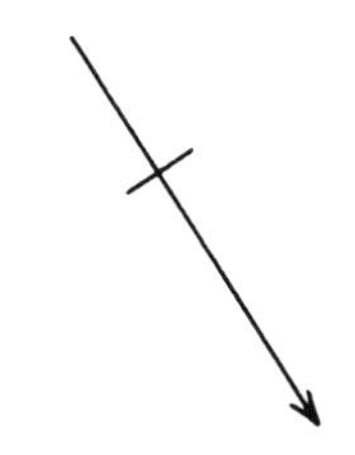

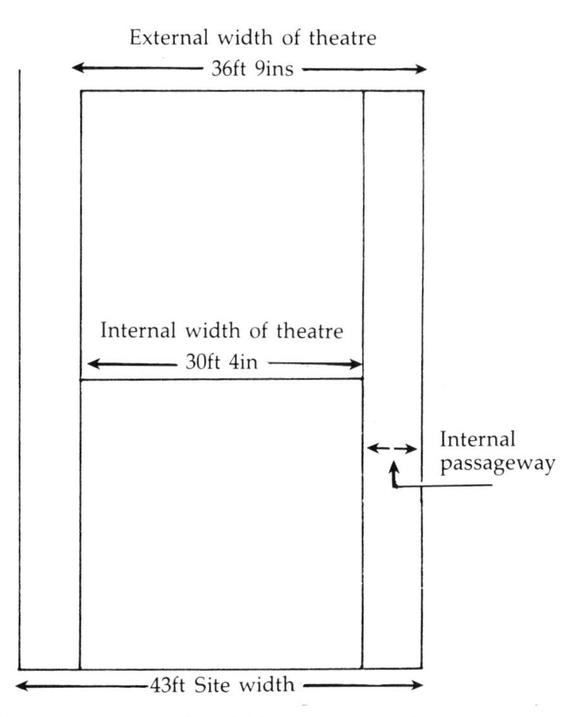


6. Jacob's Well Theatre. Plan showing double-square auditorium and stage.

above. With 1ft 9ins wide exterior walls, the theatre measured 37ft 6ins wide and 62ft long, on a site measuring 43ft wide. This agrees with our conjecture that the lease-transcript erroneously switched the theatre building's width for its site width.

With the central line of the theatre's 1ft 9ins wide exterior walls plotted by the 30ft 3.125ins square, the external side of the theatre's south wall stood exactly 5ft 6ins from the southern site boundary. Therefore, the passageway shown to the south of the theatre in the Cottage Place plan measured 5ft 6ins wide. This is within 6ins of the roughly 5ft measurement scaled from the 1817 deed plan. This lends further circumstantial support to the suggestion that numbers 11–15 Cottage Place were erected on the theatre foundations.

The conjectural reconstruction suggests that within the theatre's exterior walls a passageway ran along the north side of the double-square stage and auditorium.

The plan of Cottage Place supports this conjecture. It shows four wash houses

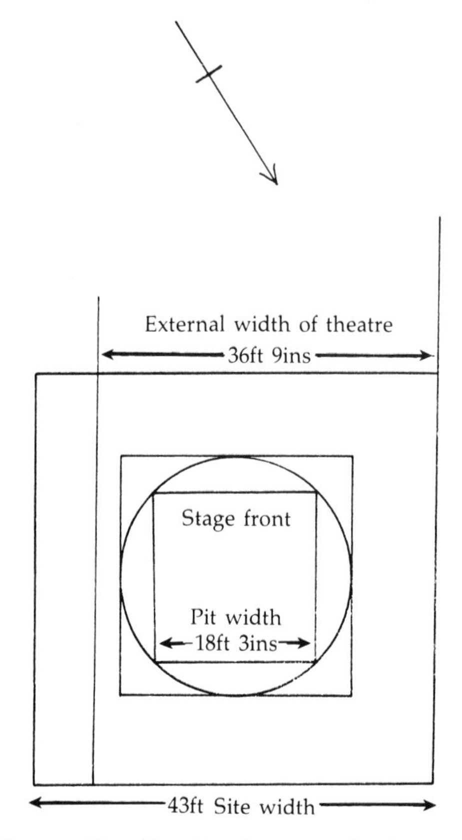


7. Jacob's Well Theatre. Plan showing theatre auditorium on site.

along the northern boundary of the site (illustration 3). According to the plan's scale, the south wall of these wash-houses stands exactly 31ft from the south wall of numbers 11-14 Cottages Place, within 8¼ins of the 30ft 3.75ins wide square which, I am arguing, plotted the width of the stage and auditorium. (It is interesting to note that the northern wall of numbers 11-14 Cottage Place stands centrally between the latter's south wall and the south wall of the wash houses.) Remembering Cottage Place may have been built on the theatre's foundations, it may be worth speculating that the south wall of the wash houses possibly plots the southern limits of a passageway which originally ran east-west along the full length of the theatre's north side. This passage may have been utilised in the theatre for backstage or dressing room space, and staircases to the pit and upper gallery. The interior width of this passageway measured, according to the *ad-quadratum* plan reconstructed above, 3ft 7ins wide internally. (If the north wall of the stage and auditorium measured less than 1ft 9ins wide, the passageway may, of course, have been wider.)

We can summarise the information about the theatre interior as follows: the theatre walls measured 1ft 9ins wide. In width, the theatre building measured 37ft 6ins externally, with a stage and auditorium measuring 28ft 6ins internally, identical to the long room-theatre at Truro. The theatre measured 62ft long externally and 58ft 6ins internally. A passageway to the north of the auditorium and stage, possibly used for backstage space, measured at least 3ft 7ins wide internally. A door in the north end of the passageway clearly marked in the 1786 deed plan gave access to the theatre from the street (illustration 2).

The architect could also use the *ad-quadratum* geometry plotting the theatre walls to plot the position of the boxes and pit - the theatre's interior arrangement. In conjecturally reconstructing the theatre's interior I adhere closely to the model at Richmond, Yorkshire.[40]

A 25ft 9½ins square (related *ad-triangulum* to the 30ft 3.75ins wide square plotting the north and south walls of the stage and auditorium) plots the position of the rear walls of the side boxes. An 18ft 3ins square (related *ad-quadratum* to the 25ft 9½ins square) plots the pit width and depth (illustration 7).

A rectangle proportioned on a 3:2 width-to-depth ratio, measuring 28ft 6ins internal width by 19ft deep, plots the stage depth from the rear stage wall to the upstage side of the proscenium doors. This proportion follows seventeenth-century theatre models. (At the surviving regular theatre built at Penzance in 1787, the 3:2 width-to-depth ratio of the stage also reaches from the theatre's rear exterior wall. This contrasts with the stage depth at Richmond, Yorkshire, which reaches from stairwells giving access to understage dressing rooms some three feet from the rear wall.[41]) This geometry suggests that the distance from the curtain line to the stage front (the forestage) measured 10ft 3ins deep. A 59ft diameter circle, centred on the forestage 3ft 9ins from the stage front, plots the position of the rear wall of the front boxes (illustration 8).

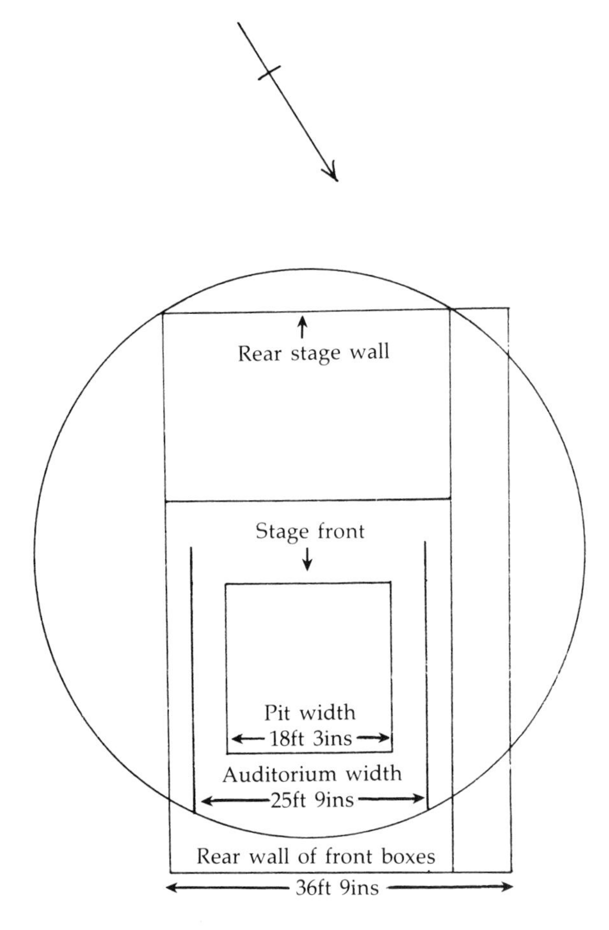


8. Jacob's Well Theatre. Plan showing geometrical arrangement.

We can apply the same geometry to the conjectural reconstruction of the sectional drawings. The 25ft 9½ins circle which plotted the auditorium width marks the pit passage floor (illustrations 10 and 11). The square which marks the pit width and depth in the plan plots the lowest level of the pit floor in the section. The highest level of the pit floor and the top level of the lowest gallery balustrade are plotted by a square measuring 12ft 11ins, related *ad-quadratum* to the 18ft 3ins wide pit. A 9ft 1½ins wide square, related *ad-quadratum* to the 12ft 11ins wide square, plots the position of the lowest gallery, box and stage floor levels. Finally, a 6ft 5½ins square related *ad-quadratum* to the 9ft 1½ins square plots the distance between the posts supporting the upper gallery. At Jacob's Well, the stage front stands exactly 29ft 6ins from the internal side of the theatre's west wall

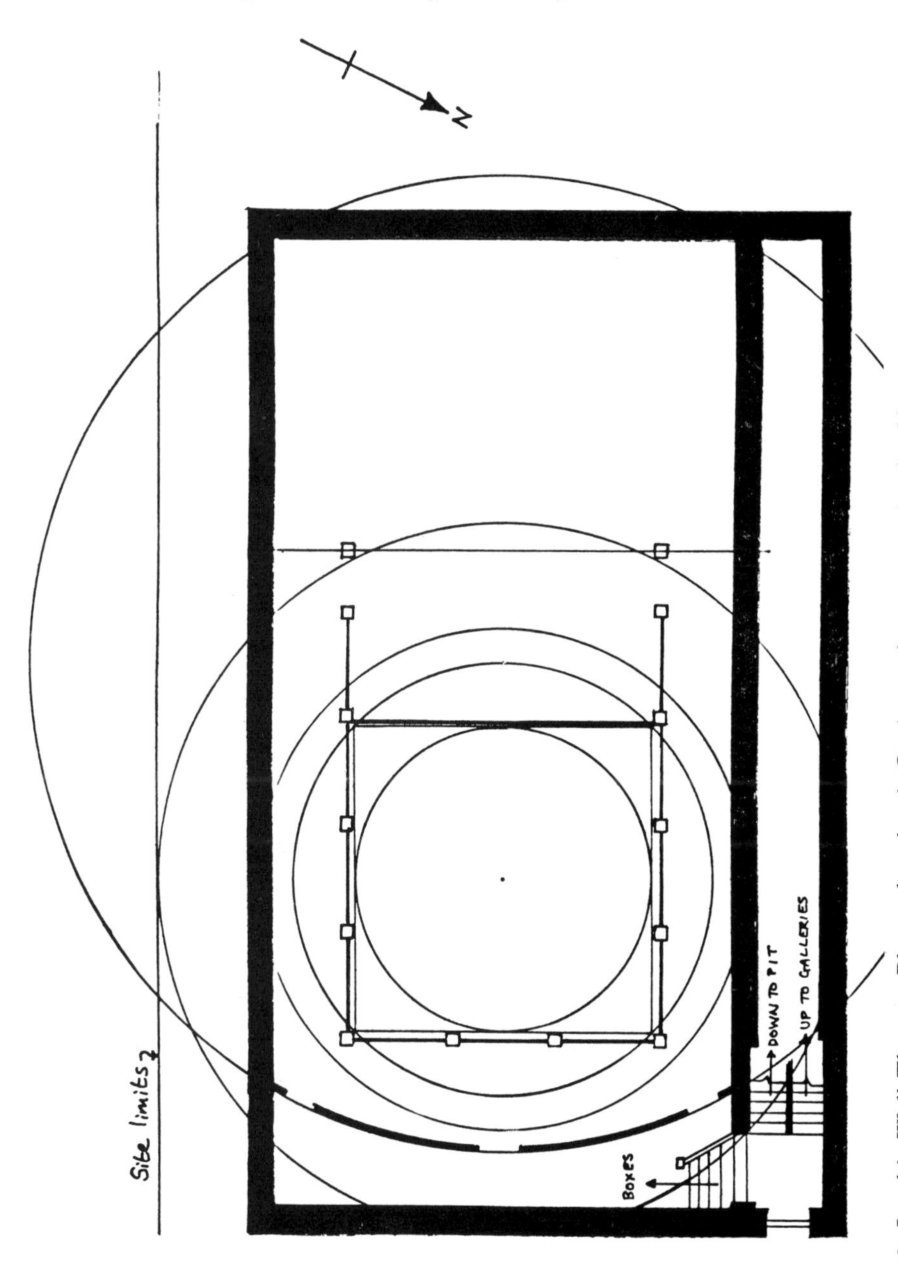


9. Jacob's Well Theatre. Plan at box level. Conjectural reconstruction by M. Howell.

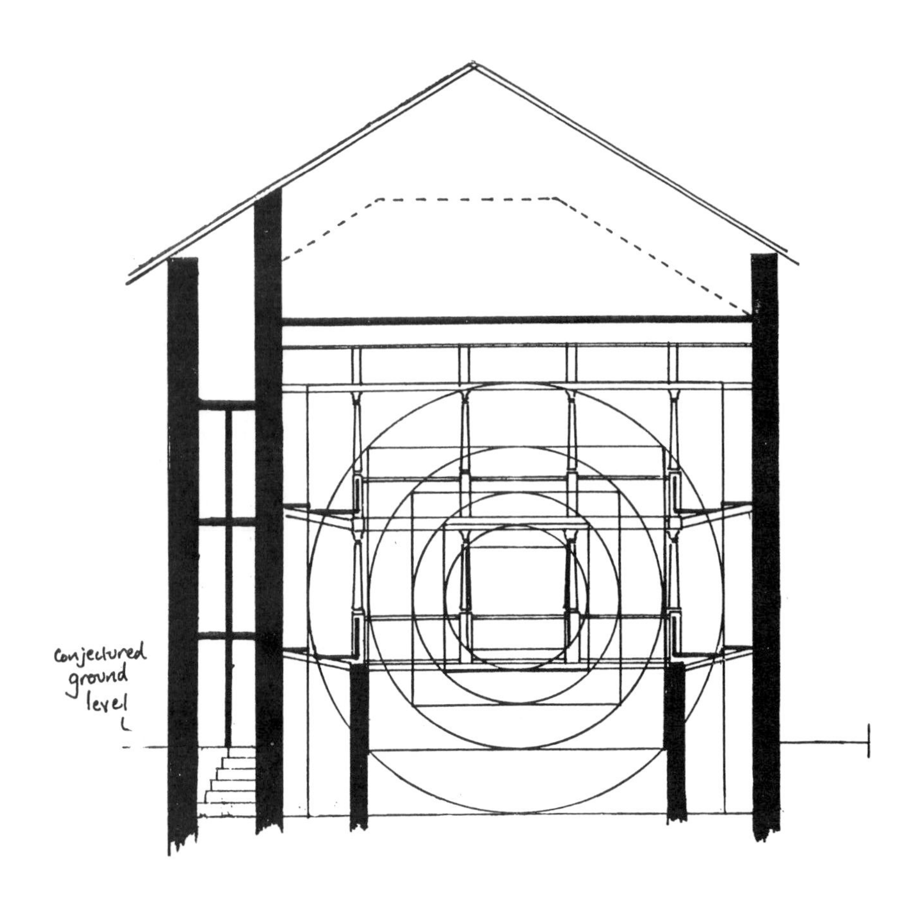


10. Jacob's Well Theatre. Cross section, looking towards auditorium. Conjectural reconstruction by M. Howell.

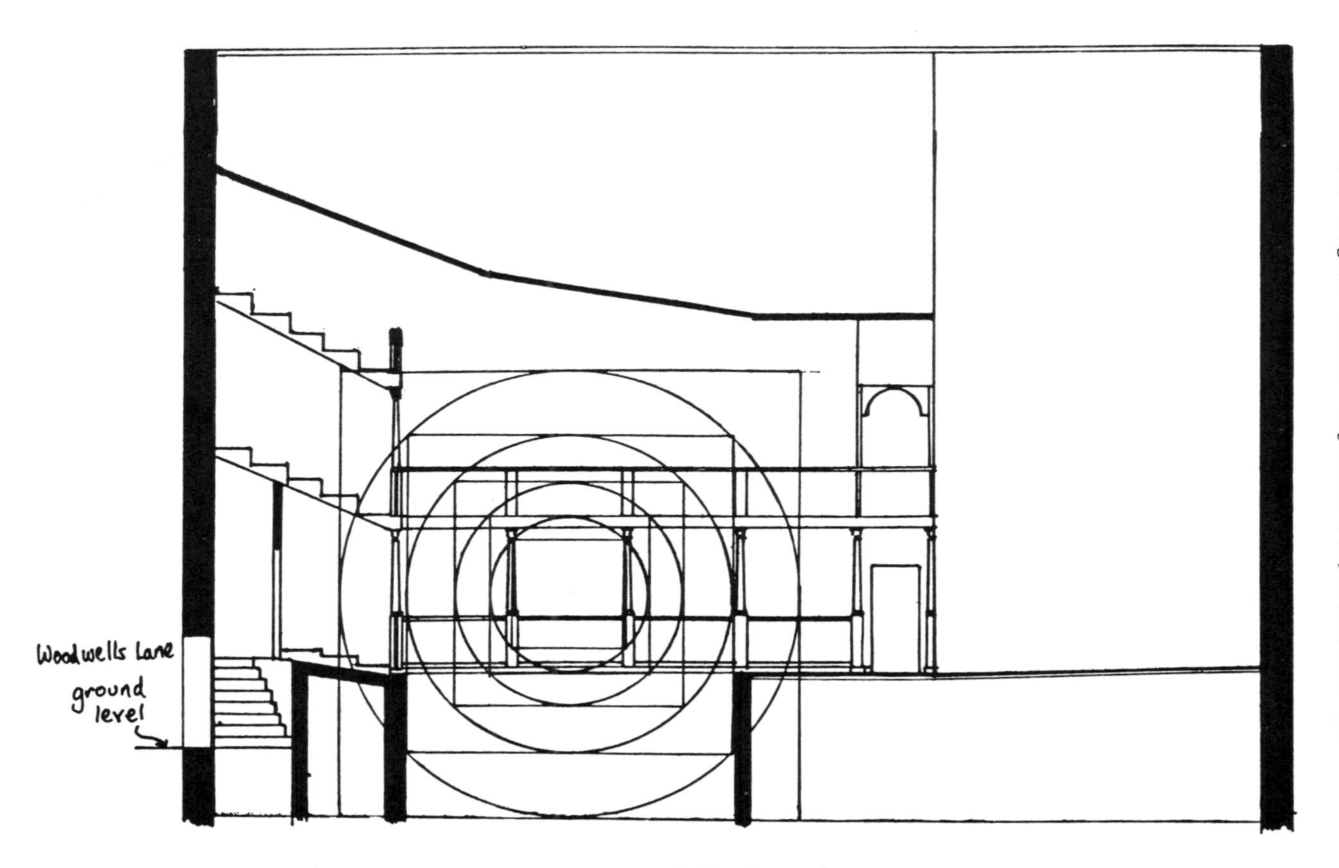


11. Jacob's Well Theatre. Longitudinal section facing south. Conjectural reconstruction by Mark Howell.

and 29ft from the internal side of the theatre's east wall.

The nineteenth-century historian Richard Jenkins' account of the theatre at Jacob's Well provides the only eye-witness description of its interior. The account bears out the diagrammatic reconstruction proposed here.

> The hall or that part allotted for the accommodation of the audience formed three sides of a square, consisting of one large front and four smaller side boxes, front and side galleries and an upper gallery . . . There was not any upper tier of boxes, but one of the side galleries was called the balcony, and over the stage door, in the proscenium, were two small boxes.[42]

The transcript deed which provided the 37ft dimension for the theatre's width includes a reference to "the Scenes Machines Curtains Decorations Boxes Seats and furniture and appurtenances whatsoever to such play house or Theatre belonging [sic]". Beyond this I know of no other evidence to colour the bare walls of the reconstruction of what was once such a popular theatre venue.

The main differences from the theatre at Richmond, Yorkshire, can be summed up as follows. Richmond has a single gallery, Jacob's Well probably had two. The second may have been added in 1747 when Bristol newspapers reported the theatre "greatly enlarged", though no direct evidence confirms this conjecture. I have drawn in a possible position for this upper gallery in the sectional drawings (illustrations 10 & 11). It is plotted by the 25ft 9½ins wide circle which also plots the width of the auditorium in the plan. The earliest of the thirty-nine surviving playbills for the Jacob's Well theatre dates from 1752. They all list a "balcony" separate from a "gallery".[43] This upper gallery may have formed a third tier without side balconies. Nothing more is known about the physical appearance of the theatre of Jacob's Well beyond the evidence used in the reconstruction here.

## Appendix 1[44]

*Plan dimensions of Regular Theatres and Long Rooms*
(All dimensions external, in feet and inches):

| *Date* | *Site* | *Building type* | *Dimensions* |
|---|---|---|---|
| c1660–c1742 | Liverpool | THEATRE | 50 x 20 |
| 1690 | Winchester | LONG ROOM | 56 x 25 |
| 1713 | King's Lynn | GREAT HALL | 107 x 29 |
| 1721 | Bristol | LONG ROOM | 90 x 35 |
| 1723 | Bath | THEATRE | 50 x 25 |

| | | | |
|---|---|---|---|
| 1727 | Wakefield | LONG ROOM | 62 x 22 |
| 1729 | Bristol | THEATRE | 62 x 37 |
| 1733 | Wells | BARN | 44 x 22 |
| c1744 | Stourhead | LONG ROOM | 60 x 30 |
| 1750 | Bath | THEATRE | 60 x 40 |
| 1751 | Bath | LONG ROOMS | |
| | | Harrison's (Simpson's) | 61.5 x 29 |
| | | Lindsey's (Wiltshire's) | 85 x 29 |
| 1758 | Plymouth | THEATRE | 68 x 32 |
| 1764 | Colchester | THEATRE | 63′ 9″ x 38′ 4″ |
| 1779 | Margate | THEATRE | 65 long |
| 1781 | Worcester | THEATRE | 66 x 36 |
| 1787 | Penzance | THEATRE | 67′ 3″ x 29′ 3″ |
| 1787 | Truro | LG. RM.-THEATRE | 63 x 28.5 |
| 1788 | Richmond, Yorks | THEATRE | 67.5 x 28 |
| 1788 | Ipswich | THEATRE | 81 x 40 |
| c1790 | Bedale | LONG ROOM | "Held 20" |
| 1792 | Ripon | THEATRE | 63 x 30 |
| 1793 | Wisbech | THEATRE | 65 x 28 |
| 1795 | Grantham | THEATRE | 52.5 x 29.5 |

*Average dimensions*

| | |
|---|---|
| Long Rooms and Regular Theatres | = 65′ 7.5″ x 30′ |
| Long Rooms | = 67′ 7″ x 24′ 9″ |
| Regular Theatres | = 65′ 9″ x 30′ 10″ |

## Appendix 2

*Plan dimensions of Theatres Royal (1737-88)*

(All dimensions external, in feet and inches, unless otherwise stated. The phrase "theatre cell" refers to the auditorium and stage with the box passages, exclusive of extra dressing rooms or rear stage space beyond these.)

| *Date* | *Site* | *Patent* | *Dimensions* |
|---|---|---|---|
| 1758 | Norwich | 1768 | 60 x 103 (site) |
| 1765 | York | 1769 | ? |
| 1765 | Richd. Sy. | 1737 | 53 x 110 int. |
| | | | 56 x 112 |
| | Theatre cell | | 38 x 74 int. |
| | | | 40 x 77 ext. |

| | | | |
|---|---|---|---|
| 1766 | Bristol | 1778 | 48.5 x 115 int. |
| | | | 55 x 120 ext. |
| | Theatre cell | | 48.5 x 98 int. |
| | | | 55 x 103 ext. |
| | | | 43 high |
| 1766 | Bath | 1768 | 43 x 84 int. |
| | | | 48 x 88 ext. |
| 1768 | Edinburgh | 1768 | 51.5 x 103 int. |
| | | | 57 x 108 ext. |
| | | | 30 high |
| ?1769 | Hull | 1769 | ? |
| 1772 | Liverpool | 1771 | ? |
| 1775 | Manchester | 1775 | 48 x 102 |
| 1786 | Margate | 1786 | ? |
| 1788 | Newcastle | 1788 | 54 x 120 |

*Average dimensions*

Theatres Royal = 107′ 6″ x 54′

# Notes

1. Only ten were built between 1737 and 1788. These were at Bath, Norwich, York, Hull, Liverpool, Manchester, Chester, Bristol, Margate and Newcastle. After 1788, when local authorities were again allowed to license theatres, Birmingham was the last provincial Theatre Royal granted a Royal Patent before 1811. See John Raithby ed., *Statutes at Large of England and Great Britain: From Magna Carta to the Union of the Kingdoms of Great Britain and Ireland*, London, 1811, V, 267 and IX, 16-17.

2. This challenges Sybil Rosenfeld and Allardyce Nicoll, *The Garrick Stage*, Manchester, 1980, 23, who described a "model" theatre of 1740-80 measuring "about 120ft long by some 50ft wide". This erroneous model only refers to Theatres Royal.

3. *The Globe Restored*, Oxford, 1968, 2nd ed., 83-4.

4. Kathleen Barker, *Bristol at Play*, Bristol, 1976, 5-11 and *The Theatre Royal, Bristol, 1766-1966: Two Centuries of Stage History*, London, Society for Theatre Research, 1974, 4-5 provide the most recent and academic records of the theatre's history. Barker's work is reprinted in a variety of local history pamphlets, including Patrick McGrath's excellent *Bristol in the Eighteenth Century*, Bristol, 1972. Ch. 10 of Sybil Rosenfeld, *Strolling Players and Drama in the Provinces*, Cambridge, 1939, is the only detailed account of the theatre's surviving account books. (The nineteenth-century historian John Latimer bound these together: during the eighteenth century they were a set of eight separate volumes.) Richard Jenkins, *Memoirs of the Bristol Stage*, Bristol 1826, includes the only possibly eye-witness account of the theatre; John Latimer, *Annals of Bristol in the Eighteenth Century*, Bristol, 1893, relates the theatre's part in his authoritative history of Bristol; M. E. Board, *The Story of the Bristol Stage*, London, 1926, G. Rennie Powell, *The Bristol Stage - Its Story*, Bristol, 1919, and Guy Tracey Watts, *Theatrical Bristol*, Bristol, 1915, all include more

anecdotal accounts of the theatre's history.

5. Bristol Central Reference Library 11204.

6. *Essay Towards a Description of Bath*, Bath, 1749, 445-446.

7. Raithby, *Statutes at Large*, 1811, IX, 16-17.

8. Barker, *Bristol at Play*, 5.

9. Barker, *Theatre Royal, Bristol*, 5.

10. Bryan Little, *The City and County of Bristol: A Study of Atlantic Civilisation*, Bristol, 1967, 230-237.

11. See McGrath, *Bristol in the Eighteenth Century*.

12. Richard Smith, "Bristol Theatre" I, ms. coll., Bristol Reference Library 7976.

13. Barker, *Theatre Royal, Bristol*, 30.

14. George Heath, *Bristol Guide*, Bristol 1797, 198.

15. Heath 197-9.

16. Barker, *Bristol at Play*, 4. Rosenfeld, *Strolling Players* 45, 170.

17. *Farley's Bristol News*, 19 July 1726, reports a "great concert of vocal and instrumental music at the Great Room near the Hotwell".

18. Tracing the origins of eighteenth-century provincial theatre buildings to Long Rooms questions the standard assumption that West End Theatres Royal provided the sole model for all provincial playhouses. The evidence for this assumption - largely from newspapers and tourist diaries - is scarce and ambiguous. In 1741, for example, John Arthur declared his new York theatre "the model of those in London" (Tate Wilkinson, *The Wandering Patentee* II, 1795, repr. 1973, 209-11). Kathleen Barker always doubted the evidence that the Theatre Royal Bristol was modelled on Drury Lane (*The Theatre Royal, Bristol* 10). In his diary, the eighteenth century tourist Sylas Neville described the Norwich Theatre Royal, built in 1758, as "a miniature Drury Lane" (Basil Cozens Hardy, *The Diary of Sylas Neville, 1768*-1788, 54, qtd. by D. H. Eshleman, *The Committee Books of the Theatre Royal, Norwich, 1768*-1825, London, Society for Theatre Research, 1970, 15. A set of 1923 photographs show the interior decoration of the Truro Assembly Room-Theatre compared with the decoration of the 1775 Drury Lane. See Mark A. Howell, "Planning Provincial Theatres Under the Stage Licensing Act", *Theatre Notebook XLIII*, 1989, 104-119. I know of no other evidence more specifically linking the designs of Regular or Royal provincial theatre buildings to West End models.

19. After 1742 many more editions survive from which, along with the theatre's account books and the surviving collection of Jacob's Well playbills in Smith, "Bristol Theatre", I compiled a "Calender of Performances for the Jacob's Well Theatre", now deposited in Bristol Reference Library, uncatalogued.

20. The following is taken from the SMV Archives "Register of Leases" and deeds in Box 9 bundle 17 (for the King and Martin deeds pre 1723), box 9, bundle 18 (for Hippisley's deed) and box 9a bundle 20 (for the site history from 1803).

21. SMV Archives Box 9 bundle 18. Also SMV "Register of Leases", I, ms., 303-309. Elizabeth Ralph, *Guide to the Archives of the Merchant Venturers*, Bristol, 1988, catalogues all the SMV Archives cited here under the title "The Manor of Clifton".

22. King was a merchant. The evidence suggests that he, like Martin, wanted to develop the whole area.

23. SMV Box 9a bundle 20.

24. SMV Box 9 bundle 18.

25. SMV "Register of Leases" II, 21 Aug. 1785. The same reference states that the SMV accepted Green's surrender of the theatre lease on the same date.

26. SMV Box 9a bundle 21.

27. John Latimer, *The Annals of Bristol During the Eighteenth Century* II, Bristol, 1900, 64.

28. Bristol University Theatre Collection, Box 40 "Provincial Eighteenth Century Theatre". Kathleen Barker transcribed notes of a lecture Turner delivered to the Bristol branch of the Society for Theatre Research in 1951. I presume these are now deposited at Bristol University Theatre Collection. The transcription adds nothing to the information given here.

29. The plan of the theatre at Richmond, Yorkshire, comprises a double square measuring 28ft wide externally and 56ft long from the exterior side of the rear stage wall to the rear wall of the front boxes and 28ft high, from the stage floor to the lowest part of the timbers forming the stage roof. The theatre interior measures 24ft high (from pit passage floor to auditorium ceiling), 24ft wide internally and 48ft long (from upstage side of the 3:2 rectangle plotting the upstage depth, to the rear wall of the front boxes). Beyond this the box lobby measures 3ft 6ins at its narrowest and 6ft 6ins at its deepest. See, Mark A. Howell, "The Theatre at Richmond, Yorkshire: New Evidence and Conjectures", *Theatre Notebook* XLVI 1992, 30-41. Charles Ebdon inscribed one of his proposal drawings for the Long Room theatre at Truro "60 x 30". See Howell, "Planning Provincial Theatres", plate 2.

30. SMV Box 19 bundle 9.

31. SMB Box 9a bundle 20.

32. This encourages me to speculate the theatre walls may have survived demolition and been retained for the external walls of some of 11-15 Cottage Place.

33. SMV, Box 9a bundle 21.

34. Richard Smith, "Jacobs Well Theatre and Other Manuscripts Relating to the Bristol Stage", ms. coll., Bristol Central Reference Library 13011.

35. SMV "Register of Leases" I, 303, SMV Box 9 bundle 18.

36. *British Architectural Books and Writers, 1556-1788*, Cambridge, 1990, 41.

37. *Palladio Londinensis*, 1738, 2nd ed., 40.

38. John Orrell, *The Quest for Shakespeare's Globe*, Cambridge, 1983, 113-117. Iain Mackintosh, *Architect, Actor and Audience*, London, 1993, 159ff, implies that the *ad quadratum* "mystery" can be found in plans for theatre buildings from Shakespeare's time to the present day.

39. Orrell, *Quest*, 113.

40. Howell, "Richmond", *Theatre Notebook* XLVI, 1992.

41. 1986 survey drawings of the surviving Penzance Theatre (1787) at the Union Hotel have been made by the architectural firm Drewitt and Drewitt, of Penzance. I was given very limited access to these copyrighted drawings and not allowed permission to reproduce them here. Research on the Penzance theatre is being conducted locally with the aim its restoration. Richard Hosley, "The Shape and Size of the Third Globe", *The Third Globe: Symposium for a Reconstruction of the Globe Playhouse* (Wayne State University 1986, p. 97, ed. by C. Walter Hodges, S. Schoenbaum and Leone found the stages of three seventeenth century theatres - the Fortune, the stage set up in Wool Hall and the plan by Inigo Jones now regarded as the Drury Lane cockpit - were all proportioned on a width-depth ratio of 3:2.

42. *Memoirs of the Bristol Stage*, 1826, 8-9.

43. Smith, "Bristol Theatre" I.

44. See Mark A. Howell "Long, Regular and Royal Rooms: Three Eighteenth Century Provincial Theatres", M.Litt. Dissertation, University of Bristol, 1992, 175-7 listing sources of dimensions given here and in Appendix 2.

# Sarah Baker: The Making of a "Character"

J. S. BRATTON

THEATRE, we are often told, is an evanescent art, its most impressive moments vanishing and leaving not a wrack behind. This is of course an exaggeration, like most theatrical cliches; vestiges of theatrical activity are often left, even after the empty drinks cans and the scribbled-over scripts have been thrown away, and the run has opened and closed. The prompt copies, the playbills, the pictures, the leases, the wills, the contracts, and most monumentally the memoirs, remain for historians to pore over and to use in constructing their versions of the work of even quite minor figures in the theatre. For the most insignificant players were public people, noticed and remembered and written about while untold numbers of their contemporaries have gone unrecorded. But how these individuals are remembered, the purposes for which their stories are told, and the kinds of history into which they are made, are by no means simple matters. What contemporary critics, nineteenth-century mythologisers or moralists and twentieth-century antiquarians have made of, say, David Garrick or Ellen Terry are discrete and several histories; and we now come to read all of them as material for another story of our own. In the process, even the generally agreed outline, the teleology of patriarchal/late-capitalist meanings, may be called into question.

My re-reading is of the story of Sarah Baker née Wakelin, 1736/7-1816, whose life work was a circuit of theatres in and around Kent. Hers was a not-unusual success story in the latter half of the eighteenth century, when it was possible to run a provincial theatre circuit with profit, offering as she did a judicious mixture of entertainments to suit most tastes, and managing the frequency and duration of the company's visits to its various locations to match the size and enthusiasm of the prospective audience. In this way a collection of medium-sized and small towns - in this case Canterbury, Rochester, Faversham, Tunbridge Wells and Maidstone, with the occasional addition of Dover, Margate, Folkstone, Deal, Sandwich and the village of Ore near Hastings - could be regularly visited by a company of modest numbers on decent salaries, travelling with their own scenery and even their own scenic artists, musicians and stage staff. Like many such ventures, this was a family business, with a high proportion of the company related to the proprietor: Sarah employed her three children Henry, Ann and Sarah, her sister Mary, her cousin Mr Ireland (as bandmaster) and his son Henry. Actors of some distinction passed through the Kentish company at various stages of their careers: Harley, Fawcett and Edmund Kean were employed by her as beginners, William Dowton came as a hired actor and married into the family, to Sarah junior, before passing on to Covent Garden and later returning, when Sarah senior wished to retire, to lease the seven theatres from her and run the circuit. Thomas Dibdin spent several seasons with her, his wife becoming a close friend of Mary Wakelin and her executor; Thomas lived to write Sarah Baker's epitaph. The audiences who remembered her and her company included Charles Dickens, who had his first experience of Shakespeare in her theatre at Rochester;[1] and the occasional stars whom the proximity of London enabled her to engage for short visits included George Frederick Cooke, Jack Palmer, Incledon, Charles Mathews, Emery, Dorothy Jordan and Grimaldi.

She created the circuit from scratch. Born into a fairground family, she was the daughter of Ann Wakelin, an acrobatic dancer who billed herself and her company of rope-dancers and tumblers as "of Sadler's Wells". Sarah married an acrobat in her mother's company who died around 1769. She became a puppeteer, travelling round the fairs of eastern England with her young family until 1772, when she announced a Sadler's Wells Company of entertainers – clowns, tumblers, rope-dancers and pantomimists – under her own management opening at Canterbury. On her mother's retirement in 1777 Sarah extended her company's repertoire to include legitimate comedy and tragedy, and set about building her circuit into a successful rival to the other Kentish managements.

The theatres she erected grew steadily from tents and fit-ups to substantial buildings with dwelling-houses attached to them for her own use and to let; they were made to a single, simple design, a rectangular space with little adornment inside or out, and a single entrance at which the owner took all the money herself, exactly as in a fairground theatre. The twin managerial pitfalls of provincial circuit theatre – on the one hand meanness, neglect and inadequacy of performances, and on the other extravagance and over-ambition in building or hiring novelties – were both avoided, and her theatres were created and run on the strength of her own energy and acumen, with no burden of debt, inflated pretensions or civic expectations. In 1815 she retired, and made her will, leaving a substantial invested and real estate above and beyond the seven theatres, altogether worth more than £15,000. This is the bare outline of her work, as extracted from contemporary records by Norma Hodgson in 1952.[2]

Norma Hodgson intended, by her careful antiquarianism, to give Sarah Baker her proper prominence, and gain recognition for her achievements. She did not succeed. Mrs Baker remains in the marginal position which history found for her right from the beginning. Hodgson prefaces her story with a tellingly phrased observation – Sarah Baker was, she says, "a singularly entertaining old character" (p. 65), but the real facts of her career are hard to come by. Of course this is no accident; the details of her career that were interesting when the memoirs were written were not those to do with "her achievements as one of the most successful circuit proprietors of her day" (p. 65) but explicitly to do with constructing her as a "character"; and it is as a character that she was built into the foundations of modern theatre history. To remove her, and to insist instead upon understanding the reasons and procedures for the marginalisation of a successful independent woman in the theatre, might – just might – begin to undermine the whole edifice.

I will begin my reading with an elucidation of the "character". The term is connected, obviously enough, both with moral and historical biography – the historical tradition that records the "lives of great men", generalised as exemplary in works such as Theophrastus' *Characters* – and with the stage; its use to designate an odd or eccentric person was new in Sarah Baker's day. The development of a new sense to a word is always likely to indicate a new cultural development; and moreover it may not be irrelevant that to the classically educated the delineation of characters has as its root sense the art of writing itself, being derived from a Greek word meaning an engraving tool or stamp. It therefore stresses the capacity to name, brand or fix meanings by the use of the pen, through sign and symbol. The theatrical "character" has been a trope in British theatre history since it began in earnest in the early nineteenth century, with the work of Genest and Collier.[3] There was a marked outburst of such mythologising, not confined to the theatre but also attempting to fix the "character" of the gentleman, the Englishman and various other types, in the 1830s.[4] At this point the battle for control of the voice of the stage was part of the more general Radical thrust to free British culture from aristocratic definition. In the heady days leading up to the 1832 Reform Acts the theatre was given a history that would make it too fit for Reform; and over the ensuing decades gentlemanly writers worked hard to refashion their new preserve in their own likeness. In the writings of such gentleman-scholars as Collier and campaigners like Lytton, the new work of middle-class self-definition created Shakespeare the professional writer and made him the representative of the Radical intelligentsia and their right to possession of the theatre (see Lytton's speech to the House of Commons, moving for a Select Committee on the state of the drama, on 31 May 1832, a bare fortnight after the Reform crisis broke). The current possessors of the theatres were cast as aristocratic villains or their toadies, whose corrupt exploitation of profits and performances was a scandal that Free Trade, a fair field and no favour, would immediately abolish. Lower class individuals who were manifestly not part of Old Corruption could be claimed as forebears or supporters of the new hegemony, but only when the class characteristics of their style had been carefully distanced from the educated gentlemen who wished to represent themselves as leading the profession. This illegitimate stagecraft included the appearance of women on and about the stage in positions of influence and power. The literary, legitimate aspirations of the new professionals would rescue the stage from these undiscriminating and sometimes dubiously moral entertainers and restore it to its proper and articulate function. The new, modern theatre was to be the theatre descended from Shakespeare's Globe, not from Astley's and Andrew Ducrow; but such stalwarts were found a niche, as guarantors of the popular roots of their educated heirs - as "characters". So Dickens edited/rewrote the memoirs of Grimaldi in 1838, as well as fixing in his journalism and novels the quaint picture of Ducrow that has been handed down, and of various old theatres in and outside London, including Sarah Baker's theatre at Rochester, his home town. "Muster Richardson" the travelling penny showman and W. G. Ross singing "Sam Hall" in the low taverns off the Strand became picturesque fixtures in Victorian visions of Regency pleasures. Vincent Crummles was born.

More urgently, before Mr Punch's cohorts got to work, individuals who had actually been part of the old theatres wrote themselves a respectable history, in memoirs that enshrined the late-eighteenth-century provincial theatre, where they had their beginnings, as a story of long ago and far away. Tate Wilkinson was probably the earliest such writer, who seems to have worked very hard, in his eccentric memoirs, at setting *himself* up as a character, one whom his readers will find amusing and original, and therefore forgive for his lack of scholarly method and gentlemanly reserve in writing about himself and his social and theatrical triumphs with such prolixity. He mocks his own pretensions to be a writer, to produce "Wilkinson's Works" bound in half calf and shelved beside Shakespeare, and deprecates his own aspirations to be anything more than a poor actor and provincial patentee. In 1827 Thomas Dibdin told his own story more seriously, detailing his life's work in a period during which it grew steadily more difficult for the working man of the theatre to identify himself and his status. It is in his work, especially, but also in the Grimaldi memoir as edited by Dickens and in the various memoirs of Charles Mathews written by Anne Mathews, his widow, in an attempt to secure his memory as a star, a gentleman and a connoisseur, that we find the "character" of the "Sole Autocratrix of the Kentish Drama", Sarah Baker.[5]

What, then, are the elements of this "character"? The first point most make seems to be that she was illiterate. Dibdin reports her (p. 94) as unable to prompt efficiently, because of the "hard words" in the text. On closer inspection, however, the "hard words" prove to be "fictitious Greek" in Hannah Cowley's farce *Who's the Dupe?*. This is a play full of somewhat fustian jokes about language, with a polyglot, often nonsensical text, culminating in a verbal duel between two pretenders to classical learning. So the subtext of the anecdote could be that while the bluestocking Cowley may have been sufficiently unwomanly to make such allusions, the sterling lower-class Sarah had not trespassed upon that preserve of masculine gentility, the classical education. Dibdin elaborates his report of her difficulty with her letters well beyond what might seem to be either credible or necessary:

> The indefatigable priestess of Thalia and Melpomene went every morning to market, and kept the box-book, on which always lay a massy silver ink-stand, which, with a superb pair of silver trumpets, several cups, tankards, and candlesticks of the same pure metal, it was the lady's honest pride to say she had paid for with her own hard earnings: she next manufactured the daily play-bill, by the help of scissors, needle, thread, and a collection of old bills; cutting a play from one, an interlude from another, a farce from a third, and sewed them neatly together; and thus precluded the necessity of pen and ink. (pp. 95-6)

The opening irony, mixing classical allusion and homely modernity, is a commonplace mock-heroic trope of the times, the basis of much theatrical burlesque, whose most familiar expression is probably in Hogarth's "Actresses Dressing in a Barn". I will return to the question of the itemised articles of plate. Norma Hodgson notes (p. 79) the contradiction in the information that Mrs Baker could keep the boxbook, but she could not write out the bills. One might infer some confirmation of the idea that she was, at least, a reluctant writer, from the evidence of the surviving correspondence of James Winston, in connection with his compilation of his survey of English provincial theatres, *The Theatric Tourist* (London 1805). He wrote to Sarah Baker, and had no reply. He then wrote to Thomas Younger, a member of her company, in whose reply of November 22 1803 (preserved in the Birmingham Central Library) there occurs the following:

> Mrs B. requests me to apologize for her not answering Your letter - by saying that it was by some means mislaid - and consequently forgotten - She tells me she has no objection to give me (for You) every information She can - therefore I have no doubt I shall be able to procure every particular You Wish . . .

Dibdin's point is not simply that she was only marginally literate, however; just as he enjoys the juxtaposition of marketing and Melpomene, he relishes the substitution of needle and thread, the tools of feminine domesticity, for the masculine managerial pen.

The matter of the "lady's honest pride" in keeping her earnings in the tangible form of silver plate is another of the apparently important aspects of her as a "character". All accounts of her stress the personal control which she maintained over her money: Anne Mathews' first words about her are that she was "a potentate of great authority, and at one time supposed to be extremely wealthy" (p. 36), which she attributes to the practice of "trusting no hand but her own to touch a shilling". She ironically recommends Mrs Baker's habit to "greater lessees, and more *losing* speculators", but her anecdotes of Mrs Baker's willingness to accept any payment from anybody, and her perpetual bustle about her own business, make clear the vulgarity of such concerns in her eyes. Both

Dibdin and Grimaldi (or Dickens in Grimaldi's voice) describe Mrs Baker as running out of ways of investing her earnings. According to Dibdin:

> No individual ever persevered more industriously or more successfully in getting money than Mrs Baker, who, as fast as she realized cash, laid it out in purchasing or building the several theatres she died possessed of. . . . she knew so little what to do with her honest gains . . . that, after vesting sums in country banks, and in the hands of respectable tradesmen at perhaps 3 per cent, and in some cases no per cent at all, with a view to its being safer than in her own hands, – she still retained considerable sums in *rouleaux* in her house and about her person. Incredible as it may appear, she had an insurmountable distrust of the Bank of England, and could never be brought to comprehend why her money would be safer or more productive there than elsewhere.

Dibdin claims to have converted her to more sensible views of cash as capital rather than currency, when she mislaid several spiceboxes full of guineas, and he was able to persuade her into buying stock. The Grimaldi memoirs, having no such personal claim to prefer, simply convert financial naivete to the nearest comic stereotype – than of the miser:

> She never put her money out at interest, or employed it in any speculative or profitable manner, but kept it in six or eight large punch-bowls, which always stood upon the top shelf of a bureau, except when she was disposed to make herself particularly happy, and then she would take them down singly, and after treating herself with a sly look at the contents, would put them up again. (p. 116)

Setting aside the impracticality of open bowls as receptacles for cash in a household frequented by all comers around a busy theatre, and moreover frequently packed up and moved on, the suggestion of miserliness seems to me to have something to do with the unacceptability of a woman who "managed all her affairs herself", and was wealthy without the help of men, or of attractiveness to them. It is, perhaps significantly, an accusation that also attached itself to Sarah Siddons. To confirm a matter-of-fact construction of Sarah Baker's simplicity in money matters – that she followed the financial practices of the fairground and the traveller until some-one filled her in about other possibilities – one might cite her will, which is an elaborately professional document setting up a series of trust funds and covering all sorts of contingencies for protecting the substantial inheritance she left from the depredations of sharks and defaulters. She certainly learnt to make full use of the finance industry, when it became available to her.

It is worth noting here that her only recorded defeat in the building of her theatrical circuit can be construed as a direct consequence of the limitation her gender placed upon her access to the networks of business and capital. James Winston records that Charles Mate, who "was sadly deficient in the qualifications requisite for successful *management*" set up a theatre in Margate in a stable owned by "Mr Cobb, then banker and magistrate" of the town. He continues the story from 1784:

> when Mrs Baker . . . commenced an opposition. She applied to Mr Cobb for permission to erect a theatre on a superior plan; but Cobb, as proprietor of the old concern, naturally gave a decided negative; whereupon the *gentle fair one* . . . told him, for all he was a Justice, she would build in spite of him. Accordingly, the following year produced a *Baker's company*, who exercised their calling near the church, and instituted a theatrical warfare. This must have proved an annihilating system to one of the belligerent powers, but for the interference of the magistrate, the mandates of whom had been so lightly regarded; nevertheless, Mate, for the present, experienced an overthrow, and had nearly left the field to the victorious *Thalestris*; when, on the 6th of August, a convention of parishioners was called by Mr Cobb, who entreated them to sign a petition that Mate had prepared, to send to parliament, for the procuration of a patent . . . Mr Robson, who was at that time an inhabitant of *Margate*, came forward to assist Mate in the prosecution of his project . . . Mate finding the expence, trouble &c. too much for an individual like him, proposed to Mr Robson a joint interest in the scheme. Thus strengthened, he applied to Sir James Luttrell, one of the representatives of *Dover*, who so far espoused his cause, as to solicit the Prince of Wales and the Metropolitan of Canterbury to forward the petition, which passed both Houses with much trouble, and an expence of £550, in the face of a counter-petition, that being unsupported, died naturally away. By virtue of the patent . . . they re-opened, and saw an order issued from the Chamberlain's office for the suspension of Mrs Baker's opposition. In consequence, she struck her theatre, which was a temporary wooden structure, and transported it to *Feversham*. Thus rid of their opponent, they purchased a piece of ground for £80, in order to erect a more respectable edifice. The foundation stone, bearing the following inscription, was laid on the 19th of September, 1786, in the presence of near five thousand persons.
>
> "This first stone for a Theatre-Royal, was laid in due form, attended by the brethren of the *Thanet* Lodge, by the proprietors, Thomas Robson and Charles Mate, the 21st of September, A.D. 1786 - A.L. 5786, in the reign of King George the Third - Duke of Cumberland, Grand-Master."
>
> The ceremony was attended by the free-masons of Margate &c in honour of Robson, Master of the Lodge, who sang several masonic songs, accompanied by a band of music; and who addressed the populace in a nervous and

> appropriate speech, amidst general acclamations.
> This Theatre, which cost about £3000, was opened the 27th of June, 1787, with *She Stoops to Conquer*, and, *All the World's a Stage*. . . . The natural easiness of Mr Mate's disposition, rendered it necessary that Mr Robson should be invested with the management. (pp. 12–14)

So the incompetent Mate, supported by the magistracy, the House of Commons, the House of Lords, the Royal Family, the Primate of All England, the Lord Chamberlain, and, not least, the Freemasons, cleared the field of the pretensions of a woman, whose only claim to present theatre in his stead was that she was better at it. Winston clearly finds this very funny; but his deployment of the language of mock-heroic battle to describe theatrical "campaigns" is by no means unusual, and is indeed the most frequently used terminology in accounts of eighteenth-century provincial theatre. In such a frame of reference, Sarah Baker is naturally cast as the Amazon; and automatically, therefore, to be defeated.

The impulse of the memoir-writers to place her as an outsider to the hurly-burly of contemporary professional theatre and its values and imperatives is not, I think, so simply negative as this might suggest. Dickens/Grimaldi, Anne Mathews, and most of all Thomas Dibdin, do not simply laugh at Sarah Baker. They are concerned to attach certain positive values to the simple way she conducted her affairs, by way of contrast to the complexities with which they themselves are obliged to grapple. The bills put together with needle and thread, between the shopping and the family dinner, have the virtue of domesticity, a feminine value in itself, and a way, perhaps, of idealising the integrity of life and work that characterised pre-industrial production. Dibdin deliberately sets up the years he spent in the Kent company as idyllic, especially the period 1796–7, when he "for about a year and a half, (brief portion of content!) . . . had little care or anxiety of any sort . . . [and] . . . had only to be industrious to insure success" (p. 203). This Golden Age came to an end for him when he achieved "real" success, with the composition of a song that was a smash hit, and so tempted him back to the insecurities of London. He represents Sarah Baker as attempting to stop him by offering the satisfactions of Arcadia, expressed in comically domestic images: after quarrelling with her and determining to leave, he came next morning to the theatre to find her marketing at her own front door:

> she clapped a Savoy leaf, containing a two-pound lump of butter, in my open palm, and said to "Take that home to your wife, and ask whether she can get half as good, or half so much, for double the price in London. If you want a week's salary in advance, take it; send away the coachman; and don't talk nonsense about going to town. The mayor, and all the 'great grand' quality, are coming tonight, and can't do without the 'Snug Little Island'. What do you write such things for? You are more trouble to me than all my actors." (p. 223)

Dibdin also makes clear the material facts of her treatment of her company that lie behind this construction: she paid salaries, not shares, and although Winston thought her benefit system not very generous, it was substantive, not the chimerical fiction lesser managers used to get actors to perform for nothing all season. Dibdin laughs about his many functions in the company, but records how he was paid for each of them; and when he first arrived to join her, as a very green aspirant, he was paid in cash in advance, so that no young man of hers should disgrace the company by running up debts in the town. He was even found a decent lodging by the family's domestic manager, Mary Wakelin. This matriarchal system stands in strong contrast to the mercenary machinations of Mate, by whom the young Dibdin was duped into walking ninety miles in pursuit of a humble job on sharing terms, and then charged unexpectedly and over the odds, for his board and lodging at an inn kept by Mate's wife.

The contrast between Charles Mate and Sarah Baker in these accounts is interesting, especially in terms of the class construction of the theatrical heritage by the early-nineteenth-century commentators. Both Kentish managers were uneducated and of the lower classes – Mate was an ex-seaman, a comic actor who was, to judge from his letters to Winston, no more literate than Baker; he was obviously much less financially capable. They both amuse by their unceremonial habits. Mate painted scenery, clad in a jacket and trousers, took snuff as he conversed – a vulgar habit by this date, as Gomersal's reputation attests – and called Dibdin and other younger men "my son". Dibdin records, on the other hand, that the Baker sisters, both trained as dancers, curtsied elegantly, and Sarah Baker had "much of the appearance and manners of a gentlewoman": but like Andrew Ducrow, her elegance was spoiled when she opened her mouth. "She could, 'in a good cause, and with the law on her side', sometimes condescend to lingual expression more idiomatic of Peckham-fair technicals than the elegance to be expected from a directress of the British drama" (p. 94). Dibdin appreciatively recorded Mary Wakelin's contribution to the company as actress, comic dancer, wardrobe-mistress and an excellent cook; but Anne Mathews, necessarily more sensitive herself to social gradations and the limits of middle-class toleration, assessed the family rather differently:

> Mrs Baker had the reputation of being exceedingly coarse and vulgar; and certainly proved herself so in her language occasionally, when thrown off her guard by any vexatious surprise or sudden anger. As a proof of this, she was in the habit, when displeased or offended by any performer, of applying to the offender, the elegant and euphonious *sobriquet* of *bugaboo*! ("You *bugaboo!*") a word not found in any polite vocabulary, but which – to be somewhat etymological – possibly took its rise from *bug-bear* – *n'importe*. The lady, however, certainly could, when she wished to do so, assume an air and tone of good manners, and was moreover very hospitable . . . and did the honours of

> her table with grace. But her sister, Miss *Molly Wakelin* as she was familiarly though not *endearingly* called – Oh! she was indeed an awful individual! but mere coarseness and vulgarity, divested of *humour*, are unworthy of record. (pp. 37–8)

The airy deployment of hard words and genteel scraps of French is enough, it seems, to distance Mrs Mathews' own educated state from the user of such vulgarities as "bugaboo"; but nothing justifies her in writing about a vulgar woman who cannot be turned into a funny story.

The comic relish of Mrs Baker, as all report it, lay in her violation of hierarchy and degree – which was also the way in which she posed a threat. She was in herself an instance of that dissonance between the classic pretensions of the drama and the brute material reality of the stage that so intrigued and shocked the middle-class commentators. She was vulgar, but wealthy; an outsider, but successful. She had very little reverence for Drama as Art. She worked very hard, in her own person, despite being in a professional managerial position which others used as a reason to assume the airs and graces of gentility. Her stage training gave her the deportment of a lady; her lack of education meant that her use of language belied that appearance. These characteristics she shared with Mate, and several other theatrical "characters" like Ducrow and Richardson; but her gender added another layer of contradiction and possible danger that made her "placing", her reduction to a literary trope, a matter of some importance in the creation of a new image for the British theatre.

Perhaps the heart of her "eccentricity", as constructed by this impulse, is the reading of her management style as "domestic". Many of the stories about her focus upon this. Not only Dibdin's fascinated account of the many activities of her day in household and theatre, but all the tales of how she managed employees and audiences, have this as their main effect. Some examples have already been given. Then the fact that she took all the money at the doors gives rise to many tales about her egalitarian attitude to her audiences, her familiar treatment of royal dukes and stage-struck streetboys all alike as paying customers:

> "Little girl! get your money ready while this gentleman pays. My Lord! I'm sure your lordship has silver; and let that little boy go in while I give his lordship change. – Shan't count after your ladyship. – Here comes the duke! make haste! His Royal Highness will please get his ticket ready while my lady – now, sir! now, your Royal Highness!" – "O, dear, Mrs Baker! I've left my ticket in another coat-pocket." – "To be sure you have! take your Royal Highness's word: let his Royal Highness pass: his Royal Highness has left his ticket in his *other* coat pocket." (Dibdin pp. 226–7)

Similarly, her refusal to be pretentious or pompous about the claims of Art is mocked, as when she reluctantly agreed to the demands of a self-important actor that a screaming baby should not be allowed to interrupt his speech, but dismissed the mother with her full money back, and the advice "don't come in another night till half-price, and then give the poor baby some Dalby's Carminative" (p. 226). Such stories, and Anne Mathews' picture of her (p. 37) at her box-office post well after the curtain had risen, bartering with small children to accept the temporary pledges of their toys in exchange for admission, aim to reduce her managerial style to a manageable model. Today one might read her practices as the product of her family fairground inheritance, a working-class entertainer catering for a working-class or mixed-class public – her Kentish theatres drew a very wide clientele, including a backbone of sailors ashore as well as a spread of middle-class art-lovers in each town she visited and a few, relatively unimportant aristocratic patrons. But for the aspiring middle-class theatre professionals of the early nineteenth century, she had to be put into a frame less suggestive of that old, disreputable tradition of catering. Urgently, therefore, she had to be stripped of its most threatening aspects: the self-sufficiency of a woman who could provide all sorts of entertainment.

One of the most telling suppressions in the tale is, of course, sexuality. Even in 1952 Norma Hodgson was unable to make use of one revelation in the newly-discovered Winston correspondence. In a letter to Winston of 22 January 1804, Mate sought to reduce Baker's importance in his correspondent's eyes by describing her early years. He said:

> a Mr Magg then was her manager her Husband Beaker was ded, thay then performed a Farce Rope dancing and concluded with a pantomime. I went to see them, when I found sum unluckie dog had wrought over Mrs Beakers dresing place as folows, Beakers wife, once in her life, had her oven Stopt up Snug, But now thay Say, instead of Clay, She stops it with a Mugg.

Sarah Baker, coming in, accused Mate of perpetrating this instance of sexual harassment in the workplace, which he strenuously denied, and took the opportunity while she was away on stage of vindicating himself by composing an equally rude rejoinder and leaving it lying on her table; for which, he concludes, "the poor deare old Girl has never yet forgiven me".

The next generation of commentators, intent upon establishing their own gentility, could not use such time-honoured methods of putting a woman in her place; but the "character" of comic matriarch has served just as well.

# *Notes*

1. See "Dullborough Town" in *The Uncommercial Traveller*, London, 1861.
2. "Sarah Baker (1736/7–1816) 'Governess-general of the Kentish Drama'" *Studies in English Theatre History*, London, Society for Theatre Research, 1952, 65–83.
3. Revd John Genest *Some Account of the English Stage*, Bath, 1832. John Payne Collier, *The History of English Dramatic Poetry to the Time of Shakespeare: and the annals of the stage to the Restoration*, London, 1831.
4. See for example Bulwer Lytton, *England and the English*, 2 vols., London and Paris 1833.
5. Tate Wilkinson, *Memoirs of his Own Life*, York, 1790; *The Wandering Patentee*, York and London, 1795. Thomas Dibdin, *The Reminiscences of Thomas Dibdin*, 2 vols., London, 1827. Anne Mathews, *Anecdotes of Actors*, London, 1844. Charles Dickens, *Memoirs of Joseph Grimaldi*, edited by "Boz", London, 1838.

# William Wyatt Dimond – Provincial Actor-Manager

ARNOLD HARE

THE professional theatre in England has had a long history – going back at least as far as the Tudor companies – of using the provinces as a convenient source of plunder when, for one reason or another, operations in London have been impossible. Not till the eighteenth century did players (and the new race of managers) choose to work permanently in the country. Of this honourable band, William Wyatt Dimond is one of the best examples. He began his acting career at Garrick's Drury Lane, but after only two years in London went to Bath, and there he remained for the rest of his days – for twenty-seven years as a leading actor until his retirement in 1801, and for nearly twenty-six years from 1786 until his death in 1812 as joint manager and proprietor; a total of forty years of varied and significant activity which represent an important element in the development of provincial culture at the turn of the eighteenth and nineteenth centuries.

Dimond was born around 1750, and as a young man, according to James Winston, was apprenticed as a "chaser" – an engraver on silver and gold.[1] But clearly his ambitions lay elsewhere. On 1 October 1772 at Drury Lane, a Young Gentleman made his first appearance on any stage as Romeo to the Juliet of Miss Mansell.[2] This was Dimond; and it was to be an auspicious start.

"He is very younge a Smart Figure good Voice and made a very tolerable first appearance he met with great applause" wrote William Hopkins in his Diary; and the *Town and Country Magazine* gave both the young players a favourable review.[3] Since the performances were repeated on the 3 and 10 October, Dimond must have been reasonably satisfied with his beginning as an actor (though the Treasurer's advance of five guineas probably gave him equal satisfaction at that time). But he had to wait three months for another part – Dorilas in Aaron Hill's *Merope*, again with Miss Mansell, who played Ismene. This had two performances in January 1773. And that, apart from his benefit on 14 May, which he shared with Miss Mansell, playing Moneses for the first time to her Selima, in Nicholas Rowe's *Tamerlane*, (and dividing with her a profit of £78.18.0.) was all that he had to show for that first season.[4] However smart the figure and good the voice of the new young man, he was caught in that common trap of the Georgian stock company – all the parts of the standard repertory were already pre-empted by senior members of the company.

He seems to have spent the summer seeking wider experience in Canterbury, but he was back at Drury Lane for the autumn of 1773. He gave nine performances as Rovewell in Shadwell's *The Fair Quaker* in November and December; three as the Dauphin in *King John*, and the rest was fustian – four performances in an unnamed part in Garrick's *A Christmas Tale*, two in Waldron's *The Maid of Kent*; and parts in home-made productions like *The Heroine of the Cave*, *The Pantheonites*, and *The Swindlers*. The only opportunity he had to show his mettle was in the benefit performance he shared with Waldron on 7 May 1774. There for the first time he was allowed to play Florizel to Mrs Smith's Perdita, and duly earned his proportion of the £124.0.6. profit.[5] But for a young man now burning to make his reputation as an actor, opportunity was clearly lacking in London. No doubt two seasons of watching Garrick at close quarters had taught him a great deal, but what use was that if he had no means of practising the larger roles? When, two years previously, John Henderson had been in a similar situation, Garrick had advised him to try the Bath theatre, and had used his influence with John Palmer, the proprietor, to get him taken on. Now Garrick did the same for Dimond, as Edward Cape Everard confirms. On 20 October 1774 Dimond opened his account in Bath, playing Tressel with the same John Henderson as Richard III. Though he could not have known it at the time, fate had settled the rest of his life for him.[6]

In fact, it was a good time to arrive in Bath. In 1766 John Palmer the Younger had taken over the proprietorship of the Orchard Street Playhouse from his father, and had begun to take the theatre, as the modern jargon has it, up-market. He had re-furbished the building, gained its Royal Patent in 1768 – the first outside London – and was steadily building up the quality of his company, making regular tours to London and the provincial cities in search of likely talent. By 1774 he had got rid of both Arthur (whose managership had been somewhat idiosyncratic) and Lee, who had presided for three years over a not very happy company; and in their place had installed Keasbury (who had been a member of the company since 1756) as his acting manager. It was probably the wisest thing Palmer ever did. Keasbury remained till his retirement in 1795, not only as a bastion of stability, but a good and popular administrator, a shrewd judge of talent, and a fine teacher of the art of acting.

When Dimond arrived in 1774 John Henderson was leading man of the company, with John Edwin (the elder) as chief, and popular, comedian, along with the young Francis Blissett, at the beginning of his thirty year association with Bath. Dimond's former Drury Lane partner, Miss Mansell, had joined the company in the previous season, and already there were stalwarts like Margaret Didier and the Summers family, with whom he was to be associated till the turn of the century.[7] Bath's reputation as a fashionable resort was at its height, as the building at this time of the Circus, the Royal Crescent and the New Assembly Rooms indicated, and Palmer and Keasbury had a growing new town to cater for. Though Dimond's first season was in the small 1750 theatre, plans were already in hand for its enlargement, and between the end of the season in June 1775, and the re-opening in September, the theatre was almost doubled in size. Moreover, within five years the joint working between Bath and Bristol was to develop, making possible a compact efficient, and prosperous circuit of only two theatres, that was to last until 1817.[7] Whether or not Dimond could discern it at the time, the omens were good.

Certainly he must have recognised very quickly the different scale of opportunity he was being offered. In that first season alone, he found himself playing a clutch of leading roles such as he had never had before - Heartfree in *The Provok'd Wife*. Lothario in *The Fair Penitent*, Jaffier in *Venice Preserv'd*, Bevil in *The Conscious Lovers*, and Shakespeare's Bassanio and Orlando, to name only half a dozen. And when in March he played Faulkland in *The Rivals* for the first time, Miss Linley who saw him, wrote enthusiastically to her sister Elizabeth, now Mrs Sheridan, about this "new actor of great merit, and a sweet figure".[8]

His elegant figure, and the pleasure he took in adorning it, are characteristics of Dimond which were frequently noted at the time - like the spangles he wore as Lothario, or the "pea-green silk with silver and foil embroidery" as Sir George Airy in *The Busybody*;[9] and the two engravings of portraits by de Wilde that

12. Mr Dimond as Philaster.

13. Mr Dimond as Don Felix.

appear in Bell's *British Theatre*, of him as Philaster and Don Felix in *The Wonder* (illustrations 12 and 13), confirm the elegance, if not the colour.[10]

In his first seasons in Bath Dimond was given more opportunity in comedy than in tragedy, and until 1777, while Henderson remained with the company, Dimond tended to play second leads – Laertes to Henderson's Hamlet, Hotspur to his Falstaff, Faulconbridge to his King John, Claudio to his Benedick, Macduff to his Macbeth. Later, as we shall see, he played Hamlet in his own right. Until 1777, Miss Mansell was his leading lady. From 1779–82 he played opposite Sarah Siddons when she, too, joined the Bath Company.

The list of his collaborations with Mrs Siddons during those years is an interesting one. Bassanio and Portia, Young Bevil and Indiana, Lord and Lady Townly, Tancred and Sigismunda, Jaffier and Belvidera, Hastings and Jane Shore, Constant and Lady Brute, Posthumous and Imogen, Faulkland and Julia, are a handful only, plucked at random from a list more than twice as long. And certainly at that date there seems to have been no sense of his being overshadowed by the great lady. *Theatricus*, writing in the *Bath Journal* of 1782, paid tribute to Mrs Siddons as "in every way so great and deserv'd a favourite", but went on to note that the company contained "other Performers of real ability", and singled out Dimond for particular comment.

> Amongst many others of real talents, I know no-one more deserving than Mr Dimond, or whose improvement has been more rapid; whether we consider him in his various walk in Tragedy, or the elegant Gentleman in Comedy. Most People of Fashion who visit us seem to unite in opinion that his taste in dress, his manners, deportment and expression, are more the Gentleman than that of anyone now on the Stage; nor is there any character which more requires these perfections than Lord Townly; a very false idea us'd to prevail in Stage Politics, in giving this as well as many other parts to what they call a Man of Weight – that is, a Man of large Figure; so that you would suppose the manager had a pair of dramatic scales, in which the body of an actor was plac'd, and weigh'd to see if he was heavy enough for the character – The immortal Garrick so effectually clear'd the Stage of this, as well as numberless other prejudices, that the World are thoroughly convinc'd, dignity no more than grace or elegance, or good acting, depend on largeness of person – Mr Dimond is I think particularly happy, where perhaps, if we retain'd the old-fashion'd idea, we might think he would be most deficient, I mean in the last act; in a manly, firm, determin'd, yet feeling conduct, to a Wife possess'd of every natural and acquir'd grace, yet sunk in folly and dissipation, and lost to the most tender Lover and affectionate Husband – I can hardly conceive anything equal on the Stage to this scene betwixt Mr Dimond and Mrs Siddons, who so greatly excels in a character where the elegant, the lively and the pathetic are so powerfully united.[11]

As a tragic actor Dimond was not content slavishly to follow tradition. Playing Hamlet in 1788, *Dramaticus* in the *Bristol Journal* found he

> gave an agreeable novelty to the character by deviating at times from the hackney'd mode of playing it - for instance, in the closet scene, instead of the threadbare trick of starting from his chair on the entrance of the Ghost, he sunk fainting into it, and on recovery dropped on his knee, in an attitude finely expressive of filial reverence; his soliloquies were also feelingly delivered, and the pauses, being well-kept, had their due effect.[12]

This careful study was part of his method. Twelve years later, near the end of his acting career, another critic reflected -

> It is impossible to hear the subject of this paper rehearse 10 lines, without conviction that he possesses a good ear, combined with a sound judgement. We are inclined to consider these qualifications in a great measure as the result of education and reflection.

But there was debit as well as credit in this.

> It has been said of Pope that he wrote more like a finished scholar than a poet, and that the fault of his verses was (pardoning the paradox) that they were faultless - in a word, that all was smooth, orderly, and correct, and in consequence he was often wanting in that fire and sublimity so characteristic of the older and even contemporary bards. Nearly the same may be said of this gentleman's playing: nothing is irregular, nothing is left to chance; every line appears to have been deeply impressed upon the memory, and every syllable in every word marked, as in a *Gradus ad Parnassum*, with its due weight and quantity. Hence it is, that if you have little to excite astonishment, you have a great deal to admire. His action, generally speaking, is not sufficiently varied, and sometimes conveys the idea of the arms being in chains; it is however, always just and impressive, occasionally very elegant, and would be much more so, could he persuade himself to rebel against the restraints imposed by too timid caution. In the estimation of many, our Manager's hero is unequal, and not always what may be expected from him; but we have received so much rational amusement from *Essex*, *Evander*, *Douglas*, *Posthumus*, *Orestes*, *Alonzo*, and many others, that we cannot tacitly subscribe to this opinion. His chief fault - *et sine culpa quis nascitur?* - is rendering sentences too prominent, which being in themselves trifling, should be kept at a distance: thus it happens that "My brave associate!" and "Shut to the door!" have attached to them precisely the same quantity of buckram. A very serious inconvenience does certainly arise in consequence, which is, that when at the climax an unusual exertion is

> necessary, the voice falters, the performer is himself exhausted, and the ear of the audience is fatigued by too much attention to minutiae not essential to the plot of the piece. The mind, like the bow of Aesop, must be now and then unstrung –
>
> . . . Lusus animo debet aliquando dari
> Ad cogitandum melior ut redeat sibi. PHAEDRUS.
> "To keep it constantly upon the stretch, is to exhaust it prematurely."
>
> In genteel Comedy, he has scarcely his equal, – certainly not a superior, – upon the English boards: *Don Felix*, *Belcour*, *Joseph Surface*, *Sir Brilliant Fashion*, *Lord Townly*, &c. beggar description, and are at once the delight and admiration of the spectators.[13]

That as an actor he was finer in comedy than in tragedy was a common opinion. Reflecting on his retirement in 1801, Genest found that it was the roles in comedy he recalled most vividly.

> his manners were perfectly those of a gentleman, and he had been very handsome – Lord Townley and Joseph Surface were perhaps his best characters he is said likewise to have acted Don Felix, Posthumus, Edgar, and several other parts very well – tho' a very sober man, he was happy in acting a drunken scene – for this reason he excelled in Charles Oakly – Sheridan told Dimond, that he played Joseph Surface in a manner more consonant to his own ideas when he wrote the part, than anybody else – *if* Sheridan said what he really thought, this was a great compliment, for Palmer was an excellent Joseph.[14]

At what point Dimond decided to stay in Bath, we can only guess. In 1775, after his first season there, he went to London and gave a couple of performances for Foote at the Haymarket, and he appeared again there in September 1778 as Edgar in *King Lear* for West Digges benefit. In the following year he played there for the whole of the summer season, giving some twenty-eight performances; so clearly he was still keeping his options open.[15] In that same year (1779) the joint Bath–Bristol operation began, and in June 1781 there is a distinct hint that Dimond might be contemplating a move. The *Bristol Journal*, at any rate, had heard something, and did not care for it.

> We hope the report of Mr Dimond's quitting our Theatre at the expiration of this season, is without foundation, as from his great merit, both in his public and private character, he would be a considerable loss to our company, which now stands in very high reputation. – If it arises from the indifference of his

> benefit last year, we will venture to pronounce him wrong; as almost every Performer of merit that have visited our city, tho' they seldom succeeded in their first year's benefit, yet have been made ample amends in successive seasons, tho' the public here are cool acquaintance, yet they are warm and constant friends, nor is there any city in the kingdom where merit is more encourag'd.[16]

Bristol, I fear, can at times be rather smug.

Dimond did not leave, however, and at some time between then and 1786 he must have made up his mind that London was not for him, for in October of that year, when Palmer found the postal service (which he was developing and reorganising) was taking up too much of his time to enable him to run the theatre properly, Dimond joined Keasberry in the management, and took a share of the property.[17] (It is possible that Mrs Dimond may have been an influence in this. She was a Norfolk girl, Matilda Martha Baker, and they had married in London in 1779. According to Winston, she was a woman of property, and this enabled Dimond to buy his share of the theatre; perhaps she, too, preferred living in Bath to London).[18] Whatever the motivation, for the next nine years Keasberry and Dimond ran the company jointly; after Keasberry's retirement in 1795 Dimond remained until 1801 as sole actor-manager. In that year he retired from acting, but with Charles Charlton as his Deputy, remained in management until his death in 1812.[19]

The great achievement of Dimond's managership, of course, was the building in 1805 of the new Theatre Royal in Beauford Square, the theatre which still survives (though now with an interior rebuilt in 1863 after destruction by fire). Ever since the beginning of the joint working of the two theatres, the Orchard Street Theatre must have suffered by comparison with King Street, Bristol. Orchard Street was small, its enlargement to some extent improvised and probably not ideally proportioned; it was on a restricted site and one which, as the new town had grown, was well away from the now fashionable areas. King Street, on the other hand, had been purpose-built to the pattern of Garrick's Drury Lane, and was in the centre of the old city. A new theatre in Bath, of the size and shape of Bristol must have seemed eminently desirable, and when a competing rival was threatened in the upper fashionable part of Bath, the matter became one of some urgency. Dimond must have been planning a new playhouse before 1801, for when in that year William Beckford sold the contents of his Palladian mansion of Fonthill Splendens to help pay for more additions to his Gothic extravaganza of Fonthill Abbey, Dimond, as well as acquiring the Fonthill state bed and chairs for his own use, bought the picture gallery ceiling decorated by Cassali, to be installed in his new theatre.[20] But at this stage search for a site was still going on, and it was not till 1804 when the Beauford Street site was decided upon, that the decision to move was made. Then matters moved quickly, and on 12 October

1805 the new playhouse was opened, and the company migrated.

In the new house the stock company continued to operate much as before, but with a greater emphasis on visiting engagements by London "stars". There had been guest appearances at Orchard Street, of course, but apart from specialists like rope dancers and whistlers, they had mostly been former members of the company who had moved elsewhere, usually to London. Now the era of the star tour was developing, and Cooke, Elliston, Munden, Bannister, the Charles Kembles, Master Betty, Miss Smith, Mrs Jordan, Incledon and John Braham, and even the great Sarah herself, on her farewell tour, all played in the new house in Dimond's last years.

How much Dimond was involved in the day-to-day management of the first six years at Beauford Square is difficult to say, since any records have now disappeared, probably in the fire of 1862. He was now a worthy and respected citizen of Bath, and a member of the city corporation; he could afford to live the life of a prosperous gentleman at his house (number 17) in Norfolk Crescent, and his son William was already a popular melodramatic playwright destined – though not very successfully – to succeed his father in management.[21] It was all a far cry from Dimond's arrival on foot at the tiny original Orchard Street Theatre in 1774. But he was not destined to retire from management, as ten years before he had formally taken leave of the stage. On Christmas Eve 1811, "while high in health and happiness, and surrounded by his family" as the *Bath Journal* put it, he had a sudden brain haemorrhage. Medical care could only delay the inevitable, and on Monday 6 January 1812, at the age of sixty-two he died.

All the Bath newspapers carried obituaries, but that in the *Bath Herald* best sums up his life and work.

> Who . . . can ever forget Mr Dimond's representation of Romeo and Lothario?
>
> Who the dignified and impressive manner of the last scenes of Lord Townly; the fire of his Posthumus; the wildness of his Edgar and Orestes; and his modest and pathetic delineation of the unfortunate Barnwell? In many characters of airy and genteel comedy he was the perfect model of the well-bred man of fashion, but his Joseph Surface, for ease, subtlety and characteristic propriety, was never excelled. In every part he played he always appeared in earnest, and was always perfect, his action was elegantly spirited and appropriate, and his voice harmonious and finely modulated. With all these qualifications, in their very zenith he retired from the stage, and devoted his mind to the duties of a Manager.

> Perhaps no situation of life is more difficult than that of a director of a theatre; he has a variety of persons to contend with and control, and few of them but have a higher opinion of their own ability, than the public award

them; yet Mr Dimond by the gentleness of his manners and his unassuming demeanour, had the power of reconciling their minds, and to make the business of his theatre go smoothly on. They obeyed him more for the regard they had for him as a friend, than the awe he might have created as a Manager.

And the *Bath Journal* ended its tribute with a simple quotation - "He never made an enemy, or lost a friend."[22]

What Dimond would have done if he had stayed in London is, of course, impossible to say. But this brief outline of his life and work may suggest some of the reasons why he did not do so. It was more than just the desire to be a big fish in a small but highly select pond - though doubtless that was some part of it. To some extent he seems consciously to have modelled himself on David Garrick - on his retirement from acting in 1801 the *Bath Journal* referred to "his old master, Garrick", and it was noted that "in person as well in manner" he bore a striking resemblance to the great man.[23] Perhaps he saw himself as doing for Bath what Garrick had already done for Drury Lane. But that, too, was not the whole of it. As we have seen, Bath gave him the opportunity to play in his own right, parts that - even as a first-rate actor - might never have come his way in London. And his audiences liked him, and said so - not only at his benefits, though that was a good enough indication of their approval - but in other ways, too. Even his company liked him. Only once, so far, have I come across a comment (from Tate Wilkinson, who liked him) suggesting that a former member of his company, Mrs Esten, bore him some animosity.[24] For the most part - and the length of time some of them stayed with the company bears this out - they were happy to work with and for him. And Bath itself was congenial to him. He loved playing "gentlemen" on the stage; in time, Bath allowed him to play one in reality. Perhaps Mrs Dimond's property helped here, but he could probably still have done it in his own right, for Bath/Bristol was a simple and efficient circuit to operate, for the most part it was prosperous during his time, and its artistic reputation was high. In Bath he could have as much, if not more, stability than he could have had in London, and on a more human scale. For all these reasons it was a wise decision that he took. Keasberry it was who laid the foundations for the Bath/Bristol period of greatness, but Dimond had the personality and the social skills to build on them, so that for thirty years that company was, without doubt, the best in the country outside London and, as John Bernard wrote, "contributed more largely to the metropolitan boards than Dublin and York put together".[25] It was no mean achievement, and one that gives Dimond a firm and justified place in English theatre history.

# *Notes*

1. J. Winston, *The Theatric Tourist*, London, 1805, Section 1.
2. G. W. Stone, ed., *The London Stage 1660*-1800, Carbondale, 1962, IV, 3, 1660.
3. *Ibid.*, 1659, 1661. See also *Town and Country Magazine*, Oct. 1772. Miss Mansell had made her first appearance on 26 Sep. as Louisa Dudley in *The West Indian*, 1659.
4. *London Stage*, IV, 3, 1686, 1723.
5. J. Genest, *Some Account of the English Stage*, Bath, 1830, V. 473, 475 etc.
6. E. C. Everard, *Memoirs of an Unfortunate Son of Thespis*, Edinburgh, 1818, 168. A. Hare, ed., *Theatre Royal Bath - The Orchard Street Calendar*, Bath, 1977, 47 et passim.
7. Hare, Introduction, passim.
8. *Bath Journal* and *Chronicle*. Genest, V, 473-5.
9. Highfill, Burnim and Langhans, *A Biographical Dictionary of Actors and Actresses*, Carbondale, 1991, IV, 421-4.
10. Bell's *British Theatre* (1791-1802) illustrations 7 and 16.
11. *Orchard Street Calendar* passim. *Bristol Journal*, 4 Feb. 1782.
12. *Felix Farley's Bristol Journal*, 26 Apr. 1788.
13. UMBRA in *ibid.*, 28 Jun 1800.
14. Genest, VIII, 527.
15. *London Stage* IV(3), 1901; V(1), 202 and 264-72.
16. *Felix Farley's Bristol Journal*, 2 Jun. 1781.
17. *Bristol Journal*. See B. S. Penley, *The Bath Stage*, London and Bath, 1892, 64-7.
18. *Bath Journal*, 6 Dec. 1779. Winston, *The Theatric Tourist*, 4.
19. A. Hare, *Bath Journal*, *Bath Chronicle* passim.
20. Penley, 97. Also *Bath Journal*. Whether the ceiling was ever installed in the theatre is not clear. It is now in the care of the National Trust at Dyrham Park.
21. Evidence of playbills and newspapers. Examples of William the Younger's plays are: *The Hero of the North* (1803), *The Hunter of the Alps* (1804), *Adrian and Orrilla* (1800), *The Foundling of the Forest* (1809). The titles speak for themselves.
22. *Bath Journal*, 6 Jan. 1812; *Bath Chronicle*, 9 Jan. 1812; *Bath Herald*, 11 Jan. 1812.
23. *Bath Journal*, 29 Jun. 1801; 6 Jan. 1812.
24. Tate Wilkinson, *The Wandering Patentee*, York and London, 1795, 3, 116-120.
25. J. Bernard, *Retrospections of the Stage*, London, 1830, 1, 34.

# The Earliest Grossmiths and their Pictorial Playbills

DEREK FORBES

In April 1824 Mr William Grossmith of Reading, Berks, took his precocious six-year-old son to London to be auditioned by the managers of the Covent Garden and Coburg theatres. Thus was Master William Robert Grossmith's career as a juvenile performer set in train. By so doing, Mr Grossmith established the foundation of a theatrical dynasty. For this he is given modest recognition in some of the chronicles of the Grossmith family, though his enterprise as the manager of a touring troupe with first one and then another "infant-phenomenon" son deserves fuller treatment than it has yet received. One intriguing feature of it seems to have been altogether neglected, namely the pictorial advertising system that William Grossmith employed. This includes a series of playbills, unprecedented in both style and extent, which are amongst the earliest illustrated theatre bills known.

In the early 1800s, before he went on the road with his first performing son, William Grossmith was a young married man living in Reading, where, as a "respectable tradesman" he made and sold picture-frames and looking-glasses. He clearly had an eye for iconography.

The pictorial advertisement to regard first is the front cover of the second and subsequent editions of the *Life* of his eldest son, *The Life and Theatrical Excursions of William Robert Grossmith, the Juvenile Actor* (Reading, 1827, *et seq.*, published anonymously). The fifth (and last?) edition of 1831 is known: its front cover, a detached document, is held by Berkshire Local Studies Library (illustration 14). It is pictorially identical to the covers of the extant second and fourth editions (the third has not been traced).[1] The influence of the picture-framer and looking-glass-maker is immediately discernible in the design of the central triptych surrounded by an oval frame and squared-off corners, all providing thirty-four panes which characterise Master William Robert in action around the figure of Shakespeare. Here is the pictorial hall-mark of William Grossmith's advertising material: abundant wood-cuts to show the boy (later boys) in postures from the act, often mounted in some form of surround.

The *Life*, a slight pamphlet of about twenty-five pages, was a souvenir for sale at performances. After a learned introduction, it chiefly concerns itself with recounting the places at which William Robert performed in early days and the tributes he received. We learn that he was born in 1818, and "was born to be an actor, so early did it appear that Nature designed him for the stage".[2] After the little boy's singing ability and various attempts at character take-off (including Richard III) had been recognised, he gave turns at the Royal Coburg (now Old Vic) in April 1824. These were followed by contributions to the summer bill during a week at the Surrey and a week at Sadler's Wells. Those reviews from London papers quoted in the *Life* were complimentary.

Back home in Reading, the stage-struck infant learnt bits from *Douglas* and *Macbeth* and begged to appear on the boards again. William Grossmith was, ostensibly, undecided, and Mrs Grossmith reluctant, until "some gentlemen of Reading . . . persuaded Mr G. to allow his son to resume". Consequently, "an evening's entertainment was got up", in which William Robert, solus, played eight characters from melodrama, sang a number of comic songs, and gave scenes from *Douglas*, *Macbeth* and *Richard III*. This was performed at Reading Town Hall on 9 and 10 and 16 November 1824.[3] They were off.

Mr William Grossmith threw his heart and skill into housing these performances:

> [He] had a small portable stage constructed, with machinery, decorations etc. at once elegant and convenient, and adapted to the age and stature of the child. This miniature theatre is fitted up with thirty changes of scenery, most of which was painted by Jones, Billing, and Greene. The front, or proscenium, is supported by gold and bronze pillars, decorated on the right and left with the figures, seven feet high, of Melpomene and Thalia, in Tuscan niches, well representing bronze statues of these two muses of the drama. The Theatre, with its apparatus, is so well executed and complete, that, without being attached to the room, it can be put up in two hours, so as to be quite ready for performance, and, the whole of the decorations being painted on very fine sheeting, the weight of it is but little more than 200 lbs, the frame included.[4]

Amongst the pictorial products later marketed by the enterprising father were prints of Master William Robert. One of them features the "miniature theatre" in the top border of a frame of twenty-six panels. The panels show the boy in action, in front of a variety of scenes which may be taken as the "changes of scenery" provided; the five scenes in the top border, we notice, have an air of *Richard III*. The whole framework of panels surrounds a central portrait (illustration 15).[5] The newspaper held by the boy in the central portrait is the *Reading Mercury*. This journal, reporting on the first Reading performances in its issue of 15 November 1824, noticed the portable theatre and its scenes as well as Master Grossmith's acting:

> Without seeing him, it is impossible to form an idea of his graceful acting, and the admirable manner in which he supports the numerous characters in his

14. Pictorial cover of *The Life and Theatrical Excursions of William Robert Grossmith, the Juvenile Actor* (fifth edition).

15. W. R. Grossmith of Reading, Berks. The Celebrated Young Roscius of the Age with the Sketch of his Characters.

> evening's performance. Mr Grossmith's Theatre is very elegant, and exceedingly well calculated for juvenile performers: it contains many fine specimens of the scenic art. The tent scene in *Richard III* is uncommonly magnificent.[6]

We notice the impact of the Tent Scene from the very beginning. This was to be the subject of a separate portrait, of which more below.

The prospect of touring must have been in William Grossmith's mind during the autumn of 1824, while preparing the scaled-down - and portable - theatre. An itinerary was planned, Mrs Grossmith's "tender scruples" were overcome, and father and little son were on tour with their show by December 1824.

We can analyse from the *Life* that their first trip took them westwards to Newbury, then back to Marlowe, Maidenhead, Windsor, Egham, Chertsey, Kingston, Wokingham and home to Reading in January 1825. This exacting schedule typifies ensuing tours. The towns visited were not normally far apart, though a long hop could occur; and while they often stayed two or three nights, or weeks, at any one place, one-night-stands were fitted in, sometimes in a series. Our sympathies are aroused by the thought of the winter journeying. The *Life* of 1827 mentions no conveyance. Costumes and their portable theatre went with them, so some form of horse-drawn transport suggests itself, unless in this first winter tour they went by canal and river or on foot with hand-cart. By 1829, the fourth edition of the *Life* claimed what we suspect from the start, that "Mr G. and his son travel in a very neat-constructed carriage, which takes in the whole of the apparatus".[7]

For their second, more leisurely, tour they took off later in January 1825. From Wallingford and Abingdon (Master W. R.'s first Shylock) they went out of the Thames valley and across the head-waters to Cirencester, Cheltenham (where they settled for three weeks), Gloucester, Stroudwater, Tewkesbury and then straight on for forty-five miles to Birmingham (whence their earliest playbill known so far, May 1825). Then on to Walsall, Wolverhampton, and Dudley. At Dudley Castle William Robert was allowed to grub about like an ordinary little boy: "the whole of his leisure hours were spent in collecting fossils, etc., from this ancient and beautiful place".[8] Stourbridge next, then Kidderminster, and Bridgnorth where Mr Grossmith "netted only £11. Shrewsbury, however, . . . amply compensated him". North again to Oswestry, then back down the marches to Ludlow, and home via Warwick and Stratford-upon-Avon, where the Young Roscius performed "with suitable emotions", and inscribed the Book of Visitors at Shakespeare's birthplace.

Later in 1825 the troupe toured the north of England "via Wales", going on from Wrexham to Chester, Liverpool, Warrington, Prescot, Manchester, Bolton, Wigan, Stockport, and Macclesfield. Readers familiar with English topography will find these lists of towns interesting as evidence of the routes that could be taken by a small theatrical enterprise in the early nineteenth century, not following the major regional circuit systems. Other readers could find the itineraries less resonant. There is little more of this to endure. Starting in March 1826, a tour of the south took in Bath, Bristol, Frome, Warminster, Devizes, Marlborough, Calne, Chippenham, Tetbury, Hungerford, and Ramsbury - tiny towns and major cities alike - then up to Cirencester, then back to the Thames valley for Abingdon, Wallingford, Maidenhead, and Reading. After a short home-visit they went down to the coast at Portsmouth and Portsea via Basingstoke, Winchester, Alresford and Romsey; across to Chichester, up to Guildford and Farnham, and home again in late October 1826. Future tours went even further afield, from playbill evidence, eventually taking them to Scotland and Ireland.

Carting his portable theatre around enabled Mr William Grossmith to be selective about premises. They did not have to use the local playhouse even if there was one, though they did sometimes, as at Wolverhampton and Bridgnorth and Winchester, and Theatres Royal at Bristol and Aberdeen. Having taken advice on the best venue, Mr Grossmith would book in his "Unique Theatre" at playhouse, or music hall, i.e. concert room (Warrington), Town Hall (Alton), Shire Hall (Hertford) or Assembly Rooms as at Dudley and Birmingham ("The Royal Hotel Assembly Room"). He emerges from between the lines as not only promoter but general factotum - working out the itinerary, seeing to bookings and publicity and organisation, and handling the takings. And did he also direct back-stage and work the scenes? There is but scant reference to assistance.[9] The implication is that William Grossmith rapidly learnt the ropes to become tour-director, house- and stage-manager, and roadie as well as accompanying father. We have to wonder if he could possibly have managed without hired help, though no doubt the son(s) had tasks. While he did exploit his children's precocity, it does not follow that he was unkind. It was an age when youngsters could be expected to contribute to bread-winning; a life on the road has a certain appeal: and young William Robert was keen to act, like his brother Benjamin after him (or "Master B.", as the younger boy was always billed).

So: the Royal Hotel Assembly Room, Birmingham, was the venue, and 5, 6, and 7 May 1825 the date, on the earliest-known Grossmith playbill. This is a somewhat haphazard broadsheet. It contains a laudatory poem, four press notices, and a description of the "Evening's Amusement" which will include a 360-ft. diorama of Italy in the interval. It has sixteen bordering pictures. These small cuts show "characters" from the repertory of "Stage-coach Adventures", *The Fugitive's Retreat* (melodrama), two musical turns and three scenes from *Douglas* and Shakespeare. The bill has been mutilated and is in separated sections, which makes its design difficult to discern.[10] It is clearly a prototype upon which later bills improved.

A lost playbill for William Robert at Bridgnorth on 26 and 30 July 1825 was described in 1888 by its then owner, George Grossmith (the second), Victorian actor, singer, and star of the D'Oyly Carte comic operas at the Savoy.[11] Observing the twenty-three tiny pictures of his infant uncle William Robert on this playbill, George Grossmith considered them, though quaint, to be "very primitive". Perhaps they were, judged by later standards. The mere fact of the art-work of these 1825 experiments tells us something about the aspirations of the enterprise, at a time when wood-block illustrations were a great rarity on playbills. George Speaight, expert on theatrical ephemera, says in a personal communication:

> Illustrations of some kind did begin to creep on to playbills from early in the nineteenth century: . . . some playbills for the New Circus at the Market Place at Hull for May and June 1803 . . . are illustrated with small woodcuts - just one illustration on each bill. These are the earliest illustrated playbills that I have ever seen. But these and the Astley playbills of the 1820s were for circus-type entertainments rather than for the legitimate theatre.

Hours spent leafing through a mere score of the British Library's fat and often fragile volumes of playbills, and further sources such as the Theatre Museum, have revealed but a handful with pictorial illustrations for the period up to 1840, though clearly a thorough search could throw up more.[12] Even well into the 1840s, playbills embellished with illustrations for straight theatre were far from common. Given, as George Speaight writes elsewhere of playbills that "Here is a subject waiting for its historian", William Grossmith's contribution deserves proper appraisal and a place in the record.[13] This paper can do no more than point the way.

The earliest Grossmith playbill that we can illustrate is one of three for William Robert's guest-appearance with the M'Cready stock-company at the Bristol Theatre Royal on 14, 15 and 17 March 1826 (illustration 16). These performances were recorded by Kathleen Barker - of course.[14] I can do nothing more fitting than to quote verbatim a note from Dr Barker, typically spare and sufficient, in which she originally supplied me with the details:

> Playbills, Theatre Royal, Bristol, recording performances of Master Grossmith.
>
> Tuesday 14 March 1826
>
> Prison Scene from *Pizarro*
> Tent-scene from *Richard III*
> Monopolylogue, *Pecks of Troubles*
> Comic Song and Piece on Musical Glasses

Wednesday 15 March 1826

as Tuesday

Friday 17 March 1826 - Benefit

Hamlet's Soliloquy on Life and Death
Quarrel Scene in *Douglas*
Comic Song and Piece on Musical Glasses
Dagger Scene in *Macbeth*
Favourite Scene in *Richard III*
Trial Scene, *Merchant of Venice*

In all cases supported by members of the Stock Company, who also gave standard pieces of their own.

The Bristol bills are illustrated by four panes of the boy in his roles, two at each edge; the first two bills of the three also have a horizontal strip showing the characters in *Pecks of Troubles*. The printing of the Bristol bills makes it clear that William Grossmith could provide local printers with his own wood-cut blocks for reproduction on bills that they were printing from scratch. Simultaneously, he carried pre-printed stock-sheets of his own for his normal practice which was to get local printers to overprint the daily details on these, as is shown by the Birmingham bill for May 1825 where the stock-sheet printer's name appears (Cowslade and Co. of Reading).

For Master William Robert to have acted with adult players as at Bristol in 1826 is otherwise unheard-of. This collaboration was suggested by the mayor (according to the *Life*), to avoid injuring the resident company's interests.[15] Until 1831, when the younger brother joined the act, William Robert's habitual style was a solo entertainment, sometimes advertised as "A LA MATHEWS".[16]

The playbill style of the early years can best be seen in the bill for Winchester on 28 September 1826, reproduced here (illustration 17).[17] A fellow to this bill, with a comparable but slightly different pattern of illustration, is extant for a Winchester performance a few days later (2 October). The bill reproduced demonstrates the settled artistic concept for William Grossmith's entire subsequent series, with its cocktail of type-size and faces, its screamers!!! - and its pictorial woodcuts in horizontal strips as well as in panels at the side-borders. The hybrid typography is normal enough for the bills of the day. The illustrations are not. They are without parallel in their time. Any graphic element in bills of this period apart from those of the Grossmiths was almost invariably a single block, centrally located at the top or in mid-text. The profusion, diversity, and sequential renewal of the pictorial element in Mr William Grossmith's playbills were characteristic of his advertising from beginning to end, and became the troupe's unique and recognisable trade-mark.[18]

Theatre-Royal, Bristol.

The Ladies and Gentlemen of Bristol Clifton, and their Vicinities, are most respectfully informed that the Celebrated

# YOUNG ROSCIUS,

Master GROSSMITH (from Reading), only EIGHT YEARS and One Month old, is engaged to perform here *three* Nights :—viz.

TUESDAY, 14th,—WEDNESDAY, 15th,—and FRIDAY, 17th inst.

## *On TUESDAY EVENING, March 14th, 1826,*

The Entertainments will commence with a PROLOGUE, by Master GROSSMITH, expressly written for the occasion ; and the

**PRISON-SCENE IN PIZARRO,**

Rolla.....Master GROSSMITH

Centinel..........Mr. GOUGH | And, Alonzo..........Mr. FLYNN.

After which, TOBIN's admired Comedy called The

# HoneyMoon

## *Or, How to Rule a Wife.*

Duke Aranza..........Mr. BARTON | Lampedo..........Mr. BAKER
Count Montalbin..........Mr. JULIAN | Jaques..........Mr. ROSS
Rolando..........Mr. FLYNN | Lopez..........Mr. DUFF
Balthazer..........Mr. GOUGH | Campillo..........Mr. SMITH
Volante..........Mrs. WILKINS
Zamora..........Miss PITT | Hostess..........Mrs. FREDERICK
And, Juliana..........Mrs. M<sup></sup>CREADY.

End of Act the First, will be presented the

## *TENT-SCENE IN RICHARD III.*

Richard the Third......Master GROSSMITH | Catesby......Mr. HOOPER.

End of the Play, the YOUNG ROSCIUS will go though his Much-admired and Laughable Comedy called

# Pecks of Troubles.

IN WHICH HE WILL PERSONATE FIVE OF THE FOLLOWING CHARACTERS, A-LA-MATTHEWS.

1 Miss Debora Grundy, (an old Maid)..........MASTER GROSSMITH!
2 Spindleshanks, (a Dandy Fortune-Hunter)..........MASTER GROSSMITH!!
3 Betty, the *Housemaid*, in love with Corporal Rattle, (with a Song, " Yes, aye, for a Soldier's Wife I'll go")..........MASTER GROSSMITH!!!
4 Corporal Rattle, as hot as Gunpowder..........MASTER GROSSMITH!!!!
5 Timothy Clodhopper, a Servant of all Work to old Grundy, (with a Song, which finishes the Piece)..........MASTER GROSSMITH!!!!!

Master GROSSMITH will sing, in the course of the Evening, his raging favourite COMIC SONG, called

**" The Farmer and Betsy Baker," presented to him by Mr. Grimaldi.**

Master GROSSMITH will conclude the whole of *his* performance with a Piece on his

## *Musical Glasses.*

To which will be added a Farce, not acted this Season, called MY

# UNCLE GABRIEL.

Uncle..........Mr. BAKER | Scrip..........Mr. HART
Ready..........Mr. BARTON | Tacit..........Mr. ROSS
Sutton..........Mr. HENRY | First Waiter..........Mr. LANSDOWN
Ostler..........Mr. LEWIS | Second Waiter..........Mr. SMITH
Mrs. T..........Mrs. WILKINS | Bar-Maid..........Miss WILKINS
And, Eliza..........Miss PITT.

*Second Night of the YOUNG ROSCIUS, Master GROSSMITH's Engagement.*

On Wednesday Evening the Entertainments will commence with a Prologue, by Master GROSSMITH, expressly written for the occasion ; and The PRISON SCENE in PIZARRO ; *Rolla* Master GROSSMITH. After which, second time, the new Comedy called LOVE'S VICTORY. End of Act the first will be presented the TENT SCENE in RICHARD III.; *Richard the Third* Master GROSSMITH. End of the Play, the Young Roscius will go through his Much-admired and Laughable Comedy called PECKS of TROUBLES. Master GROSSMITH will conclude the whole of *his* performance with a New Piece on his MUSICAL GLASSES. To which will be added a Musical Farce called ROSINA.

On Thursday Evening will be repeated, sixth time, the very popular Grand Melo-Dramatic Play called FAUSTUS. After which, second time, the new Farce called THE SCAPE GOAT, which was received on Monday with Universal Applause.

Tickets and places in the Boxes, to be had of Mr. SMITH, at the Theatre, from Eleven till Three o'Clock.

Tickets for the Pit and Gallery may be had at the General Printing-Office Narrow Wine-Street.

Somerton, Printer, 9, Narrow Wine-Street.

16. Playbill for Theatre Royal, Bristol 14 March 1826.

**Positively but for One Evening only.**

**THEATRE, WINCHESTER.**

**On THURSDAY NEXT, SEPTEMBER 28, 1826,**

THE CELEBRATED

# YOUNG ROSCIUS

**MASTER GROSSMITH, of READING, Berks,**

**ONLY EIGHT YEARS AND A QUARTER OLD,**

Will give an ENTERTAINMENT.—It being most positively the only time he will appear in WINCHESTER, Master G. feels confident he shall meet with that Support he has never failed to receive in London, Birmingham, Liverpool, Manchester, Bath, Bristol, and all the Cities and Towns he has visited.

*In the Course of the Evening Master GROSSMITH will read a few Lines from* "Milton's Paradise Lost."

PART I.

After a **PROLOGUE,** written expressly for the Purpose, Master GROSSMITH will give his **ADVENTURES IN A STAGE COACH,** when he will imitate the following CHARACTERS, viz.—

A Frenchman and a Fat Lady, an affected Lady, a Tipsy Politician, a Stage Manager, Candidates for the Stage, and his own Success, concluding the Introduction with a SONG, "*THE CAT'S MEAT MAN.*"—After which the YOUNG ROSCIUS will go through his much-admired and laughable COMEDY, called

# Pecks of Troubles

In which he will personate the following Characters, A-LA-MATHEWS:—

1 — Miss Deborah Grundy (an old Maid) ... Master GROSSMITH!
2 — Spindleshanks (a Dandy Fortune Hunter) ... Master GROSSMITH!!
3 — Monsieur Frizeur, in a Peck of Troubles, (with a Song) ... Master GROSSMITH!!!
4 — Old Grundy, in search of the Frenchman ... Master GROSSMITH!!!!
5 — Miss Adelinda Grundy ... Master GROSSMITH!!!!!
6 — Andrew Spindleshanks' Messenger ... Master GROSSMITH!!!!!!
7 — Betty, the Housemaid (in Love with Corporal Rattle) with a Song, "Yes, aye for a Soldier's Wife I'll go." ... Master GROSSMITH!!!!!!!
8 — Corporal Rattle, as hot as Gunpowder ... Master GROSSMITH!!!!!!!!
9 — Timothy Clodhopper (a Servant of All-work to Old Grundy) with a Song, which finishes the Piece ... Master GROSSMITH!!!!!!!!!

In the Course of the Evening Master GROSSMITH will sing his universally admired COMIC SONG, called "*THE FARMER AND BETSY BAKER,*" presented to him by Mr. Grimaldi, with several NEW SONGS.

PART II.

WILL CONSIST OF THE FOLLOWING SCENES:—

**The Quarrel Scene, in Douglas;**

Norval ........................ Master GROSSMITH.

**The Trial Scene, in the Merchant of Venice;**

Shylock ........................ Master GROSSMITH.

WITH THE

**TENT SCENE, IN RICHARD III.**

Richard the Third ........................ Master GROSSMITH.

The YOUNG ROSCIUS will conclude the Whole by performing a Piece, in two Parts, on his

**MUSICAL GLASSES.**

BOXES, 3s. 6d.—PIT, 2s—GALLERY, 1s.—Children under 12 Years of Age, and Schools over 15 in number, at Half-price to the Boxes and Pit only.

*Doors to be opened at half-past Seven, the Curtain will rise at Eight, and conclude at Ten.*

The whole of the WARDROBE, which is very costly and extensive, is got up by Mr. W. Shakespeare, of the Royal Haymarket Theatre, London. The SCENERY is painted expressly for the Purpose, by Messrs Jones, Billings, and Greene; which will be exhibited.

Tickets may be had at Jacob and Johnson's, County Newspaper Office, Winchester. Also a neat Pamphlet price 6d., dedicated to J. JONES, Esq. Founder of the Royal Cobourg Theatre, London, "*The Life and Proceedings of the Young Roscius.*" just published by Cowslade and Co. Mercury Office, Reading, Berks, his Birth-place.

*** Master GROSSMITH having become Purchaser of the Plate of RICHARD III. published by Mr. Greene, at 10s. 6d.; also the Portrait published by Mr. Waite, at 5s.; he intends disposing of them, and may be had as above; the print of the YOUNG ROSCIUS in the Tent Scene, at 1s. 6d.; and the Portrait, giving his Address, at 1s.

N.B. W. GROSSMITH, Sen. trusts the Inhabitants will not anticipate another Evening's Entertainment, as Master G.'s future Engagements will prevent all possibility of acceding to their wishes, should they be ever so flattering.

☞ Master G. will proceed from hence to SOUTHAMPTON, &c.

[JACOB AND JOHNSON, PRINTERS, WINCHESTER.]

17. Playbill for Winchester 28 September 1826.

18. Playbill for Bridgnorth 9 December 1831.

Sanctioned by the LORD CHAMBERLAIN, and lately patronized by the KING, QUEEN, and her Royal Highness the PRINCESS AUGUSTA, at Windsor; also, by the Rev. the VICE-CHANCELLORS of the Universities of Oxford and Cambridge (in full Term).

**POSITIVELY BUT FOR ONE NIGHT ONLY.**

# Theatre-Royal, Aberdeen,

***On FRIDAY EVENING NEXT, December 6, 1833,***

## Master B. GROSSMITH,

OF THE THEATRES ROYAL, LONDON.

**The celebrated Juvenile Actor of the present day,**

# Now but Six Years Old!

Will give his Entertainment, it being the only time:—Master G. feels confident he shall meet with that Support he has never failed to receive in LONDON, BIRMINGHAM, LIVERPOOL, MANCHESTER, BATH, BRISTOL, PORTSMOUTH, EXETER, PLYMOUTH, and all the Cities and Towns he has visited.

**PART I.**

After a PROLOGUE, written expressly for the occasion, Master GROSSMITH will give his ADVENTURES in the READING COACH, and Description of a LONDON GREEN ROOM, in which he will imitate the following Characters, Viz:—

*In the Coach.*

A meagre Frenchman, A jolly Lady, An old Scotch Lady, and himself.

*In the London Green Room.*

The Manager and his Satellites, A Youth from the Green Island, A Scotch Macbeth, Concluding with his own interview and Engagement.

After which, Master G. will give his new Laughable Entertainment, entitled the **"SEVEN AGES"** (written by D. Jerrold, Esq. and approved by Miss Mitford), assisted by his Brother,

**W. R. GROSSMITH, the celebrated Young Roscius,**

WHEN ALL THE SPLENDID NEW SCENERY AND EQUIPMENTS WILL BE EXHIBITED.

*The YOUNG ROSCIUS and Master B. GROSSMITH will proceed as follows:—*

| | |
|---|---|
| Mrs. Gibby, the Nurse (with a Baby) | Master B. GROSSMITH! |
| Tom Bentbush, Gamekeeper to 'Squire Sorrel | The YOUNG ROSCIUS! |
| Jacob Hodge, a Servant of all-work | Master B. GROSSMITH!! |
| Little Tommy, the School-Boy | Master B. GROSSMITH!!! |
| Dionysius Busby, the School-Master | The YOUNG ROSCIUS!! |
| Miss Tulia, a Lady of Fashion | Master B. GROSSMITH!!!! |
| Leander Lackpenny, the Lover | |
| Sally Primrose, from London | Master B. GROSSMITH!!!!! |
| Monsieur La Rose, a French Valet and Courier | The YOUNG ROSCIUS!!!! |
| Major Blunderbuss, the Old Soldier | The YOUNG ROSCIUS!!!!! |
| Timothy Wiseacre, the Young Soldier | Master B. GROSSMITH!!!!!! |
| Ned Knowall, Deputy to Justice Grouse | Master B. GROSSMITH!!!!!!! |
| Justice Grouse | The YOUNG ROSCIUS!!!!!! |
| John Trot, Servant to a Spendthrift | Master B. GROSSMITH!!!!!!!! |
| Old Saveall | The YOUNG ROSCIUS!!!!!!! |
| Dame Quickly, Nurse to Sir John Nestor | The YOUNG ROSCIUS!!!!!!!! |
| Young Sir John Nestor (with the Epilogue) | Master B. GROSSMITH!!!!!!!!! |

IN THE COURSE OF THE PIECE,

**A FANCY DANCE,** (arranged by Mr. WRIGHT), by Master B. GROSSMITH.

At the end of the Piece, Master B. GROSSMITH will sing his universally favourite Comic Song

**PART II.** WILL COMMENCE WITH

## A SCENE IN DOUGLAS.

Douglas ......Master B. GROSSMITH. | Glenalvon ......The YOUNG ROSCIUS.

*Masters W. R. and B. Grossmith will then go through*

SOME OF THE MOST ADMIRED SCENES IN

## *HENRY THE FOURTH.*

The YOUNG ROSCIUS, Falstaff........

Henry, Prince of Wales....Master B. GROSSMITH.

AFTER WHICH WILL BE PRODUCED, THE MOST APPROVED SCENE IN

## *RICHARD THE THIRD.*

Richard III. ....The YOUNG ROSCIUS.—Catesby ........Master B. GROSSMITH.

Prince Edward ....... .......... Master B. GROSSMITH.

*will be presented, the beauties of SHAKESPEARE's*

## MIDSUMMER NIGHT's DREAM;

*Arranged and got up expressly for Masters W. R. and B. Grossmith, in the representation of which the Audience is kept in a continual roar of laughter.*—The following are Sketches of the Characters, which are instantaneously and repeatedly changed:—

Athenian Swains getting up a Play, { Peter Quince, a Carpenter .... Master B. GROSSMITH. Nick Bottom, the Weaver, (afterwards transformed) ... The YOUNG ROSCIUS.

THE FAIRIES, { Oberon, King of the Fairies ...... The YOUNG ROSCIUS. Titania, Queen of the Fairies ...... Master B. GROSSMITH. Puck (or Robin Goodfellow) a Fairy, Master B. GROSSMITH.

In addition to Forty Changes of Scenery, a Splendid Diorama of Shakspeare's Jubilee of 1830 (at Stratford), will be exhibited after Douglas. Full particulars may be had in the Theatre, GRATIS.

**Master B. GROSSMITH, but Six Years old, will conclude the whole with his universally Favourite Song of "ALL BECAUSE 'TIS NEW."**

ADMISSION. BOXES, **2s. 6d.**—PIT, **1s. 6d.**—GALLERY, **1s.**—Children (under 14 years), BOXES, **1s. 6d.**—PIT, **1s.**—GALLERY, **6d.**

Doors to be opened at a Quarter before ... and the Drop Scene will rise at EIGHT, and conclude at Half-past Ten.——The Two Brothers will be seen previous to their Performance ... W. GROSSMITH, Sen. respectfully informs the Patrons of his Sons, their future engagements are such as to render a longer stay impossible.

*Families wishing to secure places on this occasion, may do so on applying at* RUSSEL's LIBRARY, Broad Street, *where Tickets may be had.*

Printed by G. Cornwall, Aberdeen Herald Office.

19. Playbill for Aberdeen 6 December 1833.

The celebrated **Master B. Grossmith,** (of Castle Hill, Reading, Berks.) now but **Seven Years old,** will appear for the **First and only Time,** (on his way to Cambridge, &c.) assisted by **his Brother,** (the **Young Roscius,**) who performed in **Hertford** to above **Five Hundred Persons,** a few years since, when a **new Grand Entertainment** for **1835** will be produced, with **Splendid Dresses! Scenery! &c.**

A SCENE OF THE KATSKILL MOUNTAIN

THE CAVE OF NUMBER NIPP

FOR ONE BENEFIT NIGHT ONLY, BY KIND PERMISSION,

**SHIRE HALL, HERTFORD,**

***On Thursday Evening, Oct. 15th. 1835,***

**THE CELEBRATED JUVENILE ACTOR,**

**Master B. Grossmith,**

**NOW BUT SEVEN YEARS OLD,**

Will appear in his New, Moral, and highly Interesting Entertainment of ABOVE THIRTY CHARACTERS FOR 1835 written expressly for him, by Mr. George Dibdin Pitt, Member of the Dramatic Authors' Society in London, and the Dramatique Institute, Paris; Author of "Chartley the Fatalist," "Red Banner," "Hebrew Husband," "Mountain Maid," "The Last Man," and many other Popular Pieces now performing in London.

PART THE FIRST.

*AFTER AN INTRODUCTORY ADDRESS*

**BY BOTH THE MASTERS GROSSMITH,**

**MASTER B. G. (BUT SEVEN YEARS OLD,)** will produce his **MONODRAMATIC ENTERTAINMENT,** entitled

***TRAVELLERS' TRIALS!***

***OR, CHARACTER VERSUS CARICATURE.***

In which he will give the peculiarities of, and imitate, the following Cast of Characters :—Himself!!!—Description of the Travellers!!! Aunt Peg!!!—The Sailor and his Hat!!!—The Jew!!!—Goose and Good-news!!!—The Deaf Post-boy!!!—The Little Man with the !!!—Theatrical Reminiscences!!!—Auld Reekie!!!—The Dead Letter Office!!!—Gentle George!!!—A Brown Man!!!——and conclude with A NEW COMIC SONG,

**"What Wonderful Men, what Wonderful Times, and what a Wonderful World we live in."**

PART THE SECOND.

**A Grand Melodramatic, Comic, Serio Divertisement, interspersed with Songs, &c.** (aided by the usual display of Mr. Grossmith's New Costly SCENERY and Splendid DRESSES,) in two Acts, called

**NUMBER NIPP!!**

**Or, the SPIRIT of the KATSKILL Mountain.**

| | |
|---|---|
| Numoer Nipp, the Spirit of the Mountain | Master B. Grossmith! But Seven Years Old. |
| Marco Missolonghi, the Greek Chief | Master B. Grossmith!! |
| Old Goody Gurton going to the Wedding of her Grandaughter | Master B. Grossmith!!! |
| The Thane of Fife | Master B. Grossmith!!!! |
| In the above Character Master G. will appear in his Scotch Highland Dress, presented to him by Mrs. BALFOUR, while on a Visit at her Residence, Fernie Castle, Fifeshire, Scotland. | |
| Barney Carrol, an Irish Haymaker | Master B. Grossmith!!!!! |
| Matthew Parr, aged 152 | Master B. Grossmith!!!!!! |
| Napoleon Bonaparte, with *The Hundred Days"* | Master B. Grossmith!!!!!!! |
| Cossack Cratzburg, from Siberia | Master B. Grossmith!!!!!!!! |
| Giles Grizzle, just returned from America | Master B. Grossmith!!!!!!!!! |
| Monsieur Molin, a French Cynick | Master B. Grossmith!!!!!!!!!! |
| Harlequin (when it was a Part) | Master B. Grossmith!!!!!!!!!!! |

**The Part of PEDRIGO PERLATTI, (in search of Happiness,)**

**BY MASTER W. R. GROSSMITH.**

**At the End of the PIECE, a Duet on "CONTENT," by HARLEQUIN and PERLATTI.**

PART THE THIRD.

The **ENTERTAINMENT** to conclude with a most laughable, **DRAMATIC,** Operatic, **FARCETTE,** by both the Brothers, in two Acts, entitled

***THE TWO BARBERS!!!***

OR, PHYSIC! FUN! AND FIGARO!!

In which they will exert every spring of human ingenuity to overreach each other. Any attempt to describe the Protean mystery of this Rûse contra Rûse, would prove ineffectual.

| | | | |
|---|---|---|---|
| Frank Figaro, First Barber | Mast. B. Grossmith, 7 years old. | Fred. Figaro, Second Barber | Master W. R. Grossmith. |
| Lady Loo, of the *Haut Ton* | Master B. Grossmith. | Fighting Fitzgerald | Master W. R. Grossmith. |
| Tim. Tiddlywinks, her Tiger | Master B. Grossmith. | Widow Wilkins | Master W. R. Grossmith. |
| Ephraim Mordecai, a Jew Clothesman | Master B. Grossmith. | Natty Nell, the Milk Maid | Master W. R. Grossmith |
| Bitter Bob, a knowing cove | Master B. Grossmith. | | |
| Walker, the Postman | Master B. Grossmith. | | |

THE ROOM WILL BE DIVIDED INTO THREE DISTINCT PARTS.

**Admission.—BOXES, 2s. 6d.—PIT, 1s. 6d.—GALLERY, 1s.—**

*Children under 14 Years of Age, Boxes, 1s. 6d.—Pit 1s.—Gallery 6d.*

DOORS to be opened at a ½-before 8, the Drop Scene to rise at 8 o'clock precisely.—Carriages to be ordered at a ½-past 10.

*Arrangements made for Schools with Mr. Grossmith, at the Room, on the day of Performance, from 3 till 5 o'clock.*

TICKETS MAY ALSO BE HAD AT ST. AUSTIN AND SONS, BOOKSELLERS, FORE STREET.

SCENE IN TH[E] TWO BARBERS

The instantaneous and constant change of Dress and Character being so deceptive, Master B. G ... introduced to his Auditory, previous to his appearing on the Stage, that his real size may be known.

The Masters Grossmith perform at Ware, on Friday 16th. and at Bishop's Stortford, on Monday the 19th

St. Austin & Sons, Printe[illegible]

20. Playbill for Hertford 15 October 1835.

21. Playbill for Warrington 22 March 1839.

A cognate playbill for young Grossmith at the Assembly Room, Dereham, on 20 May 1829, with some new turns from Shakespeare, "the Minor Characters to be responsed from the Wings", has been tracked down in the Theatre Museum by Cathy Haill. The illustrations follow the Winchester pattern of two horizontal strips, but have three cuts at each lower edge whose named characters are now free-standing on plinths, like Staffordshire figures. The act's art-work shows this increasing sophistication right through its lifetime. The reduction in scale imposed for publication does the playbills little justice.[19] At least the developments in variety and technique can be admired from our further examples.

The playbill next illustrated is for the troupe at Bridgnorth on 9 December 1831, "Master B." having been enrolled by now. The design has advanced to three full-width horizontal strips and six cuts at the side-edges (some characters free-standing, others with closely-detailed backing). This gives a stylish and attractive piece of printing (illustration 18). The lower extension of this bill, not reproduced, describes the show's conclusion with a Shakespearean diorama in ten itemised scenes.[20]

Two Grossmith playbills exist for performances at the Aberdeen Theatre Royal on 6 and 9 December 1833; the first is illustrated (illustration 19). Again I owe the tip-off to Kathleen Barker. Further assistance has been generously given by Dr Paul Schlicke of Aberdeen University, who noted to me: "I'm delighted to help with a project in memory of Kathleen, who was wonderfully gracious and supportive in practical ways in my research over a number of years". These Aberdeen bills share and expand on the basic structural design of the Bridgnorth bill of 1831. All have the same two main horizontal strips and side-figures. Both Aberdeen bills have further ornamentation, though the first of the two has more of it: two extra half-strips, and compression of the layout of text, render the Aberdeen bill for 6 December 1833 the most complex so far. New cuts for *A Midsummer Night's Dream* have a charming fantastication.[21]

Two years later again, a new repertory has been brought in and the pictorial design completely revised. This can be seen on the playbill for Hertford of 15 October 1835 (illustration 20). The elaboration of 1833 has given way to a classic squared surround, simple in concept but elegant in execution. In the panorama for *Number Nipp* in the top strip, which is set within and behind proscenium pillars, the figures in a curve wind back to a rolling snowscape. In contrast, the pageant at the foot is rectilinear; the *Two Barbers* and their patrons parade in front of Georgian architecture in which the formal doors and windows are all individualised. In the vertical side-panels, the sixteen cuts depict characters in *Travellers' Trials*. Each is framed within a proscenium of drapes; each, meticulously and happily, is embellished with a different swag. The immediate impact may be subliminal, but it is satisfying.[22]

Further proof that William Grossmith was carrying his own stock-sheets is provided by analogues. A replica of the Hertford bill is extant for Loughborough on 26 January 1836, identical except for local details and correction of small printer's errors.[23]

Another pictorial advance appears on 7 March 1838 for a performance at the Town Hall, Alton. The engravings on this bill are superior to anything seen before; the configuration of the blocks pays careful attention to proportion and balance; for the first time the pictures occupy more space than the written text. An analogue of this bill for Warrington on 22 March 1839 is reproduced here as illustration 21, from a reprint in the reminiscences of George Grossmith (the third), leading actor of the Gaiety.[24]

William Grossmith's marketing techniques display as much flair as his art-work. A wealth of information about these can be gleaned from successive playbills and press notices.

The Winchester bills of 1826 advertise for sale the first edition of the *Life*. They also offer a further product of Mr Grossmith's promotionalia, namely prints of two portraits of Master William Robert. One is by Waite, a guileless half-portrait.[25] The other is Hancock's study of the boy as Richard III in the Tent Scene. It is reproduced, with descriptive matter, as No. 25 in Geoffrey Ashton's *Catalogue of Paintings*. Dr Ashton's sharp eye noticed that this effigy appears on the illustrated cover of the *Life* (illustration 14), as "one of the two principal portraits, to the left of the central bust of Shakespeare".[26]

Mr Grossmith tried the entertainment out in London on at least a couple of occasions: at the Argyll Rooms with William Robert in 1827; and in 1833 advertising "Master B.", his younger phenomenon Benjamin, as "Of the Theatres Royal, London". Evidence of metropolitan success is scanty, though. It is the provincial tours that provide the best record of method and fortunes.

Before an appearance at a particular town Mr Grossmith seems to have salted the local newspaper with advance notices of his booking, sometimes for two previous issues. These contained flattering reviews of past performances, and were likely to be taken over for editorial copy, as exemplified by extant coverage for Winchester and district in September and October 1826 and Hertford in October 1828 and 1835, where the booked performances were also subsequently written up.[27]

Playbills as well as press notices recommend the desirability of advance booking, for patrons to avoid the fate of "families turned away". The fourth edition of the *Life* features a list, to 1829, of forty-four towns "that produced immense overflows".[28] This was not hyperbole; the press reviews refer to people being excluded without even the chance of a peep at the attractive portable theatre.

William Grossmith normally offered seats in boxes, pit, and gallery. These were standard playhouse demarcations which could be reproduced in Assembly Rooms: "The Room will be divided into three distinct parts". To start with, seat-prices were 3s.6d., 2s., 1s. (Winchester, 1826), later reducing to 2s.6d., 1s.6d., 1s. (1835, Hertford), and even lower at Warrington in 1839 (2s., 1s. and 6d.). The *Life* of 1829 implies that a good night's receipts were £40, £25 was acceptable in a small town but not a city, £10 induced them to move on. Half-price was offered to children (aged under twelve in 1826, under fourteen in 1835) and to school parties numbering over fifteen. The appeal of the show was wide. At Cirencester in 1825 even the Quakers came, to observe that "it was an exhibition of such talent as it behoved every person to encourage".[29] Warrington's bill of 1839 specifies the 6d. gallery as "For the Working Classes" only. The same bill advertises a new "Unique Theatre" and equipment as having been constructed for performance before King William IV and Princess Augusta. The show started at 8pm and ended two hours or so later, at 10pm for the solo act and at 10.15pm or 10.30pm when the two brothers worked together.

Publicity on the playbill includes the names of donors or authors of pieces performed – "Mr Grimaldi", "D. Jerrold Esq.", "Mr George Dibdin Pitt". A wardrobe artist is credited: "Mr W. Shakespeare, of the Royal Haymarket Theatre". Master B.'s Highland Dress for the Thane of Fife had been presented to him by the laird's lady of a Fifeshire castle. The "splendid" scenery, in first thirty then later forty changes, is "exhibited" and repeatedly billed as "New". Special drop-scenes include one of Windsor Castle. The ten-scene Shakespearean diorama was got up by Mr Grossmith "under his own direction", thus strengthening one's conjecture that it was he who was responsible for designing, if not executing, all the troupe's art-work.

Some of William Grossmith's publicity is disingenuous, though typical of show-business then as now. He avers on a preliminary bill (e.g. Winchester, 28.9.1826, and Aberdeen, 6.12.1833) that the show is "Positively but for One Evening only", then gives another performance three or four days later as a benefit. Fun can be had in spotting the slowed-down ageing of the boys from successive playbills. Of the first London reviews of 1824 quoted in the *Life*, one at least proves to be a plant.

Novelty was important. Mr Grossmith kept trying out his sons in new acts. When young Benjamin joined William Robert in 1831, the previous diet of solo extracts from Shakespeare and sequences of short turns developed into double-act scenes and playlets. By 1835 the programme was a full-scale triple bill comprising *Travellers' Trials* and two worked-over West-End pieces, *Number Nipp* (based on the Covent Garden pantomime for 1827–8) and the Figaro romp of *The Two Barbers*. By March 1838 these had been replaced by entirely new acts – *My Cousin Tom! or, Chambers in Lincoln's Inn; Poets, Proctors, and Doctors! or, A Laugh at Life;* and *Eyes Right! or, the Short-Sighted Gentleman*. Songs and a comic dialogue might also be given. Here is a repertory tailor-made for young actors – no high drama, no Shakespeare by 1835, but quick on-and-off characters and lively situations; no unsuitable casting or inept choice of play, no attempt to ape mature passions which could excite ridicule. There is no laughing at these kids but plenty of laughing with them. Certainly the young actors were talented. Equally important was the seemliness of the pieces that they performed. This, surely, is one of the most telling reasons why the popularity of the juvenile Grossmiths endured for nearly two decades.

The break-up seems to have started in the early 1840s, with William Robert going for an apprenticeship in London. "Master" Benjamin (aged seventeen?) announced the show's termination at a final performance in Reading in February 1843, nineteen years after the first Grossmith lad made his début.

Regarding them in their heyday for a moment, notice how they disarm an initial unfriendliness. The *Hertfordshire Mercury*/(*Reformer*) ends its pre-performance publicity for the Shire Hall appearance in 1835 with the statement that "The advertisement announces these heroes at our Town Hall on Thursday next" - a touch of loftiness, a touch of irony in "these heroes", "our Town Hall". Afterwards, when the act was written up, the reviewer has been won over and only respect remains: "We have never witnessed so perfect a consciousness of comic power". Master B. is described as "the retiring, gentle, but intelligent child of seven years old" in private life (he was eight or nine), but in public "he is the clever, bustling actor . . . entering with talent and with spirit" into his characterisations. The reviewer adds that Master B.

> Is admirably supported throughout by his brother, Master W.R. Grossmith: . . . and it is really quite gratifying to witness the affectionate spirit in which the latter (who is as amusing as ever) gives effect to every effort of the younger boy. (20.10.1835)

William Robert took an apprenticeship in a family firm in Fleet Street that made artificial limbs. He rose to become the master, and like his father was clearly a master-craftsman. In 1857 he published *Amputations and Artificial Limbs* in his own name as "Inventor, patentee, and manufacturer". This is the hand-book of a man of mark, expert in techniques and case-histories. He is credited by George Grossmith (III), "G.G." of the Gaiety, with inventing the glass eye as well as improvements to false limbs.[30] In old age he is said not to have looked back at his spell as a youthful actor with "much pride or pleasure".[31]

Young Benjamin took to religion. He became a missionary and went out to Africa. After this nothing more is known save that he was thought to have died from being mauled by a lion.

And the father? Mr William Grossmith is described as Pickwick-like by Tony Joseph in the family background supplied to his study of George Grossmith (II), the Savoyard, in which he draws on recollections of descendants.[32] Indefatigable, business-like, artistic and practical William must also have been. While his original business is thought to have prospered and expanded in the early 1840s, the stage kept enough hold on him for there to be tales of a theatre-managership and the composition of light music. What is unassailable is Tony Joseph's comment that "the interest William Grossmith himself took in the theatre was transmitted even more strongly to the next generation" - and, we might add, to subsequent generations.

Looking back, we bate our breath to think what a plunge William Grossmith had taken. In 1824 this young man, a sound if unsensational tradesman of thirty married to a wife "sternly opposed" to the theatre and father of an increasing family, suddenly kicked over the traces. He assembled the materials of an act, got his performing infant up to scratch, overcame his wife's objections, left the running of his business to subordinate hands. He set out on the road in the dead of winter with little to guide him but theatrical stars in his eyes and faith in the precocity of his six-year-old.

Give him credit for his skill, his vision, his energy. It was his flair that master-minded and managed a Young Roscius road-show for nearly twenty years.

Credit, also, Mrs Lucy Grossmith. Wife of the tiresomely-footloose if amiable William, mother of the precocious William Robert and Benjamin and of two more sons and at least two daughters beside, she was left to mind the shop, hold the home together, and bring up the family. She seems to have done so, wonderfully well.

There is still a lot to be found out about George the Savoyard's trouping grandfather and uncles. The aim of this preliminary investigation is to rescue a laudable little touring outfit from oblivion, demonstrating the capacity of its members and emphasising the unique quality and range of its promotional material. Further Juvenile Grossmith playbills and other records are surely there to be turned up - though not, alas, in the main archives of the Grossmith family, which suffered destruction in the blitz during Hitler's war.[33] Perhaps any reader who comes across further evidence could pass on knowledge of it via a "Note" in *Theatre Notebook*, or direct to the Theatre Museum, Covent Garden, for the file. Could we see an exhibition of pictorial playbills, one day? In any such, the Grossmiths of Reading would figure large.

William Grossmith should be remembered in theatrical annals for more than being the inspiration and founder of a family of continuing importance in the development of the British stage. Never mind that the popularity of the act he managed was restricted to provincial audiences. His sons' dramatic talents may have been light-weight, but they were not inconsiderable. Thanks to their tenacity, competence, and appeal, these Grossmiths maintained a juvenile acting venture for an unusually lengthy, perhaps unparalleled, period of time. They delighted their public in big cities and tiny towns the length and breadth of Britain from Penzance to Aberdeen. The organisation and stage-management of the act displayed style, attention to detail, intelligence, and a readiness to pay for quality.

The concept of the artwork which accompanied the act's publicity was innovative and apposite, its employment comprehensive, its subject-matter constantly renewed, and its effect constantly arresting. William Grossmith and his pictorial playbills deserve a place in theatre history.

# *Notes*

1. According to Arnott & Robinson, eds *English Theatrical Literature 1559-1900 A Bibliography,* London, 1970 (2977), the first edn of the *Life* (Reading, 1825; at Harvard) has a different title and an unillustrated cover. The authorship is ascribed to "E.C.B., his Preceptor", but dropped from subsequent editions. My references are to the 2nd edn of 1827 (British Library) and the 4th edn of 1829 (Berkshire Local Studies Library, Reading, not in A.& R.) in which the 2nd edn text is revised and extended. A full example of the 5th edn in private hands has been made available to me. It is a reprint of the 4th edn with a front cover updated to 1831. After this year the pamphlet may have been dropped, because the show took a new course in 1831 with the introduction of a second juvenile. (By kind permission, a photocopy of the 5th edn has been passed on to the Theatre Museum and to Bristol University Theatre Collection.) I am grateful to various members of staff at Reading institutions for help with identifications and photocopies, for reproduction permission, and for directing me to E. O. Farrar, *The Dramatic History of Reading,* Reading, 1926 and Daphne Phillips, *Reading Theatres, Cinemas and other Entertainments 1788-1978,* Reading, 1978: namely Katie Willis (Berkshire C.R.O.), Margaret Smith and Alan Hankin (Berkshire Local Studies Library), and Godfrey Omer-Parsons (Reading Art Gallery). Professor Michael Twyman, of the Department of Typography and Graphic Communication, University of Reading, has kindly assisted with a helpful contact.

2. *Life*, 2nd edn, 7. The 4th edn, 6, gives his year of birth as 1819. Child-stars tend to age more slowly than their years.

3. *Life*, both edns, 9-12.

4. *Life*, 4th edn, 10.

5. I am grateful to the staff of the Prints and Drawings Department, British Museum, for help and generous permission to reproduce this aquatint. Another example is in the Reading Art Gallery. The engraving is not dated. Under intensification the date on the newspaper held by the boy can be seen to be Monday January 12, 1829. (B.M. P. & D. Dept. ref. TH/5; vol. cvii/5627).

6. Quoted in Phillips, *op cit.*, 18-19. This may have been written by Mary Russell Mitford, who was contributing theatrical notices to the *Reading Mercury* at this time (Phillips, 19). "Approved by Miss Mitford" endorses a repertory item on the troupe's playbill for 6.12.1833 (Aberdeen).

7. *Life*, 4th edn, 22.

8. Information in this and the next paragraph is from the *Life*, 4th edn, 12-20.

9. After an initial announcement, a Mr Cross, to "manage the stage" and "continue the boy's education", is heard of no more. Neither is "E.C.B. his Preceptor".

10. This bill is to be found in vol. 68 of B. L. Fragmenta, 937.g.68, f. 190. So fragmented is it, indeed, with parts pasted in on two adjacent folios and the woodcuts in irregular order, that reproduction here is impracticable.

11. George Grossmith, *A Society Clown: Reminiscences*, Bristol, 1888, 40-43. His 1825 bill's engravings were said to comprise nine figures of the Introduction and seven of "Pecks of Troubles", with four blocks of the boy in private dress and three as

Shakespearean characters. A succeeding bill for the boy at Bridgnorth 2 and 3 August 1825 has just been found (John Johnson Collection, Bodleian Library), with twenty-four cuts. These all reappear on bills for 1826. In the reminiscences of George's brother Weedon Grossmith, *From Studio to Stage*, London, 1913, there is a bare mention of his father's younger brother (that is, Benjamin) who "had made a great success when a child as an actor" (27). The father of these brothers George and Weedon was also George (now called George Grossmith I). In the order of Mr William Grossmith's sons, George I came between William Robert and Benjamin. The brothers George (II) and Weedon were happily prodigal with Pooter, but we could wish them less economical with uncles.

12. A check-list of all illustrated playbills discovered in the course of this investigation will in due course be offered to *Theatre Notebook*.

13. George Speaight, *Collecting Theatre Memorabilia,* Ashbourne, 1988, 13. The history of the theatre programme has its annalists, e.g. Barbara Cavanagh, *A Century of the Programme 1860-1960,* Romsey, 1960, and posters are well documented in Catherine Haill, *Theatre Posters,* London, 1983, and other studies. The playbill, on the contrary, important forerunner of both programme and poster, doubling in duty for each, has had little attention. George Speaight's summary is on *op cit.,* 11-17, with a useful bibliography. The only monograph, Gordon Martin's *The Playbill: Development of its Typographic Style,* Chicago, 1963, is a technical diploma piece, for printers rather than theatre historians, and its reproductions very far from comprehensive. The British playbill is copiously revealing about the history of our theatre and its times from c.1710. It awaits the chronicler of its 150-year lifetime.

14. Kathleen Barker, *The Theatre Royal, Bristol, 1766-1966*, London, Society for Theatre Research, 1974, 248. The original bills are in the B.L., Playbills vol. 205. I am grateful to the authorities of the British Library for generous permission to reproduce.

15. The *Life* refers to the combined effort at Bristol without enthusiasm (4th edn, 19). The chronicler may have been influenced by the derision met by the eight-year-old "Miss Mudie" when she played with an adult cast at the time of the bursting of the Bettymania bubble, twenty years previously. This memory was kept alive in *The Percy Anecdotes* of 1822: see Allardyce Nicoll, *Early XIXth Century Drama*, vol. I, Cambridge, 1930, 21-2.

16. Suggestively, Harley had given a performance entitled "Mr Mathews At Home" in the Reading Theatre on 11 October 1822 (playbill in B.L. Playbills vol. 299).

17. I am grateful to John Cavanagh of Motley Books for alerting me to this bill, and presenting a facsimile; to Alan Dowdell for tracking down the original and its fellow in the Winchester offices of the *Hampshire Chronicle*, and contemporary press notices in Winchester Reference Library; and to Peter Whitmarsh, a director of the *Hampshire Chronicle*, for rapid and generous response to my request for photographs and permission to reproduce. These Winchester playbills were printed - or overprinted - by Messrs Jacob and Johnson, then as now printers of the *Hampshire Chronicle.*

18. The *Life* says little about the playbills themselves. The special regard in which they were held may be inferred from a remark about the imitators who ventured forth on Master William Robert's heels, "with facsimiles of his bills" (4th edn, 21). One such was "Miss M. H. Carr, the Celebrated Infant Roscia", three of whose imitative playbills for Nov.-Dec. 1828 at Bridgnorth are in the John Johnson Collection, Bodleian Library. There were, of course, several other children in the 1820s and 1830s who were child-stars in their own right, notably Clara Fisher, Master Burke, and Jean Davenport.

19. In actual size the bills have an average width of 26 cms, varying by two cms either way. The standard length is roughly half as long again as the width (e.g. Winchester, 25 x 37 cms). Some bills are twice as long as they are wide (Bridgnorth, 24 x 48 cms, and Aberdeen, 26.5 x 53 cms). Better-scale or full-size copies of these and further examples of the Grossmiths' illustrated advertisements have been presented, for more convenient

consultation by anyone interested, to the Berkshire Local Studies Library at Reading, and, including photocopies of the *Life*, to the Theatre Museum, and to the Theatre Collection of the University of Bristol.

20. I am grateful to B. R. Cleave, Esq., the bill's owner, for organising a photograph and generously giving permission to publish, and to Peter Wood, theatrical bookseller, for help with liaison.

21. This bill and its fellow for 9 December are in the A. D. Morice Collection of the Library of the University of Aberdeen, respectively folios 55 and 56. I am grateful to Iain Beavan, of the Library's Special Collections department, for help and advice on the occasion of my visit, and the generous permission to reproduce.

22. This bill was rescued from an old scrapbook of Hertford's leading printer, Messrs Stephen Austin & Sons Ltd, established 1768 and still going strong. One of the firm's directors, Richard Russell, has kindly helped me with typographical insights. The bill is now in the Hertfordshire C.R.O., ref. Acc. 2427, after expert conservation by John Lambert. A framed photograph of the bill has been donated to Hertford's Adams-designed Shire Hall, where the Assembly Room in which the 1835 performance took place still forms an impressive Reception Suite. I owe first knowledge of the bill, from which sprang this entire pursuit, to an old friend, the late Cyril Heath. I am grateful for the help in Hertford that has been given by Dr Kathryn Thompson and her staff of the Herts C.R.O. (including generous permission to reproduce), by Alan White and his staff at Hertford Library, and by the staff of "D.O.T.S." (Drawing Office Technical Service, Hertford), on all of whose expertise I have made repeated calls, never to be disappointed.

23. The Loughborough bill is reproduced in Helen and Richard Leacroft, *The Theatre in Leicestershire*, Leicester, 1986, 28. The original has now been donated to the Theatre Museum.

24. The Alton bill is in B.L. Playbills, vol. 270, too fragile to be photographed. The Warrington reprint is in George Grossmith, "*G.G.*", London, 1933, 86, approved for reproduction as out of copyright.

25. A print of Waite's portrait appears as the frontispiece of the *Life*, 2nd edn. onwards.

26. Geoffrey Ashton, ed. James Fowler, *Catalogue of Paintings at the Theatre Museum*, London, Society for Theatre Research and Victoria and Albert Museum, 1992, 36. The unpublished paper to which Dr Ashton referred (p. 38) was my "work in progress" made available to him and written in 1990 to accompany the Grossmiths' Hertford playbill on its deposit in the Herts C.R.O.; it is superseded by the present study save that further matter in it is devoted to a detailed examination of the 1835 performance at Hertford, and an account of the Infant Phenomenon industry of the early 19th century. The original Tent Scene oil-painting was donated to the Theatre Museum by Andrew Faulds Esq., M.P., with some notes on Master William Robert. In 1964 a print of this portrait appeared in the London Press, together with some correspondence about the boy, who was described from his visage in the print as a "little monster". I am grateful to James Fowler and Catherine Haill of the Theatre Museum for drawing these cuttings and further relevant information to my attention.

27. These notices are contained in the files of the *Hampshire Chronicle* held in Winchester Reference Library and the *Hertfordshire Mercury* (briefly renamed the *Reformer*) held by Herts County Record Office. The 4th edn of the *Life* contains twenty-eight further "critiques" in an appendix.

28. *Life*, 4th edn, 21, adding that "very great encouragement" met them at all the towns visited; in their first four years the troupe "completed about two-thirds of England".

29. *Life*, 4th edn, 12.

30. E. O. Farrar, *The Dramatic History of Reading*, 5, quoting a personal communication from George Grossmith (III).

31. George Grossmith (II), *A Society Clown*, 43.
32. Tony Joseph, *George Grossmith: biography of a Savoyard*, Bristol, 1982, 15–20. I am grateful to Tony Joseph for help with liaison, as well as his pages on Mr William Grossmith and the juveniles – the only known previous account which makes them flesh-and-blood.
33. This sad loss was communicated to me by John George Esq. of Edinburgh, Kintyre Pursuivant of Arms and Mr William Grossmith's great-great-great-grandson, for whose interest and support I am most obliged. From the same source we learn of a further item lost to the family which may (or may not) have been overtaken by a similar fate, namely a bust of William Grossmith mentioned in the will of George Grossmith (II) the Savoyard, who died in 1912.

# The Theatre at Grassington

SYBIL ROSENFELD

IN the grey Yorkshire village of Grassington there stand some cottages which were once the village theatre. And a unique company it was which trod the boards of this particular barn. The manager of it was Thomas Airey, the Grassington and Skipton carrier and a great character: "a little fat old man with reddish whiskers and a jolly face that Liston or John Reeve would not be ashamed to possess. In that countenance a mere tyro in physiognomy may discover a roguish slyness, a latent archness, a hidden mine of fun and good humour. Then when Airey walks, mark his stately gait, and tell me if it does not proclaim that he has worn the sock and buskin, and trod the Thespian floor." So he was described in Hone's *Table Talk* in 1838.[1]

The barn theatre appears to have been originally visited by Goldsmith and his company after they had left Skipton[2] but he used to supplement his players with local talent. After a time the company split and Airey who was among the amateurs formed a company of his own. Tradition has it that Goldsmith's and Airey's company included Edmund Kean (then acting as Carey) and Harriet Mellon among its members. This seems unlikely at the date given: 1807. Kean was certainly acting for a few months in Yorkshire in Butler's Richmond company in 1806, but there is no evidence that the company or Kean ever visited Grassington. As for Harriet Mellon, she was by that time firmly established on the London boards, and though she used to visit the provinces in the summer, it is unlikely that she would condescend to such as Grassington.

However, the real interest of the company lies not in these stars but in the fact that most of the actors were village worthies who fretted their hour upon the stage for a few weeks in the depth of winter when agricultural pursuits were at a standstill. Few of the company were still living in 1838. Hone speaks of Peter W "Whose face peeped from behind the green curtain like a full moon" and who was up to such tricks as almost blowing up the stage with gunpowder, half suffocating the audience with assafoetida and putting hot cinders in his colleagues' boots; Isaac G a fiddler and comic singer; Bill Cliff the Skipton poet and bailiff; Waddilove; Frankland of Helton; club-footed Simon Coates – all of whom were dead. There was Jack Solomon the besom maker, Tommy Summergill the barber and clock maker, Jack L the politician of Threshfield and fifteen or sixteen others from the surrounding villages.

The local schoolmaster taught the actors to pronounce in the most barbarous fashion: pomp became pump; pageantry paggyantry, fatigued fattygewed; when consulted in difficulty he would frequently, for a joke, give them an entirely wrong meaning as when he explained that piquet was French for pie cut with the consequence that they solemnly staged a business of pie cutting. Except for Elizabeth Rodwell, a Leeds milliner, the company consisted of men; Airey would strut the stage as Lady Randolph with clogs and corduroy breeches showing beneath his gown. Yet Hone says that the decorations, considering the poverty of the company, were tolerable, the scenery respectable and the barn better managed than bigger playhouses. Nevertheless sometimes the sun or moon would catch fire and expose the tallow candle behind it, whilst the dresses, though of good materials, were often not in character: Arden would appear as a Craven waggoner and a friar would wear a bobbed wig, a cocked hat and a modern surplice.

The stage was lighted by five or six halfpenny candles. The auditorium was merely a pit and gallery but when the Duke of Devonshire or Earl of Thanet came a box was improvised by railing off a part of the pit and covering the railings with brown paper painted to represent drapery. The playbills were written by hand and the parish bellman cried the plays in couplets composed by Airey such as:

> Guy in his youth our play we call
> At six to the hay-mow, hie ye all.

Yet these rude mechanicals of real life played Shakespeare, Dryden, Otway, Lillo and Rowe, favouring the older plays but omitting all indelicate sentiments or expressions. The parson, the schoolmaster and the doctor had their laugh but the crude actors kept alive in the bleak village a fire for the spirit.

## Notes

1. W. Hone, *Table Talk*, London, 1838, I, 69.
2. J. S. Fletcher, *Picturesque History of Yorkshire*, London, 1899, III, 193.

# This Multiform Modern Evil: The Annual Admonitions of the Revd Thomas Best of Sheffield

FRANCES DANN

WHEN Kathleen Barker came to Sheffield to pursue her research she told me that theatrical activity here in the nineteenth century was greatly hampered by widespread objections to it on religious grounds. So it seems appropriate to take a closer look now at some evidence of the ways in which anti-theatrical sermons set to work to keep people out of the playhouse. All my quotations are taken from the first series of the Revd Thomas Best's sermons, collected in 1831.[1]

It is immediately apparent that Thomas Best's approach to his subject was conditioned by a belief that every human creature is born with a "wrong bias within" (xii-251) which has positively to be resisted. This "inborn depravity" (xii-251) means that any theatre audience "is composed of beings who, by the very fault and corruption of their nature, are already inclined to evil" (xiv-301). Best's conviction on this point lends urgency to all his admonitions. He frequently sounds as if he is begging an invalid not to do what will worsen his condition, using words associated with the aggravation of existing disorders. His hearers, far from congratulating themselves on their spiritual health, are urged to consult at all times "an enlightened, quick, and tender conscience" (x-208).

One of Best's most basic functions, as a preacher, is to make it impossible for members of his congregation to find themselves at a theatre without having given the matter due consideration: "Bear in mind that you will never again attend the Theatre in ignorance, unadmonished and unwarned" (iv-81). A second visit, ostensibly undertaken in a right spirit, is roundly condemned with a shrewd thrust at the pleasure and excitement good people are apt to find in righteous indignation:

> to be grieved at wickedness, and to be shocked at sin, and yet go to the places where such wickedness and sin are exhibited and sanctioned; and then to hope that the pain of mind which is felt will be a mitigation of the criminality of attending; this is so palpable a delusion, that if we did not know the exceeding deceitfulness of the human heart, it would scarcely seem credible or possible; and yet, perhaps, many of you have laid this flattering unction to your consciences. (vii-141)

Best addressed his remarks, by implication, chiefly to male heads of households who are to hold themselves responsible for whatever ill effects playgoing may have on their wives, servants, apprentices and children. The modern reader recognises with a sigh a system of control and censorship which held sway from Bowdler to the trial of Lady Chatterley. But Best is no Podsnap. His disapprobation is not activated by a complacent adherence to received ideas but by his vivid sense of ever-present danger. The scenario of the fall from grace, so crucial to his view of the world, naturally dominates his thoughts about the theatre:

> God, from whom nothing is hid, has seen every youth whom the theatre has deeply injured, if not ruined, both for time and for eternity; and he has beheld every female, whose native delicacy has been deteriorated, if not destroyed, by the exhibition of scenes of vice; and by familiarity with sentiments which, under her parents' roof, would never have been permitted to reach her ear. In a word, God has been witness to all the bitter distress and remorse of parents - all the ruin of children - all the corruption of servants - all the individual, domestic and public evil of which this powerful engine of Satan has been the occasion (x-211).

Some opponents of playgoing sound, when inveighing against its effects upon the young and the impressionable, as if their real, unadmitted reasons for opposition were those of an elderly man of fixed habits who foresees expense and inconvenience to himself arising out of any deviation from established domestic routine. Best rises above this level and his Bunyanesque vision of life as a perilous progress picks up additional echoes of the epic theme of the hero in the toils of a strength-sapping enchantress. The youth who ventures into a playhouse is seduced from the narrow path of virtue into "revellings and drunkenness and foolish and frothy conversation and every kind of corrupt and corrupting communication. And all this time, the vigour and vivacity, and strength, and spirits of youth are wasted in these excesses". (xiii-276)

The preacher does not hesitate to describe the theatre's attractions in glowing terms. Did early nineteenth-century Sheffield playgoers really have their imaginations stimulated and their passions heated by so much gaiety, brilliance, exhilaration, splendour, excitement and mirth? Best himself disavows any personal experience of playgoing and one cannot help but suspect that he would have found the real thing tame and tawdry compared with the diabolical glamour of the vision in his mind.

Insofar as his notions are based upon real theatrical conditions at all they seem to reflect those of the most permissive days of Charles II, and he is not prepared to admit that things have changed for the better:

> We are told that the stage is now comparatively pure. This is a point which I

> pretend not to determine; but it is impossible to live in the world without hearing of the effects of an attendance upon the Theatre . . . The fact, I doubt not, is, that little essential improvement has taken place. (vii–138).

He has, of course, been reading the newspapers and though he is unacquainted with play texts and prevailing standards of decency on the stage itself he notices when the theatre is mentioned as the scene of a disturbance or a place to which young tearaways resort. In his day so few places (apart from public houses) were open for the entertainment of the relatively poor that the theatre was bound to become a focus of anxiety for respectable home-keeping people. If there was going to be a riot or a major accident the theatre (as more recently the football stadium) was the place where it was most likely to occur. Best does not, to his credit, gloat as some opponents of the stage do at the fate of the victims of such events, but he does not altogether eschew using them for shock effect, as here towards the end of a sermon addressed specifically to young people:

> It was during this very year that on an alarm taking place at a Theatre in a neighbouring county, *not fewer than six young persons, between the ages of twelve and eighteen, lost their lives*; and they went, from the dissipation and profligacy, and profaneness of a playhouse into the presence of a righteous, and, as it is to be justly feared, an angry God. (vii–150)

When these members of the audience were arraigned at the bar of judgement they would have to admit to having *frequented* (itself a pejorative word suggestive of slumming or at least of idleness) theatrical *amusements* (with all that that implies of time-wasting and frivolity). But beyond the preacher's concern with the wasting of precious time are more specific accusations levelled at the stage itself.

One group of objections concerns the use of the name of God on stage. Best asserts that that name is taken in vain when characters in plays pretend to pray or to swear oaths or call God to witness. In fact texts of classic plays printed from prompt copies in Best's day reveal that much of what had once been a liberal peppering of oaths had been expunged by common consent. It was usual for the Reader of Plays to see to this in London and for the changes gradually to become general. Many oath-peppered old plays did in fact slip out of the repertory in the early nineteenth century partly as a result of the drift towards decency and partly because they were superseded by more congenial modern works. Of this development Best takes no cognisance, and indeed there was probably enough praying and swearing left to shock so sensitive a conscience as his.

Another group of objections has to do with the power of example. Best, like many nineteenth-century reviewers of fiction, goes in constant dread of people's imitating the invented characters that are set before them. Thus it becomes objectionable for a villain to be shown on the stage gloating over his misdeeds.

There are, in the preacher's view, great dangers in allowing the bad people in plays to be at all attractive and it is wrong to depict revenge or ambition as goals which may be condoned or even admired. This line of argument was perhaps more relevant to the early nineteenth century than the preacher could know. The fascination of villainy, prominent in old plays such as *Richard III*, was an essential component of melodrama. The common romantic concept of the outsider driven by revenge, ambition or despair is at least as old as *Paradise Lost* and in that form must have been familiar to Best. How he would have flinched at the worldly Lord Eldon's comment on Satan: "Damn fine fellow and I hope he wins."

The third category of complaint has to do with gravity. Best objects to the presentation of pious people and the clergy as objects of derision:

> Religion is safely ridiculed under the name of hypocrisy. A preacher of God's word is, perhaps, exhibited in strong caricature. A sermon is delivered in burlesque imitation. A religious character is introduced, for the purpose of being placed in the most ludicrous points of view, and exposed as a person of weak intellect and pitiable credulity. (ix-189)

Evidently someone has told Best about *The Hypocrite*. Bickerstaff's play (a descendant of Moliere's *Tartuffe* by way of Cibber's *Non-Juror*) was ruthlessly cut up and re-formed as a vehicle for established comedians with a nice line in extemporisation. It was always a risky piece, largely because the mock sermon, itself an accretion, was frequently encored so that the actor might embark on yet more outrageous flights of grimace and mimicry. Did anyone, I wonder, imitate the Revd Thomas Best as year by year he timed his admonitions to coincide with the opening of the theatres? His complaint about the presentation of pious people as dupes goes right back through theatre history to Jonson, but does not apply with much force to the stage in his own day. Again it is the Restoration drama which is evoked, at a time when precious few examples remained in the repertory, and those few in greatly altered texts.

An inescapable accusation which the preacher levels at the theatre is that it

> upholds, and applauds, and inculcates, both by precept and example, the maxims of the world, in opposition to the word of God. The Bible enjoins upon us lowliness, meekness, patience under injuries, forgiveness and forbearance. The return of good for evil, separation from the world, a humble, contrite contented spirit, a holy, heavenly mind. (vii-136)

It is not necessary for the stage to be peopled with the rich, carefree, and unprincipled fashionables of the 1680s for this quotation to hold good. The theatre's very essence is that it reflects the world. If worldly concerns are abjured the theatre must be renounced, if not denounced. At this point its defenders might wish to point out that plays may support rather than undermine morality. Best will have none of it. In his view the occasional wholesome touch is part of the seduction process:

> In these Amusements there is much to entice and entrap; - much to excite the tenderest feelings; - much to interest the cultivated mind; - there is every thing of outward decoration, and beauty of language, to catch and to gratify the eye and the ear; - and together with all this, moral lessons and virtuous sentiments are interspersed here and there which serve to lull and pacify the conscience. All these circumstances conspire to spread over the theatre a most dangerous fascination. (iv-63).

This peroration culminates in references to beautiful serpents with venomous fangs and sparkling wine containing deadly poison. True to his vocation as the guardian of a flock all too easily led astray, Best pictures a party of homebodies venturing out at night in search of entertainment:

> On retiring from the Theatre, they are compelled to hurry themselves and their families through scenes which would not bear inspection; when the eye sees and the ear hears what can neither be defended nor excused; then, by way of unction to their consciences, they think of some moral precept, some virtuous sentiment, some of those *good things to be found in plays* which glitter on the general mass of evil and corrupt communications, like glow worms, thinly scattered amid surrounding darkness. (x-210)

He cannot fail to be aware that people who were in no other respect addicted to the drama did subscribe to the prevailing reverence for Shakspeare, whose works in editions such as Bowdler's found their way even into pious homes. Thus it became necessary, after a condemnation of plays in general, to be specific and for once mention the name of a dramatist.

> In this description of the general character and tendency of plays, I beg distinctly to be understood as meaning to include the plays of Shakspeare. And I have no fear of being contradicted by any person who is a competent judge - who knows what religion and morality are, - who forms his opinion by the rule of God's commandments, - who brings plays to the test of the Bible, - and is sincere in his scrutiny, and honest in avowing the result. (xiv-294)

At this point the preacher is aware that he carries his opposition further than is expected even of a clergyman. But irked beyond bearing by the reverence accorded to Shakspeare and determined to abide by his principles, he plunges on:

> Oh! that this truth were brought home to the consciences of those persons who are accustomed to commend, *in language of almost idolatrous regard*, such pernicious writings as the plays of Shakspeare!
>
> I shall probably be ridiculed as wanting taste to appreciate genius or talent; and shall doubtless be reproached with bigotry and uncharitableness. But what are genius and talent when employed to the dishonour of God, and to the ruin of immortal souls! (xiv–295)

Best has thought it through and, with characteristic rigour, has decided that abstention from the drama must be total to be effectual. He is quite correct. In a longer essay I could contextualise his remarks and show that, if one views the stage as a danger, access to the work of Shakespeare, even in abridged and amended form, can be the means of luring people in. But Best does not look, as I have done, at the life-stories of actors. Insofar as he considers them it is with pity from afar off, deploring the temptations to which their profession exposes them. There is no use of sensational anecdotes, as found in the most extreme religious journals, about performers dropping dead on stage just after delivering lines inviting God to judge them. As with riots and disasters, Best's attitude is one of regret, not of gleeful commination. It is greatly to his credit that he can hate the sin and simultaneously encourage his congregation to pity the actors trapped in a sinful way of life.

In my view Thomas Best's least impressive utterances are those in which he attempts to engage directly with local and recent scandals. Attempts at immediacy of this kind detract from his dignity:

> And here I would take occasion to raise my warning voice against a class of sins, which of all others, perhaps, are most fatal in their consequences, both as it regards this world and that which is to come. I will not be deterred by the captiousness of a fastidious delicacy from plainly saying *that I mean the sins of uncleanness; fornication, whoredom, and adultery.* THERE IS TOO MUCH REASON TO BELIEVE THAT THESE SINS ARE BECOME ALARMINGLY COMMON IN SHEFFIELD. (xi–236)

Something about the capital letters and the place-name does not sort well with the preacher's usual measured and balanced style of discourse. His lofty tone develops a hint of commonplace ill-humour when he descends to examples of local uncouthness:

> Large groups of rude boys and girls, and of disorderly young men and women, are allowed to assemble together, to lounge through the streets and fields, or to frequent the public-houses, without any effectual control, either on the part of parents or masters. (xii–242)

This is the voice of the grumbler, not that of the inspired preacher.

Best is at his most persuasive when he engages directly with his congregation and lets his rhetoric sweep them grandly past the doors of the theatre towards solid joys and lasting pleasures of a spiritual kind:

> Now, my dear Brethren, place for a moment the Amusement of the Theatre in comparison with the purity and holiness of God. Think of the nature of most dramatic compositions; - of the polluting language of the stage, and of the manner in which it is uttered and received. Recollect the appendages of the play-house, and the scenes which are there witnessed, and the iniquity which there abounds; and then tell me, - How must these things be regarded by a man who admires and loves the spotless purity of the divine nature, and whose very soul is won and delighted by the glory of the divine holiness; and who can say to God in the sincerity of his soul, "Thy word is very pure, therefore thy servant loveth it." (iii-47)

The preacher has another highly effective mode of speaking, in which he uses staccato short commands leading up to a weightier injunction at the end of a paragraph.

> Enter into no compromise. Make no concessions. Dread to take one approaching step. There is an important part of the original prohibition given to our first parents, mentioned by Eve in her answer to Satan; "ye shall not eat of it, *neither shall ye touch it*." Have nothing to do with the Theatre. Come out from among them and be ye separate, and *touch* not the unclean thing. (xi-238)

Best has a sure instinct for the effective closure, honed by long experience of public prayer.

> Be sober, - be vigilant. - Watch unto prayer. And may it please God to strengthen such as do stand, - to raise up them that fall, and to beat down Satan under our feet. (xi-239)

At moments like this the mantle of his fiery predecessors descends upon him with a satisfying swish - or am I responding too theatrically?

Unquestionably local theatrical ventures were valuable to Thomas Best. They gave him a focus for his hostility to worldliness and dissipation. His idea of a playhouse encapsulated all that he dreaded for the congregation in his care. In his sermons theatre-going becomes a sort of parable by means of which he can encompass all the allurements of which he has heard, including some which are beyond description. For him and for his enthralled listeners the theatre becomes a mysterious realm of unbounded luxury and licence. This kept some of them away, certainly. Pillars of the congregation could not be seen to lend their presence after hearing Best's admonitions. Being seen at the theatre would wreck one's reputation for piety. I cannot help but suspect that on the other hand clandestine nights at the play became a rite of passage for young people inclined to be impatient of parental control. I do hope they found it sufficiently shocking, after all that.

## Note

1. *Sermons on the Amusements of the Stage*, preached at St James's Church, Sheffield by the Revd T Best, London, 1831.

# "Let Glasgow Flourish"

TRACY C. DAVIS

"The greatest happiness of the greatest number."
(*An introduction to the principles of Morals and Legislation*,
Jeremy Bentham)

"The greatest number - number one."
(*Money*, Edward Bulwer)

WHEN Glasgow's Theatre Royal Queen Street (1805-29) in the Regency New Town burned to the ground, the land sold to a housing developer, while the patent was auctioned separately.[1] Its purchaser was John Henry Alexander, low comedian and proprietor/manager of the rival Dunlop Street Theatre which assumed the patent prerogatives. From that moment, Alexander vigilantly claimed the right of monopoly, turning against the "free trade" managers with whom he had formerly stood.

Alexander came to Glasgow in 1823 after serving as lessee of theatres in Dumfries and Carlisle, but only on condition that the magistrates provide written assurance that he would not be prosecuted for vagrancy under the Act of 12 Anne.[2] He established business on the basis of a minor theatre, tolerable under the law provided that he did not perform legitimate drama. While he occupied the Dominion of Fancy in the cellar of the Dunlop Street Theatre, his productions vied with Francis Seymour's upstairs, often drowning each other out. In modern terms, it was as if a regional theatre and its studio annexe existed in competition rather than co-operation, even to the extent of presenting the same pieces simultaneously. They went to court, and were ordered to amicably share the premises and perform on a roster of alternate nights.[3] After a short time, Seymour took the ultimate retribution: he obtained the lease on the Theatre Royal at Queen Street, which entitled him to prosecute Alexander for any infringement of the patent. In 1825, when business slackened during one of Glasgow's periodic recessions, the proprietors of the Theatre Royal, on Seymour's behalf, served Alexander with a suit claiming his presentation of melodramas and burlettas was a breach of the monopoly. Henceforth, according to Seymour's carpenter Mathew Mackintosh:

> On the smallest fancied infringement of his rights, he [Seymour] had Alexander and the whole company up before the Justices to answer for their misdeeds. I have known this to occur twice in one week, and the delinquents were generally amerced in the statutory penalty of £50 each. On the whole, "Alick" took no harm by this systematic persecution. The fines were never enforced, he had the public sympathy on his side, and he continued to grow and prosper.[4]

Free trade – the Act of 1737 notwithstanding – seemed to prevail, though Seymour more successfully imposed his patent rights (extending to an eight mile radius of Glasgow) on booths at Paisley Fair.

Similar skirmishes in the monopoly wars typified the Glasgow scene for almost twenty years. Seymour's tenure at Queen Street came to an end in 1829, when the theatre burned. After Alexander bought the patent and transferred it to the Dunlop Street premises he instigated a series of suits against every grade of theatrical manager that came to the city, including the bankrupt Seymour who in 1830 set up a temporary theatre in York Street, several blocks west of the newly designated Theatre Royal.[5]

The booths (or geggies, as they were known in Glasgow) at the annual chartered July fair were unlicensed, but as long as the police gave no bad reports they were freely tolerated. Sometimes they arrived well ahead of the fair and remained for several months, competing with the patent theatre. Alexander, however, allowed neither slackness from the constables nor anomalies from the judiciary. In the early 1830s, he is reported as

> prowling about our fair, and wherever he could find one or two show-folks ranting to a few mechanics, or to a few boys and girls, he immediately produced his patent, walked them off to gaol as "rogues and vagabonds", fined them in a heavy sum, or frightened them out of the place. Last year [1834], he attempted to shut up three or four of these booths during fair week; and the consequence was, that a public meeting of the Inhabitants was held, at which his conduct was characterized according to its deserving, and at which it was resolved, that his tyrannical proceedings with the poor show people, rendered him unworthy of public support.[6]

His vigilance continued unabated year-round. In 1839, for example, Alexander "made application to the Sheriff for Interdict against a person named Pindar, who it was alleged had infringed the rights of the Patentee by performing the regular drama in a tiny booth, which was used as a barber's shop during the day, and was transferred into a temple of the histrionic art in the evening".[7] The next year, lawyers wrote to Mr. Purves and David Prince Miller warning them that Alexander would prosecute any infringement of his patent involving dramatic entertainments: "operas, burlettas, melo-dramas, farces, pantomimes, and other dramatic pieces, as well as more regular tragedies, comedies, and plays; in short, it comprehends every entertainment of the stage in which either dialogue, dresses, decorations, or shifting of scenes is introduced, or a story told or plot developed".[8] Authorities ruled that the geggies must be closed down, and Miller was imprisoned for three months before friends could meet his fine.[9] In an 1841 action against John Henry Anderson's minor theatre near Glasgow Green, the majority of justices not only ruled that the rights of the patentee prevailed, but that Anderson (the magical "Wizard of the North") may not perform scenic or dramatic entertainments of *any kind* within the precincts of Glasgow.[10]

Alexander – previously the respondent to such monopolist actions, and now their instigator – lost the sympathy of the mercantile public but prospered as exclusive purveyor of theatre in the second largest city in Britain. As manager, he tolerated no lewdness, yet critics found ample cause to complain about the standards of production, most of the wrath being directed at Alexander himself. Journals like *The Theatrical Visitor* and *The Pepperbox* seemed to exist solely to decry Alexander. In the light of such invective, Alexander's theatre does not appear to be a great improvement on the rudimentary geggies.

Free trade should have been secured with the 1843 Theatres Regulation Act, yet a final episode which turns on social dynamics rather than a point of law bears some resemblance to the monopolist suits of the 1820s to early 1840s. In 1845, Anderson arrived early for the fair and began to erect a partially brick 4,000–5,000 seat theatre – the largest in Britain – in front of the prison on Glasgow Green. Cooke's Circus and Miller's Adelphi Theatre stood a few feet away in Jail Square, arousing none of the wrath afforded Anderson's City Theatre; they were wholly set back from the common land, faced toward the Green instead of the city centre, and were not built of brick, which connoted permanence. When the matter came before the city council, a quorum could not be obtained and the councillors seriously erred in not insisting on the matter being taken to a vote; instead, Anderson received informal and unauthoritative approval to proceed.[11] Had action been taken at that point, Anderson could have decamped to another site with just £50 losses. The standing committee on the Green was incensed, as was the public: 60,000 signatures (almost a fifth of the city's population) were presented in a petition against the emerging structure.

As the *Scottish Dramatic Mirror* pointed out, the quiet open air recreations of the poor in the tenements and factories around the Green should not be infringed upon because the rich, who were by then vacating Monteith Row and Great Hamilton Street along the northern edge of the Green for new suburbs in the west, sought revenue for the civic coffers:

> Have the rich not their splendid squares, ornamented with beautiful shrubbery, and improved by them at the public expense? Have they not their

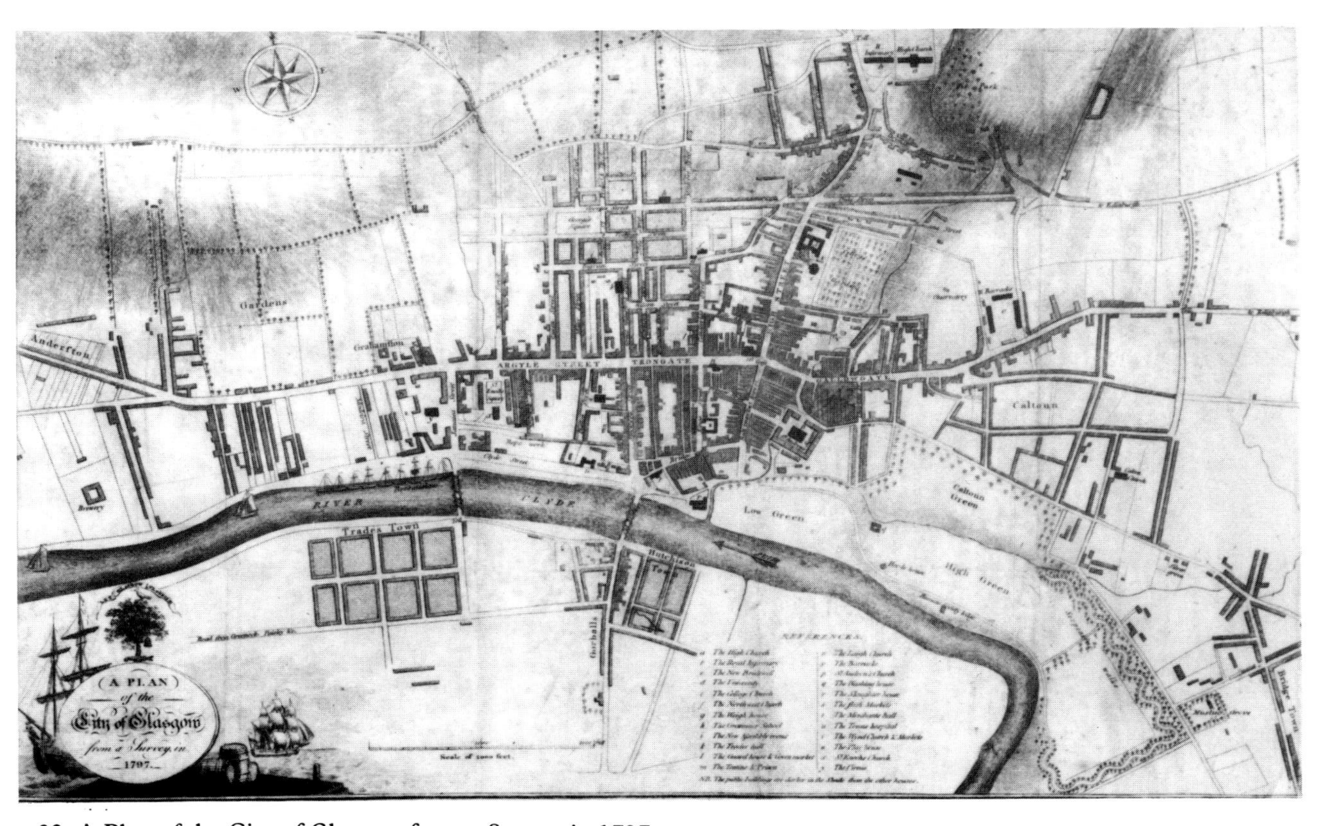


22. A Plan of the City of Glasgow from a Survey in 1797.

> Botanic Gardens in which to recreate themselves? What boots it to them that the inhabitants at the foot of Saltmarket are deafened by the jangle of drums, gongs, and trumpets, and other discordant sounds – the Bridgegate is not the New Town, and if the public Green can be made to add to the Corporation funds, already in a sufficiently imbecile state, and enable them to get up splendid portraits of Majesty in their Council Halls, *jet d'eaus* in their handsome squares, and maintain High School endowments for their pampered offspring, what matter for the Green of Glasgow? "the haunt of the idle, the lazy, and the poor".[12]

Sensitive to the opposition, the councillors voted to notify Anderson, Cooke, and Miller that at the end of one year all three structures must be removed.

Glasgow was built to an unusual degree with stone. Apart from the territorial and noise pollution controversies, the brick structure was deemed ugly. This judgement was only somewhat modified when Ionic pillars, an illuminated clock, and entablature appeared on the Jail Square facade just before the fair. The interior was the best Glasgow had seen since the Queen Street Theatre, for Anderson spent £7,000 on the structure and another £3,000 equipping the stage, despite the intense opposition and early notification that permission to remain on the Green for one year would under no circumstances be renewed. Immediately following the fair, during the brick City Theatre's first months of operation, Miller closed the neighbouring Adelphi to carry out substantial structural improvements, despite his notification of impending demolition. What gave these managers such supreme confidence? Railway speculation was at its height, and the middle classes had every reason to expect a boom. At the same time, however, newspapers reported the virtual destruction of potato crops in southern Scotland. The poorest classes had every reason to expect a famine.

In the light of the historiography of the theatrical anti-monopoly movement, and particularly Clive Barker's research on London, the class dynamics and timing of the City Theatre opposition are distinctly odd. In the light of historiography on early Victorian Reform, however, a pattern – perhaps of regional specificity – emerges. George Rowell and Michael Booth both describe the Theatres Regulation Act of 1843 as a triumph of innovations in repertoire over the artistically derelict monopolists.[13] Rowell emphasizes the failure of the Act to change the fare available at the minors once they came under the Lord Chamberlain's jurisdiction. Booth emphasizes the Act of 1843 was a mechanism allowing for freedom in repertoire while tightening censorship, an ingenious solution since it placated free traders while putting a cinch hold on the word-for-word content of what they traded in. Barker suggests "the struggle between the Patents and the Minors could well be examined in the light of a new rising class striving to take over the cultural institutions of its predecessors and of a clash of economic principles and ideologies".[14] Thus, the newly self-conscious working classes demanded theatres in their own neighbourhoods (Lambeth, Shoreditch, Islington, and the City of London) expressing their class's identity and aspirations in a diverse repertoire, against the explicit interests and wishes of the middle classes, who deliberately made their new suburbs theatre-free. Barker describes the London minors of the 1830s as an expression of Reformist sentiment and a crucible of Chartist leadership, setting the working classes against the middle classes that had so unequivocally separated since the Reform Act of 1832 extended the vote to men in households paying at least £10 in taxes.

The Glaswegian scenario suggests a different kind of involvement in Reform. Providing both the birthplace and lectern of Adam Smith, Glasgow was identified with free trade advocacy from its earliest emergence as a major trading port. Glasgow's Chamber of Commerce, the first in the world, was formed explicitly to break trade monopolies.[15] The economic theory emanating from Glasgow University was instrumental in breaking the East India Company's charter in 1813; this meant that all British ports could compete for Asian trade instead of effectively restricting business to a single partnership based in London. Given the overlap between arts sponsorship and the merchant community, this anti-mercantilism was bound to infect the theatrical speculators. Dugald Bannatyne, one of the original proprietors of the Theatre Royal, was a signatory to a 1790 report protesting Parliament's imposition of trade restrictions on grain in order to protect British farming and encourage self-sufficiency in agriculture.[16] Free trade was crucially important to men like Kirkman Finlay, a leading shareholder in the reapportioned Theatre Royal of 1821, whose muslin mills did extensive business with the Far East as well as the Bahamas, West Indies, New Orleans, and South Carolina. All of the merchants, manufacturers, and solicitors whose names appear as proprietors of the Theatre Royal were prominent civic leaders, serving as baillies, councillors, and Lords Provost, as officials of the University, on every organization promoting commerce, and as Members of Parliament. But they were staunch advocates of free trade in every matter *except* the drama. Personal, local, and regional concerns battled in the economic debate over where the national interest lay.

This complies with Barker's findings insofar as patent holders in London and Glasgow represent an upper-middle class resisting a free theatre, preferring at most a somewhat wider application of protectionist principles.[17] On the side of consumers, Marc Baer demonstrates that during the 1809 O.P. Riots, "opponents of the Covent Garden managers opposed the government-sanctioned monopoly, yet they and others were connected with petitions for a third patent theatre".[18] Protectionism for oneself and free trade for others was a common subtext in many industries, as Bulwer Lytton's variation on Jeremy Bentham's utilitarian credo recalls.

Barker's explanation may be right (for London) or it may be flawed (for Glasgow) by conflating two arms of the radical movement. He relies heavily on the 1832 Report of the Select Committee on Dramatic Literature, particularly the testimony of Francis Place, when setting "free trade in the spoken drama" within the history of Reform. But there were two distinct radical rhetorics, as Patricia Hollis emphasizes: "The older [rhetoric] was shaped in the years around 1819, and denounced aristocracy, monopoly, taxes, and corruption; the newer [circa 1835] was that of Hetherington, Carpenter, and Bronterre O'Brien, and it denounced exploitation, property, and power."[19] In addition, there are two quite distinct reformist movements with different platforms and class alignments operating in the period. Chartism, associated with the Reform Act of 1832 and its aftermath, was an artisans' movement mobilized against the privilege newly extended to a section of the middle classes (though with some middle-class reformist leaders, such as Place). For various reasons, including slightly more liberal provisions for the franchise in Scotland than in England, Chartism as the sole plank of Reform was less of a *cause célèbre* for Scottish radicals. Chartism was consciously allied with the power of theatrical representation,[20] but so too might have been the parallel reform movement concerning free trade. The Anti-Corn Law League was not opposed to extending the franchise, but in contrast to the Chartists brought about an alliance of the absolute poorest ranks of society with the wealthy merchant class who were spokespeople in favour of the abolition of tariffs and trade prohibitions. It pre- and post-dates Chartism, and was particularly contentious in Scotland in the years when minor and illegal theatres experienced the most intense persecution (1838–42), retaining currency in the years of Chartism's slump (1843–7). "Complete Suffrage" associations incorporated the free trade plank and were effective in mobilizing middle-class support in a coalition with the working classes. Members included William C. Pattison, who was prominent on the hustings during the City Theatre controversy.

By 1845, the date of the City Theatre dispute, most of the free trade questions were settled, including the matter of dramatic monopolies. The poorest classes enjoyed a range of cheap entertainments year-round in the neighbourhood just west of Glasgow Green.[21] Meanwhile, the more affluent classes enjoyed amateur dramatics in their "sporting clubs" rather than patronizing professional venues, and looked to the west coast for more extended recreation in the growing holiday resorts of Rothesay, Cumbrae, and Helensburgh. The skilled working classes enjoyed days out on the Clyde steamers, but the poorest classes had only the Green, the geggies, the free-and-easies, and the public house. They were too poor to go on holiday jaunts and too seedy to enter the West End museums and gardens. They wanted entertainment, but not at the expense of liberty, however ardent their free trade convictions.

In September 1838, the Anti-Corn Law League was founded. As in 1820, Glasgow was among the first cities to petition for repeal. Although the issue had been percolating since *The Wealth of Nations* was published in 1776, free trade propaganda was most apparent from 1838 to 1846. Between 1842 and 1846, Robert Peel's government repealed 605 duties including prohibitions on importing meat and cattle, and largely reduced 1,035 other duties which pertained to virtually every aspect of the economy. Tariffs and duties were replaced by income tax. Wage and employment rates improved, consumption rose, trade increased, the national debt was reduced, interest charges on debt fell, and the reforms were vindicated. Freer trade quelled fears of rebellion, even revolution, from among the lowest ranks of society. Glasgow had been the centre of such agitations in Scotland, usually enacted on the Green. The end of the 1837-42 depression, the quelling of severe labour unrest in 1842, and a succession of good harvests in 1842-4 increased confidence across the ranks and encouraged complacency. But signs of potato blight in 1845 raised the spectre of Irish (and Scottish) famine, the necessary impetus for Peel to push the Corn Laws before his cabinet, which supported repeal in 1846.[22] It is in this context that 60,000 signatures brought out commissioners, councillors, and leading manufacturers before the city officials in protest against the brick theatre on the Green.

They claimed the City Theatre trespassed on the rights and privileges granted in the common land. In effect, they responded to the privileged class attempting to trade unfairly: the Corporation transgressing against the people's proprietary rights to the Green was as ineffable but as important as the distinction between drama and burletta. Applying the City Theatre's rent against leisure projects in the middle-class suburbs violated the 1843 Act's point of allowing locally-based entertainment.

Newspaper sources give no hint of who the 60,000 were who petitioned against the City Theatre. Perhaps class politics allow this to be deduced. In their deputation to the town council the petitioners were supported by commissioners, councillors, and leading manufacturers, the *crême* of the merchant class.[23] But there were not 60,000 in the whole middle class.[24] The logic of arithmetic suggests that the working classes must have been the mainstay of the petition in allegiance with the artisanal and middle classes. If so, they were manipulating the concepts of free trade in the classic inverted pattern involving self-interest, though in this instance maintaining the inter-class alliances from the Anti-Corn Law and Complete Suffrage movements.[25]

The theatre monopolies controversy united both reformist planks - Chartism and Free Trade - which were otherwise sometimes antipathetic. Though the theatre controversy involved a strictly domestic context, the patent theatres were equated with the monopolizing tendencies of the old aristocratic order against which Glasgow's industrialists and unskilled labourers were similarly opposed. It presented on a neighbourhood basis what free trade between manufacturing and agricultural nations represented on an international scale. The right to determine one's culture locally - a crux of Barker's and the Chartists' arguments - played an important part in the self-determination and class-consciousness of Glaswegians, but by the late-1830s the difficulties and corruption impeding even the middle classes from registering for the vote demonstrated that suffrage per se was not the whole answer. As Eugene Macarthy, one of the 1832 Select Committee's free trade witnesses, who had been Seymour's stage manager in Glasgow before managing a Dublin minor on his own behalf, wrote: "The amusements of the people should always be encouraged as a sort of 'safety-valve', through which the elements of discord might escape."[26] In 1845, the people did the only thing they could in the aftermath of the 1843 Act: they attempted to *block* free competition in order to call attention to their grievances.

It was not the City Theatre itself that was objectionable; it was symbolic of the wider scope of Glaswegian, Scottish, and British social relations. An incident that occurred the day before the City Theatre opened demonstrates how "the brick theatre", its only title up to that moment, functioned as a simulacrum.

> It appears that a caravan, belonging to a female named Miss Owie, and painted on the outside to resemble a brick building, arrived in the course of the day, and, from some unfortunate and injudicious arrangement, was accommodated, by those in charge of the ground, within the Green itself instead of on the outside of the railing, where the other buildings, booths, and caravans, are placed. The erection of the outside work, which included a stage, wooden posts, and some pictorial representations, proceeded briskly up till about eight o'clock in the evening, when a crowd of people began gradually to surround the building, and about half-past that hour, when the mob had increased to about 2000 persons, an attack was made upon the booth. With shouts of "No Encroachment", "Down with the Bricks", and other vociferations, the crowd tore down the stage and other wood work, and, amid loud cheers, pitched a good deal of it into the Clyde.[27]

A large scale riot was narrowly averted when the authorities removed what was left of the caravan to a site off the Green and more line with Cooke's, the Adelphi, and the geggies rather than Anderson's theatre. The crowd could not rip apart Anderson's masonry, but they could and did devastate its metonymous substitute.

Baer argues that when multi-class theatres were replaced by single theatres, as occurred in London in the 1830s, theatrical rioting faded into memory. With the proliferation of the minors, fairer price setting mechanisms prevailed in theatres that no longer tried – through repertoire and decoration – to be all things to all classes. With this change, the classes no longer used the theatres to enact conflicts on aesthetic or political grounds.[28] But Glasgow had never known a riot inside a theatre. Does this mean the audiences were single-class up until the construction of the City Theatre? And what does it suggest about the mob that demolished the "brick" caravan?

When the Queen Street Theatre burned in 1829, the affluent classes lost the only venue that catered to their tastes. It had been, in some respects, a class-exclusive house that perished because of disinterest rather than competition. Revenues demonstrated that there was no cause to replace it, for even under first-class managements it could barely attract its target audience in sufficient numbers. While the Prince's Opera House (1849-67) and the Glovers' management of the Theatre Royal Dunlop Street from 1852 provided respectable venues, in effect the middle classes were left without a theatre *of their own* until the 1860s-70s, with the building of the Royal Colosseum, Gaiety, Royalty, and a new Theatre Royal in distant Sauchiehall and Cowcaddens Streets, northwest of the Regency suburb in areas newly claimed by the middle classes. Stana Nenadic's study of the Glaswegian middle classes' interests in this interim period necessarily leaves out the theatre because for the most part the middle classes were absent from it.[29] In the early Victorian period, the middle classes were increasingly privatizing their entertainments - theatre, dancing, exhibitions, and concerts alike - excluding class interaction partly through geography, particularly where the middle classes and the poorest classes are concerned.[30] When, in 1835, Robert Dennistoun argued for ending the patent system in Glasgow, he claimed unequivocally that it "hinders fair and honourable competition". While the monopoly "hinders the rich from having theatrical entertainments for themselves" it also "deprives the poor of their humble public amusements". The latter claim is a direct allusion to Alexander's persecution of the geggies, while the former refers to the impossibility of genteel women attending Dunlop Street or the Adelphi.[31] As a theatrical journal complained in 1846:

> The respectable portion of the inhabitants, those who are most able to support a theatre, may virtually be said to have none. Ladies cannot be taken to the Adelphi: at Dunlop Street they are certain of being disgusted by the unlicensed tongue, or the exhibition of buffoonery and imbecility, save when a 'star' appears; and even then the gratification is so qualified, that the desire to return is never felt. Had we a theatre worthy of support, the public would not rush to it on mere occasions of excitement; they would patronize it regularly as a rational and intellectual enjoyment: they are not the beings Mr Alexander would make us believe; they are liberal in patronizing every other amusement - they only neglect the theatre because it is contemptible.[32]

Most accounts of Glasgow Fair emphasize a working-class clientele, even though it was still a trading fair with cattle, horse, and "feeing" markets barely two blocks away; it is disputable whether the male farmers and merchants traversed the distance to the Green.[33] At the 1845 fair, the booth with Gemmill's statuary of a "Cottar's Saturday Night" was crowded with 1,800 on its first night, "much better encouragement . . . than was accorded to it when it occupied an aristocratic status in the west-end of the city", the growing residential haven of the middle classes.[34] Such exhibitions competed harmoniously with the "fifteen minute 5 act tragedies" of the neighbouring geggies, but because evidence is relatively conclusive that middle-class adults did not attend the theatrical booths is it correct to exclude them from attending the kinds of exhibitions that are known to have attracted them in the 1750s–90s and which were still being displayed in middle-class venues in Victoria's reign?[35] Why should we assume that all the exhibitions at the fair appealed to the poorest and working classes equally or exclusively? The pen and ink sketch "Glasgow Fair 1825" shows almost as many men in plaids or top hats as cloth caps; it is less easy to read class through women's garb, but some of the bonneted figures depicted decorously accompanying the middle-class men are gazing on the frontages of the menagerie, acrobats' booth, and circus (though not the theatre where the cast advertises by frolicking very energetically).[36]

Robert Reid complained that the atmosphere created by prostitutes (whom he claimed were omnipresent) and the fair's loose-limbed, rouge-painted actresses was deleterious to all who attended. Is his summary conclusion – "In short, a mixture was encouraged to commingle, whose safety lay in their being kept separate"[37] – merely a warning against the sexes co-mingling, or also the classes? The occasional balloon ascent at the Botanic Gardens (on the western extremity of the 1840s city, just beyond the nascent suburb of Hillhead) was predicted "to make for a second Fair at the other end of the city",[38] but of course it did not. There was no fair in a parallel middle-class universe, only *the* fair.

In erecting the City Theatre on the Green, Anderson may have been trying to bring about a rapprochement between the classes in keeping with the recent accomplishments of the Complete Suffrage movement. If the middle classes were attending the fair entertainments, it suggests a willingness, at least at this ancient ludic and commercial site, to breach Glasgow's increasingly distinct geographical boundaries of class. If 60,000 protested at encroachments on the Green space, and if the simulacrum of privilege and encroachment could be represented in a caravan painted to resemble brick, then certainly class anxieties were being actively contested through performances of the people. J. F. S. Gordon deplored the *assortment* of people attracted to the Green on Sunday evenings, recommending that a museum with lecture rooms be constructed.[39] His unease with class co-mingling along with the specificity of his emolument, belies a middle-class squeamishness and a Chartist-like solution of self-improvement and rational recreation along middle-class lines in segregated institutions. But Anderson not only set out to build a theatre, it was a *huge* theatre, the largest in the land, said to be particularly well decorated inside and *brick*, a material hitherto untried for a theatre in fire-prone Glasgow. It was no geggie, but neither was it the disgraced Theatre Royal Dunlop Street. Its opulence boded an increase in middle-class encroachment on the neighbourhood, running contrary to the trend towards theatres and music halls embodying exclusively working-class aspirations and ideals.[40] If Baer's thesis holds in Glasgow it is no wonder that the City Theatre was a tinderbox of class conflict. Likewise, at the Adelphi next door, where Miller hired first class talent (including the elder Mrs Glover, Samuel Phelps, Charles Mathews, Madame Vestris, Macready, Vandenhoff, Sheridan Knowles, G. V. Brooke, Miss Cushman, and Mrs Warner) for the local audience, carpenters flaunted the theatre's death sentence by carrying out an expansion. It was no longer aiming down market, on a par with Calvert's wooden Hibernian Theatre that went up two years later for an audience of "Red Republicans".[41] Like Cooke's Circus, at one moment a riding school for the middle classes and at another the site of a Chartist benefit performance of *The Trial of Robert Emmett*,[42] Miller and Anderson muddied the aspirations of a people's theatre at the historical cusp of railway mania and potato famine.

There were many reasons for the working classes to fear what the City Theatre represented: "co-mingling" on terms parallel to the middle-class Gordon's objections to the Green and the Chartists' objections to Complete Suffrage and free trade. Richard Cobden saw free trade as a way to level classes and nations to a common co-operative standard, "drawing men together, thrusting aside the antagonism of race, and creed, and language, and uniting us in the bonds of eternal peace".[43] In the case of the City Theatre this would seem to be true, though the class coalition most active on behalf of free trading judged 1845 the wrong moment – and Glasgow Green the wrong land – to fulfil the social pledge. It was the first of several attempts to encroach on the Green successfully resisted by the East End population with middle-class leadership.[44]

This analysis establishes theatre as an example of anti-mercantilist philosophy caught, in various ways, in the contradiction of self-interest. The Theatres Act of 1843 was a relatively early victory for free traders, consistent with social forces and the growing political and philosophical consensus about economic practices. Such an analysis would be impossible without combining various ways to examine the theatre in economic terms, including industrial and human geography, and the empirical application of economic theory as it was debated and tried in a culture of tremendous privilege as well as privation. Narratives about the theatre and the economy need to be told in tandem, their patterns of growth and retraction correlated, and social allegiances measured, particularly where questions of identity formation and class interest may be involved. However, while explaining the possible ways in which people resisted oppressive tendencies while others exploited economic opportunities it remains open to question whether this is purely a context-specific argument or whether it can be extrapolated to a wider narrative of theatre history and Reformist politics elsewhere in Britain.

The theatrical monopolies controversy united rhetorics about freedom of speech with a free press and access to education. Behind it all, at least in Glasgow, was a coherent politic of economic interests derived, historically, from the state of trade and manufacturing on the Clyde and the people it drew to the city. Dorothy Thompson argues that the working classes "showed a strong inclination to follow leaders who preached a very simple doctrine of class hostility" whether the purpose was Chartist or anti-mercantilist, but Glaswegian entertainment suggests a more complicated scenario.[45] While theatre took its place among the industries and manufacturers of Strathclyde, sharing their dilemmas to trade, protect, streamline, and meet debts, it also took a share in the human geography and social history of the city.

## Notes

1. The letter from Archibald Campbell (M.P. for Glasgow Burghs) to Robert Peel, 31 March 1829, requesting changes in the patent for the Theatre Royal Glasgow on behalf of the proprietors (whose appended petition does not survive) most likely asked that the patent not be attached to the property at Queen Street. This enabled it to be sold separately from other assets in the June 1829 auction (Strathclyde Regional Archives, TD 106). A new patent was issued to Alexander in 1830, valid for seventeen years.

2. Copy of Deed of Suspension and Interdict for Henry Alexander, 1823 (Theatre Royal Queen Street), papers in Peter Mackenzie deposit, William Patrick Library, Kirkintilloch, T20 G11).

3. [Matthew Mackintosh] An Old Stager, *Stage Reminiscences: being Recollections, Chiefly Personal, of celebrated Theatrical & Musical Performers during the last Forty Years*, Glasgow, 1866, 93.

4. Mackintosh, 1866, 100.

5. He counted on Fanny Kemble to recover some of his charred fortune. Upon being informed of the nature of Seymour's premises, she cancelled the engagement and was instead announced for Dunlop Street, the newly designated Theatre Royal. What Alexander achieved in 1830 by underhanded business tactics and a £100 cash settlement he later left to solicitors. Mackintosh, 1866, 234-5.

6. Walter Dennistoun, *Letter to the Lord Provost, Magistrates, and Town Council of Glasgow, on the Present State of the Theatre Royal, and the Duties Incumbent Upon Them Regarding its Patent*, Glasgow, 1835, 6.

7. "Poor Pindar Peppered", *The Pepper-box* 28 Mar. 1840.

8. *The Pepperbox* 25 July 1840.

9. William Glover and J. Stewart, "Some Stage Reminiscences: Local and General", (Glasgow) *Evening Times* 20 June 1889.

10. Alexander *v.* Anderson, *Court of Session Cases*, Edinburgh 1841-2, 4: 1525-32.

11. *Glasgow Herald* 9 May 1845; 4 July 1845; and 8 Aug. 1845.

12. "Brick Theatre on the Green of Glasgow", *Scottish Dramatic Mirror* 2 May 1845.

13. George Rowell, *The Victorian Theatre 1798-1914*, Cambridge, 1956; Michael R. Booth, *Theatre in the Victorian Age*, Cambridge, 1991.

14. Clive Barker, "A Theatre for the People", *Nineteenth-Century British Theatre*, eds Kenneth Richards and Peter Thomson, London, 1971, 10. See also Clive Barker, "The Chartists, Theatre, Reform and Research", *Theatre Quarterly* 1.4 (Oct.-Dec. 1971), 3-10.

15. The original purposes of the Chamber of Commerce, as stated by Dugald Bannatyne were:

"1. Labouring zealously to procure Free Trade;
2. Maintaining a uniform measure of value so that paper currency can be immediately convertible into the precious metals; and
3. Reforming Commercial Law (particularly with reference to Bankruptcy), to make it more acceptable and sure, and its administration more expeditious."

*Glasgow Chamber of Commerce Journal*, May 1970, 247.

16. *Report of the Committee of the Chamber of Commerce and Manufacturers of Glasgow on the Bill . . . for Regulating the Importation and Exportation of Corn &c.*, Glasgow, 1790.

17. Barker, 1971a, 15.

18. Marc Baer, *Theatre and Disorder in Late Georgian London*, Oxford, 1992, 26.

19. Patricia Hollis, *The Pauper Press: a Study in Working-Class Radicalism of the 1830s*, Oxford, 1970, viii.

20. Dorothy Thompson, *The Chartists: Popular Politics in the Industrial Revolution*, Aldershot, 1984, 117-18; and Alexander Wilson, *The Chartist Movement in Scotland*, New York, 1970.

21. The Glasgow magistrates' licensing books for such drinking establishments do not survive, so the dates of the free-and-easies cannot be precisely ascribed. The press gives little coverage to the singing saloons, though the *Glasgow Dramatic Review* conclusively documents that many were in existence by 1845. The repertoire consisted of comics, comic dancers, female serio-vocalists, ethiopian singers, and all the trademarks of minstrelsy. See also *Glasgow Theatrical Review*, 30 Dec. 1846.

22. Llewellyn Woodward, *The Age of Reform 1815-70*, 2nd edn Oxford 1992, 122-3.

23. *Scottish Dramatic Mirror*, 2 May 1845; and 14 June 1845.

24. Estimated Glasgow middle class income distribution for 1860:

| *No. of families* | *Income per year* | *Average* |
|---|---|---|
| 50 ( 0.2%) | Over £5000 | £21,144 |
| 500 ( 2.3%) | £1000 to £5000 | 3,000 |
| 1,650 ( 7.5%) | £300 to £1000 | 650 |
| 8,800 (40.0%) | £100 to £300 | 200 |
| 11,000 (50.0%) | Under £100 | 60 |

Stana Stella Nenadic, "The Structure, Values and Influence of the Scottish Urban Middie Class; Glasgow 1800 to 1870", Ph.D. dissertation, Strathclyde University, 1986, 149.

25. Wilson, 1970, 167-80.

26. Eugene Macarthy, *A Letter to the King, on the Question now at Issue, Between the 'Major', and 'Minor' Theatres*, London, 1832, 15.

27. *Glasgow Herald*, 14 July 1845.

28. Baer, 1992, 187.

29. "The manner in which wealth was consumed and displayed - through fine housing, entertaining, a glamorous social circle, cultural activity, a generally opulent life-style, and particularly through financial generosity in support of city institutions and charities - was repeatedly stressed [in nineteenth century sources]. Involvement in culture, education, literary creativity and scientific endeavour was seen as particularly important since it contributed to the greater achievements of Glasgow as a centre of beauty and intellectualism." (301) This would seem to be an open-ended statement about the arts, but her examples of prominent manufacturers, merchants, and Sheriffs making major contributions to the arts supported fine art, literature, and music but never theatre. Nenadic, 1986, 301-2.

30. "In contrast, however, to the hardening of middle class attitudes to the very poor or

'residuum', was the development of a new set of relationships with elements of the more prosperous and apparently more 'respectable' working classes. The growth of workers' soirees and testimonial dinners in the 1840's, widely reported in the press, at which members of the workforce of large prestigious factories were entertained by their employers and vice-versa, was only one of the many signs of a new rapprochement between the middle classes and elements of the working class after the difficulties of the 1820's and early 1830's." Nenadic, 1986, 356-7.

31. Dennistoun, 1835, 9.

32. "New Theatre", *Glasgow Dramatic Review*, 24 June 1846.

33. The cattle market, formerly at the end of Stockwell Bridge (a site of the Fair more than a century before and again between 1795 and the commencement of Clyde dredging and embanking), was moved in 1818 to Graham Square at the east end of Gallowgate. A. MacGeorge, *Old Glasgow: The Place and the People*, Glasgow, 1880, 189. N.B. elsewhere the date is given as 1826. J. F. S. Gordon, ed., *Glasghu Facies: A View of the City of Glasgow*, Glasgow, 1872. The "feeing" market in which servants from town and country changed employers may also have endured to this period. If so, it offers additional evidence of the presence of the middle classes. Mackintosh, 1866, 212-13.

34. "Glasgow Fair", *Glasgow Herald*, 18 July 1845.

35. "A peep at the audience is one of the least nice sights which it is possible to conceive. Imagine a thin slip of boards, supported on posts, running round three sides of the booth, and which, during the fair, is dignified as the twopenny boxes: - below, the heads and shoulders of the audience are seen looming through drifts of rising dust and tobacco smoke, and sweating up an odour as far as possible removed from that which is wafted from the 'spicy shores of Araby the blest'. There are squallid women with more squallid infants; dirty men; and, above all, masses of mere children of both sexes, whose countenances are lighted up into extraordinary excitement - some fighting, some swearing, some laughing, and the majority masticating *speldings* with great ferocity." *Glasgow Herald*, 18 July 1845. See also *Glasgow Dramatic Review*, 30 July 1845; *Glasgow Theatrical Review*, 14 July 1847. Compare the advertisements from 1750-90 reported in "The Glasgow Shows of Olden Time", 8 July 1861, reprinted in [Robert Reid] "Senex", *Glasgow Past and Present*, Glasgow, 1884, III, 313-69.

36. Reproduced in Gordon, 1872, between I, 576-7.

37. Gordon, 1872, I, 581.

38. *Glasgow Theatrical Review*, 23 June 1847.

39. Gordon, 1872, I, 581. This account was written decades earlier.

40. Its repertoire also aimed for an up-market audience. During the fair, a variety bill was offered but immediately afterward, when it had acquired a dramatic licence, it opened with *The Bohemian Girl.*

41. Reid, 1884, I, 116-17.

42. Wilson, 1970, 201.

43. Richard Cobden, *Manchester Guardian*, 16 Jan. 1846; quoted in Norman McCord, *Free Trade: Theory and Practice from Adam Smith to Keynes*, Newton Abbot, 1970, 74.

44. In 1847, a proposal to build a viaduct across the Green to connect to a railway bridge across the Clyde was strongly opposed. Gordon, 1872, I: 600-1. In 1858, the city proposed to extract the coal from deep under the Green in order to finance the interest on its purchase, eight years previously, of Woodlands, Kelvingrove, and adjoining lands for the West End Park. James Moir, a Gallowgate grocer who had been seen on the hustings in 1845 and shortly after became a councillor, strenuously objected: "I have not spoken to one working man who would not willingly pay a tax of one penny per pound on his rental rather than have the Green so destroyed". He argued that "some deference ought to be

shown to the present hostile attitude of the working classes, especially when the people at the east end would pay a tax . . . to avoid the Green being ruined." Indeed, when Glasgow sought permission from Parliament to levy such an assessment it was unopposed. Reid, 1884, III, 60–1 and I, xxxv. Again, in 1868, Moir led a popular movement to stop the council from appropriating 2,216 square yards of the Green for Greenhead Street. Gordon, 1872, 601–3.

45. Thompson, 1984, 251.

# The Faucit Saville Brothers; or, Theatre and Family

CAROL J. CARLISLE

AMONG the most striking phenomena of the nineteenth-century British stage is the theatrical family, stretching over several generations and spreading out, sometimes, over a large geographical area. As several scholars have pointed out, membership in such a family was a tremendous advantage since it ensured opportunities for the novice and provided a support system (not exclusively financial) unavailable to actors who had to make their own way.[1] For a provincial manager, too, there were decided benefits: his children could be pressed into service at little expense while learning their trade, and mature relatives who had attained a reputation elsewhere could add lustre to his theatre with starring visits.

A noteworthy but neglected example is the Faucit Saville family, which, though it produced only one star comparable to the major Kembles and the best of the Terrys - Helen Faucit - contributed steadily and substantially to the theatrical life of England for many decades. It began with John (ca.1783-1853) and his wife, Harriet Elizabeth, née Diddear (1789-1857), continued with their six children, and extended to several grandchildren. (There were also "second families" as a result of new unions for both Harriet and John.)[2] Their combined careers covered most of the nineteenth century, and if those of related Diddears and Farrens were included, the family's theatre history would begin in the eighteenth century and stretch into the twentieth.

Obviously that story cannot be told here. This paper will concentrate on the three eldest sons of the original Faucit Saville couple, men who were connected almost exclusively with British provincial theatres and the London minors: John jun. (1807-55), Edmund Henry (1811-57), and Alfred (1812-??). The daughters will be mentioned only when relevant to their brothers' careers: Harriet (1808-47), a talented actress who has already been the subject of a study,[3] and Helena, or Helen as she was known on the stage (1814-98), whose experiences were very different from her brothers'. The youngest son, Charles (1816-??), never acted in England, apparently, though he may have played a minor part in Australian theatre.[4] Since even three careers are too much for a thorough study, I propose, after some necessary family background, to give a brief overview of each career, with emphasis on the importance of family ties but with enough theatrical details to suggest what the profession was like at the level of stock company and minor (mainly "illegitimate") theatre.

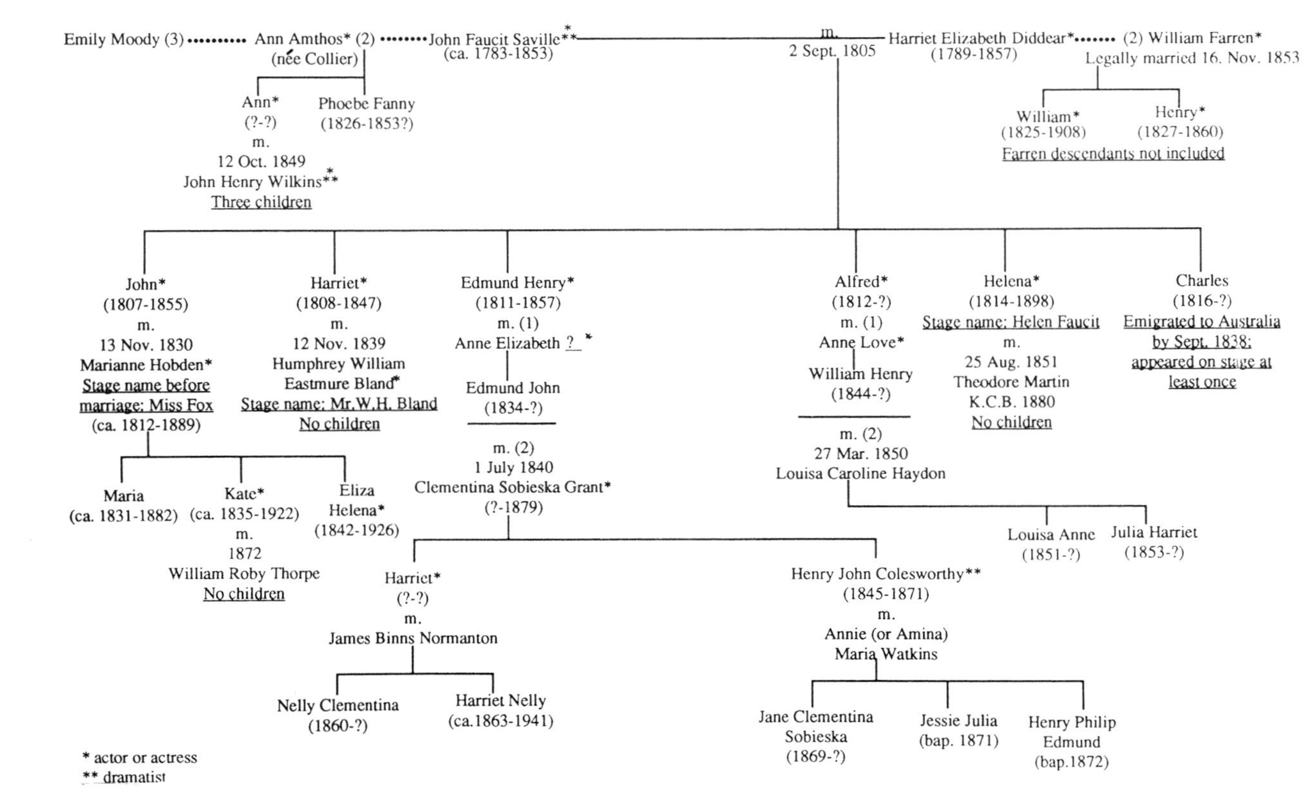

23. The Faucit Saville Family.

On 29 May 1813 six-year-old "Master Faucit" made a brief appearance on the Norwich stage as the Child in *Nature and Art*.[5] This can be looked on as a theatrical debut for the Faucit Saville brothers, for the child was John jun.; his parents, actors on the circuit, were billed as Mr and Mrs Faucit. Later that year they moved to London to take up the engagements at Covent Garden that the wife's notable talents had won for the couple. Mrs Faucit remained at the major London theatres, but Mr Faucit, or Saville Faucit, as he often signed his name, spent an increasing amount of time managing the theatres at Greenwich and Margate (later he would add others in Kent); he was also beginning his career as a playwright. At least once, in January 1819, eight-year-old Edmund and six-year-old Alfred appeared on their father's Greenwich stage - as the children in *The Stranger*.[6]

By 1821 Mrs Faucit had left her husband for the famous comedian William Farren. The separation was no gentle dissolving of ties: the wife even tried - unsuccessfully, of course - to have her fifteen-year marriage annulled; the husband's grief over her faithlessness was well publicized.[7] (Although theatrical liaisons were never uncommon, particularly in that day of stringent divorce laws, the Faucit-Farren relationship would be the butt of censure and jesting in the press for years to come, and as late as 1837 the theatrical diarist Charles Rice would identify the elder John Faucit Saville as "the victim of Mr W. Farren's lust".[8] The union would finally be legalized in 1853, shortly after "the victim's" death.)

The children were divided into separate households. The two girls became a part of the family unit of their mother and Farren; eventually they had two half-brothers, William and Henry Farren. Since Mrs Faucit retained her professional name, the daughters were also called Faucit. The father headed the other household - Mr Faucit Saville, as he now called himself, disavowing association with his wife by reversing the order of the names he had previously used. Fourteen-year-old John jun. evidently went with him immediately; the younger boys, possibly after a period with their Diddear grandparents, eventually joined him[9] - perhaps when he had acquired a new mother for them. (That "Mrs Faucit Saville", Ann Amthos, née Collier, began appearing in the Margate playbills in 1822.) There would be at least two half-sisters, Ann and Phoebe.[10] One might have expected circumstances to estrange the sons from their mother, her second partner, and their sisters. But in later years the two eldest (especially John) had close ties with Harriet and Helen, and all were apparently on good terms with Mrs Faucit and Farren. Their careers showed the usual co-operation among members of a theatrical family. Self-interest was largely involved, no doubt, but one senses as well the loyalty of a theatrical clan.

A vexing problem in studying this family is the shifting use of names. Perhaps, as has usually been assumed, Saville Faucit was the elder John's actual name, but there is reason to suppose that his later reversal was, in fact, a return to the proper form.[11] Curiously, both John jun., and Edmund used "Faucit" as the surname during their early careers in provincial theatres, then changed permanently to "Saville" with the first London engagement. (There seems to have been no particular pattern in Alfred's usage.) These Wildean shifts of identity between country and town reflected, I suppose, a combination of divided loyalties and professional expediency. As new and unknown actors, the brothers chose the family name with the greatest advertising value – that is, the one associated with their mother and the London theatres; but in London, where the family story was well known and an open alliance with Mrs Faucit and Farren might embarrass their father, they adopted his current choice, which they then retained to avoid further confusion. Even with the same surname there were various permutations (with and without Christian names or initials), but the brothers were most often known, finally, as J. F., E. F., and A. F. Saville.

John jun. evidently began his adult career at twenty (in 1827), with engagements at Worthing, then Bath, acting such roles as Paris in *Romeo and Juliet*.[12] In the next few years, acting utility at Brighton, he had parts in a wide variety of dramas, even opera. Here, in November 1830, he married a talented young actress billed as "Miss Fox" but actually named Marianne Hobden. Sometimes they were lucky and had engagements together, as in several seasons at Edinburgh; other times they were as far apart as Dublin and Dundee.

From mid-1836 to mid-1841 John acted mainly in London, with occasional engagements at Liverpool (where his sister Harriet was leading lady) and Brighton. His first London engagement – at the Haymarket, the only "legitimate" metropolitan theatre besides Drury Lane and Covent Garden – was probably due to the influence of William Farren, a longtime favourite here and brother of the stage manager; apparently John did not take full advantage of his opportunities, for he was engaged only two seasons. The other London theatres where he acted generally featured "burlettas", so called to escape licensing problems: the newly opened St James's offered a variety of entertainments; the Adelphi (where he stayed four seasons) favoured dramas combining the sensational and the realistic; the Strand, *inter alia*, introduced his father's popular farce *The Aldgate Pump*.

John's last thirteen years were devoted to provincial theatre management. His three-season venture at the Theatre Royal, Brighton, in partnership with Harroway (1841–2 through 1843–4), was carried out with vigour and ingenuity. His family connections were fully exploited: his wife was the leading lady, and he himself took secondary parts; his uncle, Charles Diddear, was principal tragedian; his little daughters, Maria and Kate, appeared in pantomimes; Helen Faucit and William Farren made starring visits. The largest "family reunion" was in the first part of the final season: sister Harriet and her husband, W. H. Bland, augmented the company for a while; Helen remained after her own engagement to see brother Edmund star as Hamlet and to play Juliet to his Romeo. But the theatre was not just a family project: legitimate dramas often featured stars like

Charles Kean and Mrs Nisbett, and performances of melodrama, ballet, tightrope acrobatics, etc. catered to "illegitimate" tastes. Financial problems beyond John's control, however, made it impossible to continue management. As Kathleen Barker says, he "failed at Brighton, but not for want of enterprise".[13]

He was more fortunate in his management of the Theatres Royal Nottingham and Derby, which he undertook in the autumn of 1844; he retained Nottingham for the rest of his life and Derby almost as long. Using the same company for both theatres, he alternated periods of performance. Later he took on additional theatres (Buxton, Chesterfield, Leicester, Sheffield), some briefly, some for longer periods. Sometimes he evidently had a second company: early in 1849, James R. Anderson, who starred at several of John's theatres, complained that at Sheffield the wardrobe keeper was "the best actor in the bunch", but, although he grumbled about the Nottingham company too, he considered Mrs Saville a "very good actress".[14] Reviews of productions in the local newspapers were, maugre Anderson, very favourable throughout John's tenure. His family contributed heavily to his success: his wife was a versatile, highly competent actress, and their daughters were all useful - Maria, though not an actress, helped to operate the theatre; Kate was a much-applauded child actress who retained her popularity as she grew older; and Eliza Helena, the youngest, inherited some of Kate's earlier roles. (Mrs J. F. Saville acted at other theatres besides her husband's: for example, she supported Macready on his farewell tour; the daughters, especially Kate, had successful careers at major provincial theatres and in London.) Helen Faucit not only acted for her brother but took him to York as her co-star. As at Brighton, John offered a varied bill of fare - something for every taste; he did try to reserve Fridays for legitimate comedy but had to give up the experiment in favour of plays like *Don Caesar de Bazan*.

Various influential citizens and groups patronized the performances. In John's first year at Nottingham the mayor, an enthusiastic supporter, invited the Savilles to a grand ball that astonished journalists with its elegant decorations, lavish refreshments, and gorgeously-attired guests. The Saville family were, in fact, respected as exemplary citizens, an asset to the community socially as well as artistically.

Early in 1854, when John reopened his Nottingham theatre, he was no longer simply its lessee but its owner. After his death, on 31 December 1855, his wife continued the management; in 1865 she closed her theatre and joined the company at a newly constructed Theatre Royal, which she took over two years later and managed, with Kate's help, until her retirement in 1870. Like her husband, she drew on family resources: her bill of fare included plays especially written for her by Edmund's dramatist son, Henry.

According to a critical sketch published in 1838 but probably valid throughout his career, J. F. Saville had a "strongly expressive" eye, a speech somewhat marred by a nasal tone but notable for "great correctness and good emphasis", and an unembarrassed "action", which, however, was "rather too set from habit, looking a little of the spouting club". His inclination was toward heroic parts, but he was a "gentleman performer in comedy of great respectability", and his "firmness of acting in tragedy forcibly [held] an audience in his interest".[15]

Edmund, though not "intended for the stage", proved to be the brother with the greatest histrionic talent. If, as a contemporary article says, he was a student at Christ's Hospital between the ages of nine and fifteen, he was rarely at home after his parents' separation; yet his later career brought him closer to his father than any of his brothers were. He reportedly served an apprenticeship with a surgeon at Reading but was too interested in theatre to practice medicine. At about nineteen, he made an amateur appearance in a benefit performance of Mary Russell Mitford's *Foscari* (Reading, 1830), and a year or so later he began his professional career with engagements at "various places in the Midland counties";[16] thus he was probably the "Mr Faucit" who acted at Nottingham, Derby, and other towns on Tom Manly's circuit in 1831-32. He evidently had a good singing voice, for, in addition to minor roles in the plays he had parts in musical dramas when vocalists were starring. (Such casting continued in several later engagements.) When only twenty-one, he managed the Theatre Royal, Kingston (Hull), from late 1832 to the spring of 1833. His wife, Mary Elizabeth, was his leading lady; with managerial commonsense, he played Mercutio, not Romeo, to her Juliet.

In the summer of 1833 Edmund and his wife were at the Royal Pavilion Theatre, Whitechapel Road, Stepney; thus he was the first of the brothers to have a London engagement. Despite its "illegitimate" status, the theatre boldly produced a series of Shakespearean plays, but the good roles were still out of Edmund's reach. The Savilles may have had a second London engagement in 1834, but by the late autumn Edmund was at Birmingham. The illness of Mude gave him a chance to act the villainous usurper in a grand revival of the "Melo-Dramatic Spectacle" *The Wood Demon*. Apparently he was very successful; the play had a good run, and he kept his part until he left Birmingham. At Bath, where he was engaged for several seasons, he had more substantial roles than formerly, much to Macready's displeasure on one occasion: "acted Werner", wrote the disgruntled star, "as well as the . . . vulgar rant of Mr Saville [as Ulric] . . . would let me".[17]

Obviously he impressed some people more favourably, for in 1837 he was brought to the Surrey in London to act the hero to Mrs Yates's heroine in a much-heralded production of Buckstone's new drama *Abelard and Heloise*. Splendidly mounted, with "historically accurate costumes", and with actors from the Adelphi as well as the Surrey companies (they had temporarily joined forces for this play), the production opened on 8 May and was a resounding success. Edmund remained at the Surrey for almost four successive years and in London for sixteen. During the first few, his brother John, also in London, was acting at

West End theatres; but, though the productions there may have been more sophisticated in treatment than at the transpontine Surrey, they were often of the same genre. When John left to manage the Brighton theatre, he was still, at best, secondary in rank, whereas Edmund had become established as one of the most popular actors on the "Surrey side". Edmund was the only one of the Faucit Saville men who would be mainly identified with metropolitan theatres.

After his first wife died, Edmund married, in July 1840, a Surrey actress, Clementina Sobieska Grant. When he abruptly left the Surrey in 1841, following a dispute over his refusal to act a role, his wife remained in their old company but, according to a hint in the *Theatrical Journal* (6 March), was suspected of malingering in sympathetic protest. After a brief stay at Sadler's Wells, Edmund acted at the Victoria for two years, then at the Surrey again for a year; later he had shorter engagements at the City of London and the New Standard as well as at all his recent venues; his last five and a half years in London were at the City of London.

At all these theatres melodrama was the staple offering. (This remained true, except at Sadler's Wells, even after 1843, when it became legal for all to produce the elite drama.) The plays might differ in quality, but, whether they were dramatizations of Dickens and Ainsworth or original creations by Rede, Buckstone, Fitzball, Wilks, or Faucit Saville, and whether their themes were historic, domestic, nautical, or criminal, they had many of the same ingredients and demanded much the same kind of acting. Edmund was a melodramatic actor *par excellence.* Not that he lacked versatility: he portrayed the patriotic hero of *Hofer, the Tell of the Tyrol* in a "discreet and manly style", and as Oliver Nick in *Black Whisker* he made the audience laugh "boisterously"; but he was most appreciated in bold sailors who were "a match for half a dozen pirates or smugglers" and in characters that aroused strong emotional responses, like Bill Sikes, the "savage and reckless housebreaker" in *Oliver Twist.*

The latter was one of his most famous characterizations. John Hollingshead's well-known description of the murder scene, though an obvious caricature of both actor and audience, does suggest the source of Saville's power: Sikes drags Nancy round the stage by her hair, then looks up defiantly at the gallery, which responds, chorus-like, with a "fearful curse"; he drags her about again, then again, "like Ajax defying the lightning"; finally, working up to a climax, he seems to dash her brains out – thus provoking a violent, Bedlam-like explosion in which "a thousand enraged voices" threaten to "tear his sanguinary entrails from his sanguinary body".[10] However exaggerated by Hollingshead, Saville's challenge to the gallery and their half-ritualistic, half-maniacal response are a striking reminder of the basic compact between actor and audience in all drama, which is simply most obvious in melodrama.

Now and again there was a chance to act legitimate roles. When Osbaldiston, manager of the Victoria, gratified his own ambitions by playing Lear or Othello,

Edmund was cast as Edgar or Cassio. Occasionally he himself acted Shakespearean heroes, as at Sadler's Wells in 1841 and at the City of London in later years. In the summer of 1845 the latter theatre announced that E. F. Saville would appear, "By desire", in a legitimate play every night that week; and apparently an annual period of such plays became customary there. According to critics, however, the long, almost exclusive practice of melodramatic acting had stifled the development of Saville's undoubted potentialities in legitimate drama. Although usually commended for his conception of character, he was considered deficient in ease and naturalness. He was best in the heavy parts: when he was cast as Gratiano, a reviewer, who wished he had acted Shylock, compared his attempt at light comedy to a raven's swooping down from Macbeth's battlements to "play the Canary bird at Portia's window".[19]

The intertwining of theatre and family took a somewhat different form in Edmund's career than in John's. While at the Surrey Edmund helped launch several new plays by his father, who wrote expressly for that theatre: in 1837, *Wapping Old Stairs* (13 November); in 1844, *The Last Shilling* (26 February) (illustration 24), *The Eve of Battle* (7 October), and *Young Nick and Old Nick* (a one-act piece introduced for Edmund's benefit, 19 November). Later, at the City of London, several of Faucit Saville's plays were revived with his permission. At this theatre, more than anywhere else, there was a gathering of the clan. In addition to Edmund and his wife, a minor actress called "Miss Saville" was in the company for a while - probably Edmund's half-sister Ann. His little daughter Harriet made her debut here on 11 April 1848, dancing a *pas seul* for her parents' benefit; before long, acting as well as dancing, she became a popular addition to the company. Even Edmund's father was on hand: having given up management, he had a post in the City's "treasorial department".[20]

Edmund's association with this theatre, which included managing the summer seasons, had to be broken off in 1852 because of serious illness. Although valued for his "respectability" and his kindly, affectionate nature,[21] he had one besetting weakness: addiction to alcohol. The resulting liver disease often incapacitated him during his last five years and eventually killed him at the age of forty-six. His financial problems were acute: a giant benefit was given him at Sadler's Wells on 25 June 1853, but he still had to apply to the Royal General Theatrical Fund for assistance; his sister Helen repaid the disbursements, however.[22]

His last professional efforts were in the provinces. At Margate, where he and his wife had three seasons (two of which they managed), Edmund's father made his last appearance on the stage, on 28 September 1853, acting Benjamin Bowbell in *The Illustrious Stranger* for his son's benefit; on 31 October the old man died. Early in 1856 Edmund was reportedly engaged as stage manager for a "handsome portable theatre" which had been constructed for Mr Douglas, proprietor of the Boston theatre; it was to tour the principal towns of England. As with another Edmund, though less ominously, a wheel had come full circle: for his father had

24. E. F. Saville as Paul Peril in *The Last Shilling*, by (his father) John Faucit Saville, first performed at the Surrey Theatre, 26 February 1844.

begun his career with "Muster Richardson's" travelling booth and, in recent years, had invented a cast-iron portable theatre of his own, put together with bolts for easy taking apart and reassembling.[23] If Edmund did take this engagement, it was probably his last. He died on 20 November 1857. Mrs E. F. Saville acted for at least ten years more, at Dublin, Nottingham etc.; Harriet probably left the stage when she married.

Alfred, the least distinguished of the three brothers, is therefore the hardest to trace professionally; but, despite some gaps in his known career, its general shape is discernible. Personally, too, he is more elusive than the other two. As far as career was concerned, William Farren was his most important family connection.

Alfred is almost certainly the "Mr Faucit" who acted at Deptford in late 1832 and early 1833; he would have been twenty years old. Notable in this engagement was a locally set drama "founded on fact", *The Miser of Deptford Ferry*, in which Alfred played a character named Dagger. There would be other such plays in later engagements. Although the careers of all three brothers attest to the popularity of both "factual" plots and familiar settings, Alfred's has some particularly interesting examples. At Dover, where he acted the following year, this combination of interests evidently inspired an unusual revival of the Elizabethan play *Arden of Feversham*, "founded on a circumstance which occurred in this County".

By 1835, at the latest, Alfred was married, presumably to the Ann Love by whom he had a son in 1844, and the couple were engaged at Ramsgate. Here occurred a typical provincial dilemma: the manager, Poole, lacked the money to pay the actors' salaries for the previous week - unless he used some of the proceeds from his own benefit; unwilling to do this, he promised to pay as much as he could after the next performance and the rest when receipts had proved sufficient. The actors published a bill proclaiming his perfidy and refused to play in that night's production, announcing instead a programme of their own featuring songs and recitations.[24] Eight actors (no actresses) signed the bill, but presumably they spoke for any others not connected with the management; if the due sum, nine pounds, were divided among only ten people, the salaries at that small theatre would have been eighteen shillings a week. Back at Ramsgate after a short engagement at Northampton, there were dramas, allegedly founded on legends, that combined local and supernatural interests: *Margate in Ancient Times* and *The Haunted Hovel of Ramsgate Beach*.

For a while after this, Alfred acted mainly on the Robertson circuit - at Wisbech, Leicester, Grantham, Boston, Sheffield, Doncaster. Now using the name Saville consistently, he had also fixed upon a specific line of parts, the Old Man: Adam in *As You Like It*, Polonius in *Hamlet*, Old Bundle in *The Waterman*, the title role in *Grandfather Whitehead*, etc. This was the Farren line, of course, and some of the parts, especially the last, were identified mainly with that actor. Alfred now added to his repertoire the song "The Fine Old English Gentleman", advertised "as originally sung by W. Farren, Esq.". In 1843 the *Theatrical Journal* (London) published a two-part article, "A Peep in the Provinces" (23 September and 6 October) describing poor theatrical conditions in the counties where Robertson's company acted (half-salaries for the actors during the previous week, etc.) and giving an unflattering picture of his productions. In a performance of *The Belle's Stratagem*, Alfred, as Hardy, reportedly acted the old gentleman in "imitation of Farren, whose left-off theatrical wardrobe [was] duly forwarded to him". The writer unkindly added: "with the coat ends all comparison". Alfred was better appreciated on the circuit, however: a fellow member of Robertson's company, John Coleman, later recalled him as a "very good" old man, one of the "public favourites" – "his Hardcastle and Old Rapid were capital performances, while his Grandfather Whitehead was not a long way behind his prototype and relative".[25]

In 1850 Alfred, now a widower, married Louisa Caroline Haydon. In 1851 he had his first London engagement (as far as I know), at the Pavilion in Whitechapel Road, the East London theatre where Edmund had made his metropolitan debut some seventeen years earlier. Now that he was a London actor, the *Theatrical Journal* mentioned him among those deserving commendation (24 April 1851), and later, in announcing his engagement at the Marylebone, called him "the popular personator of old men" (26 May 1852). Other London minors where he acted were the City of London (the year after Edmund left) and the Victoria. In the summer of 1858 he was at Margate, playing Doggrass in *Black-Eyed Susan* to the Susan of Sarah Thorne, with whom he had acted at the Pavilion, and for a period in the 1860s he was back at the latter theatre. My last reference to him is at the Queen's Theatre, Hull, in 1867, where he had roles in two dramas written by Morton Price for the local company, both "founded on fact": *The Dauntless*, an American Civil War drama, and *The Bushranger*. Among the other actors were "Miss Louise Diddear", Alfred's cousin, and "Mr McFadyen", evidently her husband, James McFadyen. It is pleasant to end this account with another family group from the Faucit Saville album.

## Notes

1. See, for example, Michael Booth, "Going on Stage", *The Mind and Art of Victorian England*, ed. Josef L. Altholz, Minneapolis, 1976, 108–10. Tracy C. Davis emphasizes the particular advantages of family support systems for women and the vulnerability of actresses who lacked them. See *Actresses as Working Women: Their Social Identity in Victorian Culture*, London and New York, 1991, 7.

2. See the genealogical chart. Sources: Records in St. Catherine's House; *International Genealogical Index*, Church of Jesus Christ of Latter-Day Saints, Columbia, S.C.; parish registers for (1) All Saints, Norwich (Norwich and Norfolk Public Record Office) – births and baptisms of John jun., Harriet, Edmund Henry, and Alfred; (2) St. Alfege, Greenwich

- birth and baptism of Charles; (3) St. Mary Abbot, Kensington - baptisms of William and Henry Farren; (4) Brighthelmston (Sussex Public Record Office, Lewes) - marriage of John jun. and baptism of his daughter Eliza Helena. For Helena's birth date, see Carol J. Carlisle, "Two Notes on Helen Faucit", *Theatre Notebook*, XXX, 1976, 101.

3. Carol J. Carlisle, "The Other Miss Faucit", *Nineteenth Century Theatre Research*, 6, 1978, 71-88.

4. See Eric Irvin, "'From the London Theatres'", *Theatre Notebook*, XXII, 1968, 171-72. "Mr Charles Faucit", advertised as the "well-known celebrity on the London boards", appeared in Sept. 1838 at the Royal Victoria Theatre, Sydney, but proved by his ludicrous ineptness that he was a novice. Charles may have persisted in his efforts, however, shifting, as his brothers did, from "Faucit" to "Saville" as a stage name. In a letter of 1 Jan. 1983, Mr Irvin told me that a "Mr Saville" was a member of George Darrell's company in Dunedin, N.Z. in the 1870's.

5. Playbill in the Local History Library, Central Public Libraries, Norwich.

6. Walter Donaldson, *Recollections of an Actor*, London, 1865, 107-9.

7. See records of the case "Diddear falsely called Faucit, otherwise Savill against Faucit", tried in the Consistorial and Episcopal Court of London, 11 May 1821-13 July 1821, in Assignation Book 1820: DL/C/129, London County Hall. A description of John Faucit's agitation on learning of his wife's infidelity is in "Memoir of William Farren", *Oxberry's Dramatic Biography and Histrionic Anecdotes*, London, 1825, III, 43-4.

8. Charles Rice, The Dramatic Register of the Patent Theatres. &c. vol. 7, p. 162. MS in the Harvard Theatre Collection.

9. According to "Memoir of Mrs Faucit", *Oxberry's Dramatic Biography*, III, 133 (published in 1825, several years after the events it reports as current), Mrs Faucit "contributes largely to the support of her children, most of whom are with her, or under her controul [*sic*]". The last phrase suggests that some were with their maternal grandparents. Sir Theodore Martin says, in *Helena Faucit (Lady Martin)*, Edinburgh, 1900, 2, that the girls lived with their mother, the boys with their father.

10. An obituary, "The Late John Saville Faucitt", states that he was legally divorced from his first wife and that he remarried twice: Mrs Amthos, widow of an actor; and, after her death, the daughter of a Yorkshire clergyman (unidentified clipping in the Library of Performing Arts, New York Public Library, Lincoln Center). The divorce must have been a polite fiction (the cost alone would almost certainly have been prohibitive), but John may have gone through marriage ceremonies with both women. There is a record of his marriage with an Emily Moody (evidently his third partner) at St Clement Danes on 11 Apr. 1829. (*International Genealogical Index*)

11. Carlisle, "Two Notes on Helen Faucit", 100.

12. Mary Theresa Odell, *The Old Theatre, Worthing: The Theatre Royal, 1807-1855*, Aylesbury, 1938, 80; Playbills (Bath), Huntington Library. N.B.: To avoid repetitious notes, other major sources for the rest of this paper are now cited: PLAYBILLS in the following libraries: (1) British Library (Vols. 181, 193, 198, 202, 203, 213, 271, 273, 274, 275, 276, 277, 278, 281, 293, 296, 298, 299, 327, 363, 396); (2) National Library of Scotland (Edinburgh); (3) Folger Shakespeare Library (Bath, Grantham; London - Haymarket, St James's, Adelphi, Sadler's Wells, City of London, Victoria); (4) Harvard Theatre Collection (Bath, Belfast, Sheffield, Queen's Theatre in Hull); (5) Local History Collections in the Central Public Libraries of Brighton, Liverpool, Margate, and Norwich; (6) Shakespeare Library, Central Public Libraries, Birmingham, (playbills for performances in many places, in volumes for individual plays). BOOKS: Henry C. Porter, *The History of the Theatres of Brighton from 1774 to 1885*, Brighton, 1886, 59, 70-80, 92; Malcolm Morley, *Margate and Its Theatres 1730-1865*, London, 1966, 70-72, 75.

NEWSPAPERS: *Brighton Herald*, *Brighton Gazette*, *Nottingham Mercury*, *Derby and Chesterfield Reporter*, *Buxton Herald*; clippings in the Saville Scrapbooks, Nottingham Public Library, Vol. I, f.34 (obituaries of Mrs J. F. Saville), f.42 ("Old Nottingham Theatre/Stock Company Days/Memories of the Saville Family", 2-part article signed "G.H.", from *Nottingham Evening News*, 20 and 21 June 1906). THEATRICAL JOURNALS: *Theatrical Times*, *Theatrical Chronicle and Dramatic Review*, *Dramatic Mirror*, and especially *Theatrical Journal* (weekly, 1843-73).

13. "The Decline and Rise of the Brighton Theatre 1840-1860", *Nineteenth Century Theatre Research*, 8, 1980, 35.

14. See his Theatrical Eng & Memd[a] [Engagements and Memoranda], MS in the Harvard Theatre Collection.

15. "Theatrical Sketches: Mr. J.F. Saville", *Actors by Daylight: or Pencilings in the Pit*, I, 13 Oct. 1838, 264.

16. "Mr. Edward [*sic*] Faucit Saville", *Theatrical Journal*, 11 Mar. 1843, 79; "Memoir of Mr. E.F. Saville", *Theatrical Times*, 29 Aug. 1846, [89]-90.

17. *Diaries of William Charles Macready 1833-1851*, ed. William Toynbee, London, 1912, I, 211.

18. John Hollingshead, *My Lifetime*, London, 1895, I, 188-9. The comments on Hofer and Nick are in *Theatrical Journal*, 11 June 1842, 186 and 11 Mar. 1843, 79, respectively; the description of a stage sailor, which occurs in a review of *Signal Rocket*, is in *Theatrical Chronicle*, 1 May 1841, 136.

19. "Murder at the Victoria Theatre", *Theatrical Chronicle*, 20 Aug. 1842, 150-51.

20. Mentioned in an obituary, "Sudden Death of a Veteran Actor", *Sunday Times*, 6 Nov. 1853.

21. See "Mr Edward [*sic*] Faucit Saville", 79; also Hanley's "Lines on Mr. E.F. Saville", *Theatrical Journal*, 3 Dec. 1851, a verse tribute to Saville's personal merits as well as his histrionic abilities.

22. See Helena F. Martin's letters to William Cullenford, Secretary of the Royal General Theatrical Fund: one dated only "Nov. 25th", MS in the Enthoven Collection, London Theatre Museum; and one dated "March 5th", Folger Shakespeare Library, MS. Y.d.3.(94).

23. Edmund's engagement for the portable theatre: *Theatrical Journal*, 2 Jan. 1856, 7. His father's cast-iron theatre: "The Late John Saville Faucitt" (see note 10, above); see also playbills for Saville's New Portable Royal Kent Theatre, Deal, in British Library Playbills 276.

24. The Ramsgate playbills dated Fri. 27th Feb., Fri. 6 Mar. etc., with no year given (in British Library Playbills, Vol. 298), must be for 1835, when the days of week and month would coincide. A bill issued by Poole about his controversy with the actors is puzzlingly dated 1 Apr. 1834, even though it seems to be from the same season. If Poole's reference to the "liberal patronage" of "Tuesday night" is the same as a reference to his Benefit "last night" in the actors' reply, undated but obviously issued immediately, 1 Apr. was on a Wednesday - as in 1835.

25. John Coleman, *Fifty Years of an Actor's Life*, London, 1904, I, 161.

# Charles Kean at Bristol and Bath*

M. GLEN WILSON

CHARLES KEAN, debuting at Drury Lane on 1 October 1827, was not yet seventeen and totally inexperienced. The engagement, ill-advised otherwise as well, was a failure and drew demoralizing notices. When Kean turned to the provinces the following spring, he was treated harshly there as well. The *Bristol Journal* of 6 September 1828 wrote of him in *Richard III*:

> Mr Kean, Jun., the son of the "lion-tamer", made his first bow to a Bristol audience. . . . He is no more like Mr Kean, Sen., than "Hyperion to a satyr". . . . anyone familiar with the peculiar style of his father's acting could not fail of observing the attempt at imitation.

Other performances were received with equal disfavour. The same critic asserted, "The truth is, we fear Mr K. has mistaken his forte - he certainly possesses none of Macklin's indispensable requisites for the stage", and advised the tyro to "adopt some less arduous but perhaps equally lucrative profession". The *Bristol Gazette* tersely reiterated the same views. When Kean returned to Bristol two years later for five nights, beginning with *Richard III*, reviews again denounced his acting, focusing mainly on imitation of his father. The *Gazette* declared him "a very inapt representation of the 'crook-backed Tyrant' . . . due to poor voice, small physique, and obvious imitation".[1] Thus it was for Kean at Bristol in his apprentice years.

After a fairly successful American tour and a mediocre engagement at Covent Garden in 1833, Kean left London for the provinces that summer, vowing never to act there again until he could command £50 nightly. Five years later, he had created such a reputation in the provinces that Drury Lane engaged him at that salary.[2] His triumph there in *Hamlet*, in opposition to William Charles Macready's management at Covent Garden, established him as Macready's major rival and incurred the older actor's enmity. To those who have read widely the press notices on Kean's remaining career, it does seem clear that Macready's

* Typical of Kathleen Barker's selfless dedication to British theatre history, in 1970 she gave her transcriptions of Bristol newspaper coverage of Charles Kean's appearance there to this writer for copying. Her direct and significant contribution to this article is acknowledged with warm appreciation.

journalistic friends served him well, in London mainly but in some provincial journals as well.[3] At Bristol, where Macready had both strong family and theatrical ties, the press remained dominantly anti-Kean until 1862 when misfortune of the manager evoked such support that the old enmity to Kean was replaced by general eulogism. Comparison of Kean's success, critical and popular, in two cities of such proximity as Bath and Bristol may evidence the probability that Macready's influence, whether direct or indirect, did result in negative press for Kean. Such an account will, of course, also inform on the contributions of Charles Kean as a provincial star.

There is no record of Kean's appearing in Bristol between 1830 and February 1836, when he acted four nights, preceded by eight nights at Bath, his first appearance there, and he returned after Bristol for a re-engagement of four nights. Bath at once became a major provincial theatre for Kean, and he enjoyed success there like that at Brighton, Dublin, and Edinburgh. For whatever reason, he was not so welcome at Bristol as at Bath.

The free list was suspended for Kean's first appearance at Bath on 7 February 1836, in *Richard III* and then for his benefit in the same role. He also acted *Othello*, *Hamlet* (twice), *Macbeth*, *King John*, *The Merchant of Venice*, *The Iron Chest*, *A New Way to Pay Old Debts*, *Pizarro*, and *Sardanapaulus*.[4]

The *Bath Herald* and the *Bath Journal* reported a "house crowded to the roof" for the opening,[5] and their reviews were lengthy and flattering. Subsequent notices followed in kind, with the *Journal* being more enthusiastic, but a temperate letter to the *Herald* on 20 February deemed Kean "on the whole a good actor, and will be still a better, when he learns to tone down his impassioned scenes and read his authors more critically", adding that but for comparison to his father his fame would have equalled the father.

Kean's account book shows he received an average of £16.13.0. for his twelve nights, on terms of £10 nightly, half the benefit, and a third of the final night.[6] The benefit had grossed £149.15.0. He wrote his mother after opening that he rued declining the manager's offer of half after £30, for opening night would have brought him £50 with great promise thereafter.[7]

In the same letter Kean anticipated doing poorly in Bristol, for the season had gone badly and he was to follow engagements by Young and Macready. However, he averaged just under £16 for four nights at £10 nightly and half the benefit. The Bristol press was at best coolly reserved. "It is impossible to speak of Mr Kean without reference to his father," wrote the *Journal*, and other notices repeated the theme.[6] The *Gazette* was typical; granting that while his performance was "a superior piece of acting," it did not measure up to either Young or Macready. His voice was "much against him, being singularly harsh and dissonant" and his stature was inadequate.

On 6 February 1837 Kean opened for eight nights at Bath, and the engagement was extended to twelve. On terms of half after £25 and half the benefit gross, he received £256, a nightly average of over £21, from receipts of £762. Attendance was excellent and notices enthusiastic without qualifications. The *Bath Chronicle* declared in one notice that "in extremes of sensibility" he was without rival, and in another compared him to Macready to the latter's disadvantage.[9] Following Kean at Bath and drawing mediocre houses, Macready was made acutely aware of Kean and fretted about it in his diary.[10]

Kean did not play Bristol in 1837, for he was visibly ill at the end of *Macbeth*, his last night at Bath. It was smallpox. Upon "medical advice", he did not act for three weeks. But he gave presents to Bath theatre personnel and received presents from Bath patrons: bouquets, poetry, items of considerable value, and "locks of hair".[11]

Kean's great success at Drury Lane as Hamlet in 1838 burgeoned provincial demand. He opened in *Hamlet* at Bath on 7 January 1839, playing the first four nights for a third of receipts, the next four for half, and, re-engaged, four more nights for half. He received £534.10.0., averaging £44.10.0. per performance. Reporting packed houses and great enthusiasm, the *Bath Journal* praised the performance in eulogistic terms.[12] At the last night he announced his return for another two weeks beginning 18 February, whereupon there was "great sensation, the house rising and immense cheering". Despite many competing events, he drew £258 for those eight performances. He had acted thirteen roles: six were Shakespearean for nine nights, and *The Lady of Lyons* - his first time in Bath - was acted three times.[13] It had been a triumphant engagement with the manager averaging £46 nightly.

After Bath in 1839, Kean opened at Bristol on 12 March, receiving £200 for six nights at a third for two nights and half on the others, while Mrs Macready, the manager, averaged £43 nightly. But there was no extension of the engagement. Local press was, in the main, grudging.[14] Despite the usual reservations, the *Mirror* considered his acting "a rich treat" but the *Gazette* refused to join "in praises so lavishly showered" but admitted audiences did not share that view: "His voice is as hoarse as the night-raven's, and his manner as harsh, abrupt, and wanting in dignity, and his conception of the character . . . faulty". The *Mirror* of 16 March "with every friendly disposition", declined to "join in the adulatory commendations" of current criticism and called him "greatly over-rated". Comparisons to Macready and Edmund Kean were unfavourable, and the old charge of imitation was reiterated. Then, "having said this much of Mr Kean's demerits", the reviewer stated there was "much to be admired" and cited several points of excellence in *Hamlet*. It would seem the Bristol press was striving to be loyal to Macready while yet acknowledging Kean's competence. It being the first Bristol engagement after Kean's 1838 triumph over Macready in London, it may have been the Macready influence that accounted for the markedly contrasting criticism in Bath and Bristol in 1839.

After an American tour and a lengthy Haymarket engagement, Kean began 21

September 1840, at Bristol for six nights. His share was only £141.19.6., the weather being "very wet and inclement".[15] While it has been reported the manager took less than £25 for expenses,[16] Kean's account book shows slightly more than £29. Kean made a donation to "The Grateful Society" in appreciation of local support. Despite the contrary evidence, four Bristol newspapers reported excellent houses and warm reception, but again they cavilled, in varying degrees, with his acting.

Kean's account book shows no accompanying Bath engagement that fall, nor did the Bath press carry notices. He did begin again at Bath on 11 January 1841, for a third of receipts for four nights and half for the final four. Romeo was a new role, and reviews were lengthy and detailed.[18] While tragic scenes were praised, there were reservations on Kean as a romantic lover, mainly due to physique. The *Herald* praised his Hamlet and noted there were many virtues in his acting, but it cited voice as a major shortcoming:

> neither extensive, sonorous nor mellow – deficient in harmony and softness, incapable of many necessary intonations, at times creaking and, when urged to extreme loudness, coarse and harsh.[19]

On 18 January, his thirtieth birthday, he acted *Richard III* as a free night for Mrs Macready and then four more nights. He then returned to Bath for a free night in *The Stranger* and four other nights. For the sharing performances he averaged £32 at Bath and £34 at Bristol.

Writing to Ellen Tree on 17 January, Kean reported "a crowded house last night" at Bath, but the engagement was not so lucrative as the previous year, "only 250£".[20] Returning to Bath on 4 March for four nights and two at Bristol, his average share was £22.11.0. at Bath and £34.15.0. at Bristol. A struggling management, some critical reservations in the Bath press, and playing only two nights at Bristol may account for the fact that this time Bristol gave better average return than at Bath. Bristol reviews were favourable although without enthusiasm. Four notices conceded his popularity, noted enthusiastic audiences, and gave some limited praise. The *Standard* pointed out, however, that never having created "an absolutely new character", his place "in the high walk of drama" was questionable.[21] The *Mirror*, after chastising his imitation of his father, took him to task for acting *The Stranger* at all and greatly disdained his costume as unbecoming one of his stature.[22]

In October following, Kean wrote the new manager at Bath he had expected to by-pass that theatre, having been there too much.[23] While that may in part explain lowered receipts in the previous Bath engagement, the change in management and Kean's letter suggest the problem was with the theatre and its management. Kean agreed to go on the new manager's account but for five nights only. On 1 February 1842 he began six nights there while his bride of two days,

Ellen Tree, acted at Bristol.[24]

Kean opened at Bristol on 15 February for four nights. The *Mirror* condemned audience taste for supporting him and derided his imitative acting: "He is, in fact, so entirely a double of his father that likenesses and dislikenesses are matters of inheritance." A week later it reported the theatre "full to the bung" for the benefit and "Mr Kean exerted his usual tact and knowledge of the stage to make his palpable hits".[25] For the six nights at Bath, Kean's share averaged £28, and the four nights in Bristol averaged over £33.[26] Again, he had drawn better in Bristol for fewer nights. He had played his standard roles, but at Bath on 19 February, he acted both Shylock and Claude Melnotte for a single performance. The following June, asked for a gratuitous appearance to aid the struggling Bath company and unable to do so, Kean sent £20.[27]

Mr and Mrs Charles Kean began at Bath on 7 January 1843, in *Much Ado About Nothing* to rave reviews.[28] Benedict was a new role for Kean, and he sent glowing reviews to Edinburgh for press release there.[29] But Bristol critics were mixed in judgements the following week, the *Mercury* being particularly harsh:

> Mr Charles Kean, as Benedict, was far from being successful. We have never been among the "thick-and-thin" admirers of this gentleman, and when it was more fashionable to regard him as the paragon of actors than it is at present, we were at a loss to discover those bright emanations of genius which the million, whom he has so enthusiastically followed, perceived (or fancied they perceived) in his effort . . . His Benedict was scarcely a second rate representation.[30]

The *Gazette* compared him unfavourably to Kemble and Macready, physically and intellectually, charging he depended on stage tricks, body jerks, facial contortions, and rolling eyes. It also quoted *Punch*: "Mr Kean may justly appeal against the income tax on the ground of being over-rated."[31] (Interestingly, Kean was just at this point, under influence of his wife, changing his style toward greater restraint and realism.[32]) The *Bristol Times* and *Bath Advocate*, on the other hand, citing necessity for a good Benedict, declared Kean had "fully done justice" to the role, noting his fine flashes of comedy and total lack of buffoonery. (Kean's Benedict was, of course, to become his greatest success in Shakespearean comedy.) However, in *The Stranger* the *Advocate* agreed with the recurring Bristol criticism of Kean's "out-doing Termagant".[33] The benefit brought a crowded house, making *amende honorable* for previous mediocre attendance, and reservedly favourable notices cited an enthusiastic audience.[34]

On 18 February 1843, the Keans were again at Bath in *As You Like It*, following with *Richard III*, *Hamlet* and their recent London success, *The Rose of Arragon*, plus *The Honeymoon*, as the benefit. They brought prosperity to the theatre, but Ellen's health obviated further performances there as well as in Bristol the rest of that year.

At Bristol from 8 to 15 January 1844, the Keans drew "very fair houses every night and elicited great applause", according to the *Mirror*.[35] There was no Bath engagement, for they returned to London to prepare special staging of *Richard III* at Drury Lane under Kean's supervision; it was in "the Macready manner" - historical accuracy, careful rehearsal, and specially conceived staging for a specific play. When they returned to the provinces, Kean took with them costumes and properties for supporting players and supernumeraries. A letter by Ellen informs that while in Belfast Kean acquired thirty-six special costumes and properties for supernumeraries in *Macbeth* for £200: "I think it will repay him in *Cash* - if not it will in satisfaction", she wrote.[36] Whether the costumes had arrived from London in time for use at Belfast is uncertain, so Bath and Bristol may have seen the first production of *Macbeth* in the new manner.

On Saturday 11 January 1845, the Keans acted *Money* in Bath, *Hamlet* on Monday, and then three nights in *Richard III* with "magnificence hitherto unknown at the Bath theatre".[37] With three rehearsals, unusual for a provincial theatre, and with new scenery and Kean's costumes and properties, Bath was introduced to the new mode of production. (The *Chronicle* informed readers that the production was "got up under Mr Kean's personal superintendence".[38]) After a benefit in *The Merchant of Venice* with *Don Caesar de Bazan*, they were announced for *Macbeth* for three nights with scenic splendour, preceded by four days of preparation. After its opening one review reported the "promise" had been "fully realized" even though "the moving wood of Burnam astonished Macbeth more than it did the audience".[39] Another writer objected to new music and inept scene shifting,[40] but six notices during the Bath engagement were unqualified in praise of the productions and the acting of both Keans.

After the last showing of *Richard III* in Bath on Friday, the production was moved to Bristol for one night on Monday 20 January; however, as result of a fine reception, the playbill the next day announced repetition on Wednesday and Friday. (The theatre had closed the preceding Thursday for rehearsal.) It being a time of severe economic distress in Bristol, the press rallied in vigorous support of the theatre with lengthy announcements promising "entirely new Scenery, Dresses, Decorations, etc". On 18 January the *Mercury* reported scene painters had been at work for "several weeks", fifty supers were engaged, and Kean was providing "correct costumes and accessories" at personal cost of £500. Its review on 25 January praised production - staging was in "admirable style" - but Kean's Gloucester was "too melodramatic and artificial". Other notices praised scenery and costumes, but Kean's performance received scant attention. One reviewer of the benefit on Saturday did note that Kean drew great applause in *The Gamester*, "proving how true to life was his representation of the infatuated and ruined Beverley".[41] But the second piece, *Don Caesar de Bazan*, drew no comment despite its being a new play with new scenery in Bristol.

After great success with the new stagings at Exeter and Plymouth,[42] the Keans returned to Bristol on 3 March, repeating *Richard III* for three nights, and then brought out *Macbeth* "in a manner never witnessed outside London". Newspapers and playbills announced there would be extensive programme notes on antiquarian staging and costumes. Weather was bad and, with hard times, audiences were disappointing; the *Mercury*, noting the engagement was not "liberally supported", hoped the mayor's patronage and the benefit would make up "for the deficiencies of the week".[43] There was generally perfunctory attention to the acting by the press, with reserved approval for Kean. Staging was lauded by all four newspapers although the *Mercury* regretted that "bungling of the scene shifters" had marred the change from "the blasted heath to a moonlight view".[44]

After two years in America and a triumphant run of *The Wife's Secret* at the Haymarket, the first showing in London of their new play, the Keans acted it one night in Bristol on 3 March 1848. The *Bristol Mirror*, despite the previous great success of the play in America and at the Haymarket, to say nothing of its prominence and success in the Keans' repertoire to the end of their careers, denounced the play as "exceedingly unnatural and overdone", and declared,

> Mr Kean's style of acting possesses all its former faults and merits. If he has added to the latter, he has not still decreased the former, and, consequently, those who have ever admired him will do so still - those with whom he has not been so popular, will yet find a something wanting to prevent them considering him a favourite.[45]

*The Bristol Times* discussed Ellen's "matchless" performance in detail, but thought Kean, while fine in parts, tended

> to turn every passage into a passionate one. This tendency to rant has been his great fault and we regret that it appears to be almost incurable. Let him but master it and his Sir Walter will be one of the finest performances of the day.[46]

Such was the grudging criticism in Bristol in what had already proven to be Kean's first undeniable success in an original role on both sides of the Atlantic.

As resident stars at the Haymarket the next two seasons, the Keans did little provincial acting, and after assuming management of the Princess's Theatre in 1850, they acted only there and at Windsor Castle until after leaving management in 1859. They again took to the provinces.

James Chute, son-in-law of Mrs Macready, assumed management of both the Bristol and Bath theatres in 1852. He had given Ellen in marriage and remained in close association with Kean, even to the point of bringing out five productions at Bath and Bristol that were copied from Kean's staging of the plays at the Princess's. In 1860 he engaged the Keans for a fortnight, alternating between the two theatres, to open at Bath on 9 April. They played *The Wife's Secret*, *Louis XI.*, *Hamlet*, *The Corsican Brothers*, and, for their benefit, *The Merchant of Venice* - all major successes during their Princess's tenure. The Bath press was unequivocal in its lengthy and eulogistic reports of performances and of crowded, enthusiastic houses.

On 7 April Bristol's *Gazette*, *Mercury* and *Times* gave fulsome publicity for their appearances the following week. But Bristol again gave them a cool reception. The *Times* and the *Mercury* reported houses were below expectation,[47] and on 21 April the *Mirror* stated, "It is evident he will never be a favourite in Bristol", but a week earlier, while admitting some excellence, it noted he was "throwing off much of that mannerism which so seriously mars the effect of every character he strives to delineate". The *Mercury* deemed Kean very uneven in *The Wife's Secret* but praised his Louis XI - "indeed a remarkable piece of acting".[48]

In this engagement as in his other provincial appearances, Kean's terms almost doubled standard admissions, with no second prices. And with some justification, since he brought his wife and a "petite company" of three supporting players with their costumes and properties. The *Mercury* cited reasons for raising prices, blaming neither the stars nor the management,[49] but in "money-conscious" Bristol, the result was poor houses and a loss to the manager.

On 12 January 1861 the Keans returned to Bath, *Keene's Bath Journal* heralding them as "a burst of sunshine" despite the raised prices; its subsequent review proclaimed them as popular and accomplished as ever.[50] Kean's Hamlet was described as a "non-declamatory, deeply studied, . . . minutely detailed" performance; Louis XI was declared his masterpiece, and at the benefit in *Henry VIII* and *The Wonder* his dash and spirit "quite surprised" the audience. Both notices in *Keene's Bath Journal* were full columns of unqualified praise. The Keans did not appear that year in Bristol; they left Bath to prepare the opening of a Drury Lane engagement on 2 January.

Beginning on 14 January 1862, the Keans were at Bath for four nights. Again Bristol did not see them, for they went to London for another Drury Lane engagement. Scheduled again at Bath in early May, they happened to be there when the theatre burned on 18 April. They watched the fire, and it was Kean who telegraphed Chute in Bristol of the calamity.[51] They did open on 5 May in Bristol in *Hamlet* and acted five nights. This time all four Bristol newspapers vied in praising Kean. Evidently sympathy for Chute's loss at Bath had brought an outpouring of support that obliterated the prevailing hostility to Kean in the Bristol press, and the engagement was a brilliant success, critically and financially. The *Mirror* reported many Bath playgoers came to see the Keans at Bristol.[52] The *Western Daily Press* pointed out that Kean had repeatedly demonstrated his acting skill and power "beyond the possibility of cavil or dispute". It reviewed his Princess's management, the protracted controversy about his acting merits, the charges of upholstery to mask acting deficiencies, and then praised his Hamlet at length. Kean had "last night proved to the Bristol public - if, indeed, such proof had been necessary - that as a histrionic artist Mr Charles Kean has . . . no compeer on the English stage". While not so subtle as Fechter or his elocution so "harmonious" as Macready's, merits of his performance "place it upon a higher altitude, both as regards conception and execution, than any representation of the part we have seen anywhere". Citing Kean's "psychological" interpretation, his power and detailed excellence throughout, the care and earnest study in the "most trifling interlocutory remarks", the writer declared:

> all is great, and we are led to the greater and the greatest by such natural and imperceptible gradation that we experience none of those spasmodic starts and surprises which, in representations of other distinguished actors, sometimes startles us.[53]

Despite obvious overstatement, this review does evidence Kean's mature acting style and suggests the level of achievement that recent scholarship on Kean has described and documented.[54] All Bristol reviewers lauded both the Keans in lengthy columns for the "bumper" benefit in *Henry VIII.*

After touring Australia and America, the Keans returned to England in 1866, acting in London and other provincial theatres before opening at Bath on 14 January 1867. They came with the same "petite company" that had accompanied them earlier as well as during their tour abroad, but now they needed it more than ever. Not yet fifty-six, Kean was chronically ill, crotchety and dispirited, old before his time. Ellen, three years older, was quite matronly and plain, ill-fitted visually for many roles she essayed. However much they retained of acting skill and despite occasional bursts of excellence, they were conspicuously in decline. Nonetheless, in the hearts of many Victorian theatre-goers they were about the last of a memorable generation of stars. They were warmly welcomed after their three years' absence.

At Bath they acted *Louis XI.*, *Hamlet*, *The Merchant of Venice*, *Henry VIII*, and, for the benefit, *Richard II* and *The Jealous Wife*. Bad weather and "conflicting private parties" diminished attendance, according to *Keene's Bath Journal* in its eighteen-inch column of eulogism on *Henry VIII*, but it considered Kean's Hamlet too conventionalized, not comparable to some recent but un-named actors of the role. Moreover, Kean was deemed less effective in comedy than in tragedy. The notice was on 18 January, Kean's fifty-sixth birthday. On the 29 January, the Keans celebrated their silver wedding anniversary with a fine party. It was appropriate that it was in Bath, where they had honeymooned and where they had enjoyed such great success, artistically and socially.

Concluding at Bath on 21 January to a full house and generous praise in the press, the Keans acted the same roles in Bristol the following week. On 23

January despite advanced prices, bad weather, and competing private theatricals, balls, and other fashionable events, a crowded house enthusiastically greeted Kean's entrance in *Louis XI.*, repeating it at the end. Reviews were unanimous in enthusiastic praise of Kean, although Ellen's Portia was gently chided for want of vocal range and flexibility.[55] They closed on 28 January, the benefit, in *Henry VIII* and *The Jealous Wife* to a crowded house and glowing notices.[56]

Four months later, on 18 May 1867, in Liverpool, Kean suffered a heart attack after performing *Louis XI.* and remained a helpless invalid until his death the following January.

Of Charles Kean in Bristol, Kathleen Barker wrote: "While never entirely winning round the critics, Charles Kean usually received good support from the public."[57] It has been shown here that he did win critical support in his three last engagements, apparently due to a surge of support for the troubled manager. In Bath he was more successful with both press and audiences. For almost thirty years he usually acted contiguous engagements, in the same repertory with few exceptions, at these two theatres of close proximity. While Bath press evaluation generally parallelled that of Dublin, Brighton, Edinburgh, and other provincial towns, Bristol was an exception, and one cannot but speculate on the reason for such persisting negativism, often acrimonious, in view of Kean's success elsewhere in the provinces and of his evolving and salutary change in acting style under influence of his wife. The most likely hypothesis - and it can only be hypothesis - is that Macready, directly or indirectly, influenced the Bristol press.

The prevailing negativism of the Bristol press was seldom parallelled at the box office, and Kean's extant account books show he proved advantageous to managers in both cities, given allowance for local conditions, rather consistently. Whether his terms were comparable to other touring stars remains unknown, but Bristol reviewers made no charges of excessive prices and frequently reported good attendance. Their focus of attack was on Kean as an actor. Whatever his terms, managers and, with few exceptions, audiences in both Bristol and Bath welcomed Kean whether he was introducing new staging, acting new roles, or repeating proven successes.

Perhaps most important to history of provincial theatre is Kean's general influence on dramatic production there. His personal supervision of rehearsals in the 1840s, his introduction of specialized and historically accurate staging (before, and indirectly during and after his Princess's management), and his contribution to scenic and lighting advances have been evidenced in varying degrees here and in other research.[58] The data here on Bristol and Bath can only partially support this claim, but it hopefully will encourage research on the subject at other provincial theatres.

# Notes

1. 18 Mar.·1830.
2. See this writer's article, "Charles Kean in the Provinces, 1833-38", *Theatre History Studies*, I (1981), 39-49.
3. One need only read *Diaries of William Charles Macready*, ed. E. Toynbee, London, 1912, and *Macready's Reminiscences*, ed. F. Pollock, London, 1866, and peruse theatrical press columns to which his friends contributed. Clement Scott, in *Hours with the Players*, London, 1881, was one who affirmed the fact: "For many years the admirers and private friends of Macready had been among the most hostile of Charles Kean's critics." (I, 232) As for those who have researched Kean's press coverage and his correspondence, see the published works of Prof. Virginia Francesco and myself as cited in a lengthy footnote in Dr Francesco's "Mr Charles Kean, Actor: A Re-evaluation", *Theatre History Studies*, IX, 1989, 55-68.

As to Macready's influence at Bristol, he had a financial interest in the theatre after death, in 1828, of his father, who had been manager, and his stepmother subsequently managed from 1834 to 1852. See Kathleen Barker, *The Theatre Royal, Bristol, 1766-1966*, London, Society for Theatre Research, 1974, chs. 3-5.

4. "Charles Kean Account Book, 1835-1837", Folger Shakespeare Library. Kean's account book listed for each night the plays acted, the gross receipts, his share, and occasional pertinent notes. Figures, etc., cited herein for subsequent engagements in 1836 and 1837 are from this source.
5. 5 Feb. 1836.
6. These were Kean's usual terms at principal theatres that season.
7. ALS to Mary Kean, Bath Reference Library.
8. *Bristol Gazette*, 25 Feb. 1836 and *Bristol Journal*, 20 Feb. 1836; *Bristol Mercury* and *Bristol Mirror* also had notices on 20 Feb. 1836.
9. 16 and 23 Feb. 1837.
10. Macready, *Diaries*, *op. cit.*; see entries of late February 1837.
11. ALS, Kean to David Buchanan, 27 Mar. 1837, Folger Shakespeare Library.
12. 14 Jan. 1838; see also 28 Jan., 25 Feb, and 5 Mar. *Bath Chronicle* also carried notices on 28 Jan., 21 Feb. and 1 Mar.
13. "Charles Kean's Journal of Receipts and Expenses, 1838-1839", Harvard Theatre Collection. Terms, receipts, and roles cited herein for 1839 are from this source.
14. *Bristol Mercury*, 16 Mar. 1939; *Bristol Mirror*, 16 Mar. 1839; *Bristol Gazette*, 14 and 21 Mar. 1839.
15. "Charles Kean Receipt Book, 1840-1841", Harvard Theatre Collection. Figures for both years cited here are from it.
16. Kathleen Barker, *The Theatre Royal, Bristol, 1766-1966*, 112.
17. *Bristol Standard*, 24 Sep. and 1 Oct. 1840; *Bristol Gazette*, 1 Oct. 1840; *Bristol Mirror*, 26 Sep. 1840.
18. *Bath Herald*, 16 Jan. 1841; *Bath Chronicle*, 14 Jan. 1841.
19. 26 Jan. 1841.
20. ALS, 17 Jan. 1841, Folger Shakespeare Library. (This letter has been incorrectly dated as 26 Sep. 1840, but Kean was not then at Bath.)
21. 28 Jan. 1841.
22. 6 Mar. 1841.
23. ALS, 16 Oct. 1841, University of Rochester Library.
24. The marriage in Dublin was unannounced to prepare Kean's mother, who had long opposed the match, but *Bristol Mercury* carried the news on 2 Feb. and other newspapers

soon followed. On 28 Feb. in Glasgow, Ellen Tree became Mrs Charles Kean professionally. Of course, she was a major star herself, but thereafter Mr and Mrs Charles Kean were an acting team; only when one was ill did they act separately.

25. 19 and 26 Feb. 1842.

26. "Charles Kean Account Book, 1841-1842", Harvard Theatre Collection. There are no extant account books for the next six years.

27. *Dramatic and Musical Review*, 11 June 1842. Kean's account book has an entry for 16 April 1842, at Bath, but no figures or plays are entered, and no reviews have been found. Whether the Keans acted remains questionable.

28. *Bath Herald*, 14 Jan. 1843; *Bath Chronicle*, 14 Jan. 1843.

29. ALS to David Buchanan, 14 Jan. 1843, Folger Shakespeare Library.

30. 21 Jan. 1843.

31. 19 Jan. 1843.

32. See Virginia Francesco, "Mr Charles Kean, Actor: A Re-evaluation", cited in fn. 3 above.

33. 21 Jan. 1843.

34. *Bristol Mirror*, 28 Jan. 1843. See also the *Mercury* and *Advocate* of the same date and *Mirror* of 18 Feb.

35. 13 Jan. 1844. See also *Mercury* of that date and the *Gazette* of 18 Jan.

36. ALS to unidentified person, 28 Dec. 1844, Missouri Historical Society.

37. *Bath Chronicle*, 16 Jan. 1845.

38. 23 Jan. 1845. John Coleman provides an account of Kean's supervising rehearsals in Belfast just prior to the Keans' coming to Bath; see his *Fifty Years of an Actor's Life* London, 1904, 182-99.

39. *Keene's Bath Journal*, 31 Jan. 1845.

40. *Bath Herald*, 1 Feb. 1845.

41. *Bristol Mirror*, 1 Feb. 1845. *Bristol Mercury* and *Bristol Gazette* printed long notices in praise of the production of *Richard III* but ignored the new play for the benefit.

42. Kean wrote James Hackett from Plymouth, "In 14 nights, I shall clear nearly £700!!! & no mistake", and gloated on his success despite the "malignant press". ALS, n.d., Folger Shakespeare Library.

43. 8 Mar. 1845.

44. 15 Mar. 1845. See also *Bristol Journal*, *Bristol Gazette*, and *Bristol Mirror* of the same date.

45. 4 Mar. 1848.

46. 4 Mar. 1848.

47. 21 Apr. 1860.

48. 14 Apr. 1860.

49. 21 Apr. 1860. George Everett, James Cathcart, and Patty Chapman were Kean's supporting players, so there were five in the touring company. Cathcart and Everett had been in the Princess's company and, knowing Kean's wishes, supervised rehearsals as well as acting key supporting roles. Miss Chapman, Kean's beloved niece, had debuted at Bath and Bristol under a pseudonym as Jessica in preparation for Kean's production of *The Merchant of Venice* at the Princess's in 1858. Another niece travelled with them for off-stage assistance. These three played with the Keans in acting performances to the end of their careers.

50. 19 and 26 Jan. 1861.

51. ALS, Kean to unidentified person, n.d., Norman Philbrick Library (now at Pomona College); ALS, Ellen Kean to Mr Levy, n.d. (written from Plymouth where they next played), in Stead scrapbook, Theatre Collection, New York Public Library at Lincoln

Center. Chute had been uninsured, but the theatre was rebuilt and opened on 4 Mar. 1863, with a production of *A Midsummer Night's Dream* that copied Kean's production at the Princess's.

52. 10 May 1862.

53. 6 May 1862. The Keans liked this notice well enough to paste a clipping in a scrapbook now at Folger Shakespeare Library.

54. Francesco, *op. cit.*

55. *Saturday Times & Mirror*, 26 Jan. 1867.

56. *Daily Bristol Times & Mirror*, 29 Jan. 1867; *Saturday Times & Mirror*, 2 Feb. 1867; and *Bristol Mercury*, 2 Feb. 1867.

57. Barker, *op. cit.*, p. 112. The statement is made in the context of Bristol theatre of the 1840s.

58. Russell Jackson, in "Shakespeare in Liverpool: Edward Saker's Revival, 1876-81", *Theatre Notebook*, XXXIII, 3, 100-9, has written that Kean's influence was more significant in the provinces than in London. My article in the same journal, XXXIV, 1, 18-21, "Edward Saker's Revivals and Charles Kean; An Addendum", cites a *Frazier Magazine* (Feb. 1858) report that provincial theatres were following Kean's examples of "upholstering" Shakespeare. *Brighton Herald*, 4 Oct. 1848, described a box set in its review of *The Wife's Secret*, the first reference to such in the provinces that I've seen, and reported Kean had sent designs to provincial managers. It called him "a reformer of the stage".

# Charles Dillon: A Provincial Tragedian in the Former Colonies

## *An Open Letter to Kathleen Barker*

GAYLE T. HARRIS

DEAR KATHLEEN,

You had so hoped to return to the States to further your research for a book about your favourite provincial actor, Charles Dillon. But, so sadly for us, it was not to be. You had sketched out the general framework for this period of his life, but it remains only a sketch, and I hope that what follows will be in some small way useful to someone who may one day take your notes forward and produce that full-length biography.

You did, however, publish an article wherein you wrote:

> when eventually Charles Dillon followed the example of so many provincial stars in setting off for America, it seems to have been totally on impulse, with no pre-planning, and could hardly have been worse timed. Surely no one but he would have taken ship for New York in the middle of winter, without a single advance contact, and with a Civil War in imminent prospect at his destination. To add, undeservedly, to all this, he broke his ankle during a terrible storm on the passage out, and was still limping when he arrived in New York early in January 1861.[1]

But those difficulties were perhaps the least of his troubles. In the early days of that 1861-2 United States tour, had it not been - to coin a phrase - for bad luck, poor Dillon would have had no luck at all.

To have a look at those early months of 1861 in the United States from the perspective of a working actor is instructive. The slavery issue with its underlying economic stresses had been smouldering for many years, waiting for the final spark that would make Civil War inevitable. That spark was to be the election of President Abraham Lincoln who was firmly pro-Union and anti-slavery. While no one in America at the time could be totally oblivious to sectional tensions, in early 1861 the war had not yet begun and there could be no predicting when - or even if - it would. That Charles Dillon came on in spite of whatever warnings he may have had should not necessarily reflect upon his judgment or lack thereof;

American actors were themselves soldiering on as they always had. No one, least of all a visiting Englishman, could or should necessarily have known in early 1861 what dangers were imminent.

Dillon arrived in New York on 3 January 1861, on the Cunard liner *Australasian*, following a nearly disastrous voyage. During a storm at sea, nine men had been washed overboard and drowned, and Dillon himself sustained the injury to his leg.[2] We may assume, however, that he probably had some medical assistance, since among the thirty-eight survivors of the voyage were two surgeons.[3] He checked into the New York Hotel, and began to look for work. A massive snowstorm and bitterly cold temperatures undoubtedly hampered his search. Two weeks later, still unemployed and owing $35 to the hotel, he pawned his watch - with some great difficulty - for $40.[4]

In the meantime, the United States were coming undone. South Carolina, good to its word that it would secede from the Union if Abraham Lincoln were elected President, had done so on 20 December 1860. By the end of January 1861 Mississippi, Florida, Alabama, Georgia, and Louisiana had joined the exodus, forming the nucleus of the Confederacy.

Finally, Dillon secured an engagement at the Winter Garden Theatre on lower Broadway for Thursday 24 January. Edwin Booth was in the midst of a long run, but with an option to play either four or six nights per week. That he agreed to surrender two nights during the week to Dillon was quite likely due to the kindly offices of Dillon's new-found friend, Sam Cowell, who Booth would have known as a neighbour in Baltimore in an earlier time. The deal was for Dillon to play *Belphegor*, and share the receipts, after $250. He, of course, was responsible for the printing of his own bills and tickets. At the end, he suffered a net loss.

As Dillon's day dawned, a blizzard struck: four inches of snow fell, followed by sleet and freezing rain. A small but hearty band of first-nighters, however, braved the storm, and Dillon earned considerable critical acclaim:

> This fine artist's success was one of the most distinct we have ever placed on record . . . The whole performance was characterized by originality and power, and under favorable circumstances would secure for the piece a long run. We trust that Mr Dillon will have another opportunity of appearing before our public.[5]

Edwin Booth, however, did not share the critics' enthusiasm. He withdrew his agreement to allow a second night that week, citing financial need, and Dillon was thus limited to a one-night stand.[6]

A New York paper at this time reported:

> Secession, snow squalls, slosh, and New York mud, all combine to tax the patience and pockets of the gentlemen who cater for our amusement. By the

> most strenuous exertions, assisted by a lavish distribution of "free parses" on stormy evenings, managers have managed to "keep up appearances" thus far, but there is no concealing the fact that the "treasury box" is becoming tighter and tighter every day, and cash pay out-able is beginning to get the whip hand of receipts at the box office.[7]

Not until 11 February did Dillon appear again on a New York stage. This time, James Simmonds, an agent who had previously represented Joseph Jefferson, took the French Theatre for one night to present Dillon in *Belphegor*. Little critical note was taken of this performance. Dillon did at this time, however, have the prospect of an engagement at the Philadelphia Arch Street Theatre in March.[8] On the same day, President-elect Abraham Lincoln boarded a train in his home-town of Springfield, Illinois, en route to Washington, and Jefferson Davis left his plantation on the Mississippi for Montgomery, Alabama - one to be inaugurated President of the Union, the other to be inaugurated President of the Confederacy.

At liberty until the March engagement, Dillon accompanied Sam Cowell to Boston, where his fortunes seemed to take a turn for the better. He played the week of 18 to 23 February at the Boston Museum, playing *Belphegor* five nights and *Othello* one. A local critic enthused:

> Mr Dillon pulls new wires. He is quiet when quiet is demanded, - he is intense when intensity is in keeping with his situation; but he never lets one inclination interfere with, interrupt, or o'errun the other. He disappoints you at every turn, yet although your expectations may have been based upon the principles of a just conception, it is difficult to find fault when there instinctively leaps to your tongue the exclamation - "*How natural!*" He is a man of rare ability.[9]

Mrs Cowell reported that Dillon had made a very handsome $500 on the week, but also there had been a considerable amount of "spreeing" by Dillon and Sam Cowell in Boston, which, perhaps, suggests a reasonable cause for at least some of Dillon's "illnesses".[10]

As President-elect Lincoln traversed the friendly northern tier of states by train on his journey to Washington, he was greeted by cheering crowds. The last leg of the journey, however, from Philadelphia to Washington, required passage through the hostile slave-holding state of Maryland. In Baltimore, the mood was particularly ugly. Assassination threats against Lincoln were taken so seriously that he was guarded on the train by Detective Allan Pinkerton and the car on which he was riding was silently switched to another train as it reached the city at 4 a.m. - on Friday 23 February.

Dillon opened at Baltimore's Holliday Street Theatre on Tuesday 26 February - playing *Belphegor* four times and *Louis XI* once. He was not reviewed, apart from the succinct comment "business *very* poor".[11] During this week, however,

Dillon happened to be dining at the public table of the hotel, and found himself playing a scene which provides a sense of public sentiment. Seated next to Dillon was a "dark, fierce looking stranger" whose sharp demands on the black waiter seemed to be more effective than Dillon's quiet requests. Suddenly, the stranger thrust his arm out to Dillon, demanding "You shall pull this arm from its socket, sir" to which Dillon replied: "No, sir, I have no intention." Responded the stranger "you shall pull it out sir - pull it from its socket before you make me own a d——d nigger equally good flesh and blood as I am."[12]

On Monday 4 March Abraham Lincoln delivered his Inaugural Address in Washington. He left no doubt of his basic intentions in the coming conflict:

> I shall take care, as the Constitution itself expressly enjoins upon me, that the laws of the Union be faithfully executed in all the states. . . . In your hands, my dissatisfied countrymen, and not in mine, is the momentous issue of civil war. The government will not assail you. You can have no conflict without being yourselves the aggressors. You have no oath registered in heaven, while I have the most solemn one to "preserve, protect and defend it".

Mrs Cowell reported:

> "The Panic" is now universal! Lincoln was formally inaugurated at Washington yesterday, and his speech is rather equivocal. Every one fears that war will soon take place between the Northern States, and the Southern Confederacy . . . "Stocks" are falling frightfully, and in spite of the enormous sums imported, money is scarcer than ever . . . Theatricals are awfully bad now, in New York, as well as elsewhere.[13]

On 11 March Dillon began a three-week run at Philadelphia's Arch Street Theatre. The old Arch Street, built in 1827, had just recently been purchased on borrowed monies by the adroit actress turned manageress, Mrs Louisa Lane Drew. The first year of her management, 1861, she cajoled major stars such as Edwin Booth and Joe Jefferson into appearing on her stage. She evidently had sufficient faith in Dillon to include him in her galaxy, and she supported him on the stage as well. The venture would have been a gamble during the best of economic times; in 1861, the probability of a new theatre – much less one managed by a woman – succeeding must have seemed remote indeed.[14]

Dillon's run was evidently successful, despite the fact that he was playing against the popular Joey Gougenheim at the Walnut Street Theatre for the first two weeks of the run. In *Belphegor*, on opening night, "his success was as brilliantly complete as it was merited".[15] During the second week of the run, he "added new laurels to his wreath"[16] with *Louis XI*. In addition to *Belphegor* and *Louis XI.*, he offered during the three-week run *The King's Musketeers*, *Othello*,

*Virginius*, and Westland Marston's *The Hard Struggle*.

While war fever evidently did not disturb Dillon's run at the Arch Street, during the last week of his run a near riot occurred at the nearby Philadelphia Concert Hall. The band had opened with "The Star Spangled Banner" (a patriotic number based on the tune of an old British drinking song which had not yet become the American national anthem). From there, the band struck up "Dixie", written a few years earlier for a New York minstrel show, but with obvious links to the South. Yells and hisses followed. Sensibly, the band leader called for a quick and judicious segue into "Yankee Doodle", and this elicited screams of delight from the Yankee audience - perhaps averting a disaster.[17]

For several months, Union forces had, despite a blockade, tenuously held Fort Sumter on the South Carolina coast against a blockade by Confederate naval forces. On Saturday 13 April the Fort was bombarded by heavy mortar fire. On Sunday 14 April the Fort surrendered. On Monday 15 April, President Lincoln issued a formal proclamation of war, calling for 75,000 volunteer troops - and on the same day Charles Dillon opened a two-week run at the Boston Museum.

He presented *Belphegor, Louis XI., Virginius, The King's Musketeers,* and *Damon and Pythias,* but we can never know how he was received nor how business ran, for the Boston newspapers of those two weeks carried nothing but up-to-the-minute war news received over the telegraphic wires. There was no mention of theatrical activities – even though Charlotte Cushman, the grande dame of the American Theatre, was playing at the Howard Theatre against Dillon.

Closing in Boston, he managed to secure one night at Troy, New York. By 7 May he was back in New York where Mrs Cowell reported that he was "penniless, parted with his agent Simmons, who got Dillon's last receipts, and kept them, as 'owing to him'".[18] The following day, Dillon had an interview with Laura Keene who was authorized by Knowles of Manchester to offer him any amount of money he desired to return to England. After dithering for a week, Dillon refused the offer, unable to face returning penniless to his home shores.[19]

He was next offered an engagement in St Louis, but having read of a fearful clash between military troops and citizens, he decided for safety's sake against that as well.[20] Instead, undoubtedly wisely, he chose to forsake the dangerous and un-United States for the moment in favour of a Canadian tour including Toronto, Montreal, and Quebec where evidence that you collected shows that he did inordinately well, financially as well as romantically, for it was in Montreal that he took up with Eliza Webb. The pair moved on to California, where they played successfully between October 1861 and June 1862.

Dillon eventually returned to America in December 1865, after the Civil War had ended, and, by all accounts, repaired his reputation as well as lining his pockets somewhat more generously than he had on the first tour. That, however, will be a tale for another time.

But it should not be taken from this short sketch of the 1861 Dillon tour that the Civil War had a totally deleterious effect on the theatre in America. In fact, theatre did seem to thrive in spite of the odds against it. Americans, particularly those from urban areas, were generally accustomed to theatre-going, and in the larger towns and cities of both North and South the theatres thrived - Washington, DC being a prime example. In 1861, the city was served by one very small, very dirty, and very ill-equipped house of drama; two years later, at least six houses of entertainment were in generally regular operation to serve the demands of the troops stationed there. And, of course, President Lincoln met his end in one of those theatres, at the hand of an actor as you will remember from our visit to Ford's Theatre.

I would venture to say that most of those who may share this letter may be unaware of the funny delight you took in certain peculiarly American things - one such being baseball. You seemed to think that the language of the sport was something in a world of its own, as, indeed, it is. I think I probably neglected to tell you about a legendary baseball manager by the name of Charles Dillon ("Casey") Stengel (no relation, incidentally, to our Charles), whose tongue frequently engaged his brain in strange and wondrous ways, e.g. "It ain't over 'til it's over."

It will never be over. You gave so very much so very joyously to so many people that you live in our hearts forevermore.

Very much love,

Gayle

Gayle

# Notes

1. Kathleen Baker, "Charles Dillon: A Provincial Tragedian", in *Shakespeare and the Victorian Stage*, ed. Richard Foulkes, Cambridge, 1986, 289.

2. Mrs Sam Cowell, *The Cowells in America*, London, 1934, 241. In view of the fact that he was on the stage within a few weeks, it seems somewhat questionable that the leg was actually broken; it may, instead, have been sprained.

3. US National Archives and Records Administration. *Passenger Lists*, New York, 1861, M237.

4. Mrs Sam Cowell, *The Cowells in America*, 242.

5. *New York Times*, 26 Jan. 1861.

6. Mrs Sam Cowell, *The Cowells in America* 244-5. Several days later, the Cowells saw Booth in *Richelieu*, "and down came *that* statue from its pedestal. He looked like an old

woman, and played alternately as if in the last agonies of death from exhaustion, and the raging passion of a man in full health. I like him so little that I shall say no more about him" (247).

7. *New York Clipper*, 2 Feb. 1861.

8. *Spirit of the Times*, 9 Feb. 1861.

9. *Boston Post*, 19 Feb. 1861.

10. "The first night there, Dillon got so awfully tipsy that when he was led to his room and left at the door, he could not strike a light, nor find the bed, so went groping about in the dark, till he stumbled and fell, in a sitting posture in the middle of the room. - He described this situation very funnily, and his shame preventing him calling for a light. Three quarters of an hour 'at least' he sat there, shivering - then he felt about in all directions, until he caught the bed, where he threw himself 'in trousers and boots' and then the bed began to dance and whirl as it usually seems to do, when tipsy people lie on it." - Mrs Sam Cowell, *The Cowells in America*, 258.

11. *Daily Baltimore Republican*, 1 March 1861.

12. Mrs Cowell, *The Cowells in America*, 325.

13. *Ibid.*, 265.

14. Mrs Drew eventually turned the Arch Street into a handsomely profitable operation. Eventually, too, she would be grandmother to Maurice, Ethel, and John Barrymore.

15. *Philadelphia Inquirer*, 11 Mar. 1861.

16. *Philadelphia Inquirer*, 21 Mar. 1861.

17. *New York Clipper*, 30 Mar. 1861.

18. Mrs Cowell, *The Cowells in America*, 324.

19. *Ibid.*, 342.

20. *Ibid.*, 341.

# Dangerous Acts

## GEORGE SPEAIGHT

FROM time immemorial, minstrels and other travelling entertainers have amazed their audiences with remarkable feats of skill. English civic documents from the sixteenth century often record the visits of travelling entertainers who passed through the town: between the years 1570 and 1663, for example, there are records of twenty-two rope dancers, thirteen tumblers, seven vaulters, and five jugglers who requested permission to perform from the mayors of English provincial towns.[1] During the eighteenth century the fairs, which had originally been founded for trading purposes, became largely occasions for entertainment, and in these entertainments feats of skill bordering on danger were increasingly featured. Vaulters leaped over a squad of soldiers with drawn swords; rope dancers balanced with chains round their ankles; women spun round with swords apparently sticking in their eyes; strong men lifted enormous weights; strong women drank boiling oil; and a stone-eater provided an alternative to fire-eating.[2] These were the kind of entertainers who drew gaping spectators at the great provincial fairs like Stourbridge, near Cambridge, and throughout the country.

Towards the end of the eighteenth century displays of trick horse riding developed into the circus, and buildings specifically intended to house this type of entertainment sprang up all over Britain in the early years of the next century. At first existing riding schools were adapted for this purpose, but it was not long before amphitheatres and circuses, so named, were erected. We can find them in Birmingham in 1787, in Edinburgh in 1788, in Bristol in 1792, in Manchester in 1793, in Liverpool in 1798, in Nottingham in 1803, in Glasgow and Newcastle in 1822, in Salford in 1823, in Brighton in 1836, and in Leicester in 1840. These were all permanent, or at least semi-permanent buildings, but in 1842 Richard Sands' American circus introduced the use of transportable canvas tents, and from then on the tenting circus became a familiar feature of the English provincial and country scene.

In all these places - fairgrounds, circuses, pleasure gardens, exhibition halls, and evolving music halls - entertainers traded upon the fact that the public has always been attracted - even when it has been repelled - by witnessing a performer attempting what appears to be a dangerous feat. To quote a few examples: Signora Josephine Giradelli "put boiling melted lead in her mouth, emitting the same with the imprint of her teeth" in 1814; Ivan Ivanitz Chabert drank boiling oil and entered a blazing oven while a steak was being cooked in 1829; and Eugene Rivalli was entering a fiery furnace on the stage of the Victoria Concert Hall in West Hartlepool in 1869. All these performers seem to have emerged unharmed after repeating their feats over many years, but an American called Samuel Scott, who made a speciality of diving from great heights in 1840 – 100 feet at Manchester, 167 feet at Liverpool, from the top-gallant yard of *HMS St Joseph* at Devonport – slipped from his scaffolding on Waterloo Bridge in 1841 and hanged himself.[3]

In the second half of the nineteenth century public opinion began to be expressed at the undesirability of dangerous acts being performed as public spectacles. In 1883 the Revd Edward Z. Lyttel wrote to the Home Secretary "in the interests of some little girls whose bodies are being subjugated to various painful contortions for the amusement of sightseers at Eastbourne and other places. One of these children is exhibited as a 'human serpent' and is made to double herself up in an unnatural and disgusting manner." In 1885 a Petition from the Royal and Parliamentary Burgesses of Scotland was presented to the Home Secretary asking that "in view of the numerous fatal injuries that have recently occurred . . . Parliament should pass a Bill declaring it illegal for individuals to perform with wild Beasts within their Cages or Dens . . . and that the performances gone through with wild animals in public are demoralizing in their tendencies and should be prohibited".[4]

The Home Secretary responded cautiously to these and similar demands, but pressure was kept up, especially in cases where children were involved. Attempts to frame legislation failed in 1872 and 1873, but finally suitable wording was found acceptable and the Children's Dangerous Performances Bill received the Royal Assent in 1879. Under this it was enacted that "no child under 14 should take part in any public exhibitions or performance which in the opinion of the Court would be dangerous to life or limb" (42 & 43 Vict. c. 34).

This however, did not satisfy all the campaigners, and the next year a movement was launched by a Member of Parliament, Mr E. Jenkins, to persuade the government to bring into law a bill "to prevent the exhibition in places of amusement of acrobatic performances dangerous to life and limb". A popular magazine called *The Penny Illustrated Paper* published a double page illustration in its issue of 13 March 1880 depicting a number of recent and contemporary acts that would become illegal under the proposed legislation. Mr Jenkins' proposal never reached the statute book, but it may be of interest, at this distance of time, to examine just how dangerous were the acts depicted in *The Penny Illustrated Paper* (illustration 25) and what was the fate of the artistes concerned. Let us take them from top left to bottom right.

Several women tightrope artistes adopted the name of "the Female Blondin" in the 1860s. The earliest seems to have been Selina Young, the niece of James Wild, the portable theatre proprietor,[5] who first appeared as Pauline Violante and was

25. "Dangerous Performances". *The Penny Illustrated Paper* 13 March 1880.

then persuaded by the impresario Van Hare to adopt the name of the Female Blondin.[6] She acquired some fame in 1861 from crossing the Thames on a tightrope from Battersea to Cremorne Gardens.[7] Later that year she fell from the rope at Highbury Barn, injuring her hip, and was forced to retire from performing. She was soon followed by Mrs Powell, performing originally as Madame Genevieve but adopting the name of the Female Blondin, who fell to her death at Aston Park in Birmingham in 1863 while walking a tightrope at a height of thirty feet, while shackled in chains, her feet encased in baskets, and her head and body enveloped in a sack. This was particularly sad, as she was pregnant at the time and left seven children dependent on her earnings. The cause of her death was no lack of skill on her part but was due to the breaking of the rope. Indeed the majority of fatal accidents sustained by circus acrobats are found to be due to faulty equipment rather than inadequate expertise. The Clergy, Magistrates and Bankers of Birmingham presented a Memorial to the Secretary of State in connection with this accident, urging "that such Exhibitions are in the highest degree degrading and injurious to the well being of Society".[8]

Another "Female Blondin" (Madame Salvi) was performing at the Amphitheatre in Leeds in 1862 and, probably, at Quaglieni's Circus in Nottingham the same year. Also in 1862 a sixteen-year-old girl called Abbot was appearing at Leamington as a Female Blondin. Perhaps the last Female Blondin was Madame Caroline who appeared with Pablo Fanque's Circus at Bolton in 1869. She walked along a rope stretched at a height of thirty feet from the fourth storey of the Coronation Mills to the summit of the circus tent in Ashburner Street. Halfway across, however, she came to a big knot in the rope, and in attempting to step over it she lost her balance and her balance pole. She managed to cling to the rope, which was lowered a few feet, and she then fell into the arms of a number of men below. She was shaken, but not seriously injured and "the same evening she went through a performance at the circus and received a perfect ovation".[9]

Vincent de Groof was an aeronautical pioneer rather than a circus performer. He tried to emulate Icarus with a home-made flying machine that was lifted into the air by a balloon, but he fell to his death while displaying it in Cremorne Gardens in 1874.[10]

Lu Lu was actually a boy, adopted by his manager Farini, who passed as a girl for many years. He made his debut in London in 1871, and the highlight of his act was an enormous leap from the stage to a trapeze bar twenty-five feet above; this was achieved with the aid of a concealed spring. He, or more probably his manager, wrote a long letter to the *Era* in 1876, replying to critics who wanted to ban "dangerous performances". A safety net was fitted in case he failed to grasp the trapeze bar.[11]

Zazel was the first person to be shot from a cannon. She introduced this feat at the Westminster Aquarium in 1877, though the cannon was, of course, not activated by gunpowder but by a spring, similar to that employed by Lu Lu. The Home Secretary was bombarded with letters complaining about this "dangerous and objectionable performance", but a civil servant minuted that "I don't believe there is any risk in it . . . The cannon is all gammon . . . it is spring trick and fireworks".[12] Zazel was, in fact, slightly injured in a circus at Portsmouth in 1879, when the net in which she landed broke and she fell to the floor, but she continued to perform the act for many years. There are conflicting accounts regarding her later career and misadventures.

Emma Juteau was, perhaps, the originator of what is known as the "iron jaw" act. In this act the artiste supports either herself (it is usually performed by women) or another artiste by her teeth. In fact, the weight is not normally carried directly by the teeth but by a mouth grip. Emma Juteau had made her debut in Paris in 1878 and arrived in London at the Oxford Music Hall in 1880. The act was widely copied. The well-known painting by Degas in the National Gallery shows La La (a mulatto acrobat) performing it at the Cirque Fernando in 1879. Emma Juteau is represented in this picture as biting a short rod, and there is a story that this rod twisted during a performance at the Hippodrome de l'Alma, breaking her jaw. If this is the case, Emma did not, in fact, make use of a mouth grip.[13]

Léona Dare, a Spanish-American from the Antilles, on the other hand certainly was using a mouth grip. She had appeared at the Folies-Bergère in Paris in 1877 in a "straight" aerial act on the *corde lisse*, but by 1878 she had apparently developed the iron-jaw act as depicted in the drawing, and was presenting it at the Oxford Music Hall. The act attracted the usual consternation and letters to the Home Secretary, and a police inspector was asked to report. His report is of some interest as it provides the fullest description of her act that has been preserved, and such detailed descriptions are rare in circus records. It reads as follows:

> She is a woman about 30 years old and very strongly built, and dressed in the ordinary costume of an acrobat; she commences her performance by hauling herself up from the stage by some instrument which she puts in her mouth, holding it by her teeth, and so pulls herself up to a trapeze . . . about 40 feet from the ground, when she goes through various performances such as hanging head downwards by her feet, holding with one leg and hand, and by the same apparatus as mentioned above swings to the trapeze by her teeth . . .During this part of the entertainment she makes several false drops but catches herself by her feet, head downwards. These acts caused several women among the audience to scream but the majority of the spectators applauded her. The performer next mounts a kind of swinging stand . . . and she is now accompanied by a male acrobat; from this stand she mounts another trapeze and swings herself from that to the first trapeze, under which a small net had been placed, into which she alights for about a second, the spring from

> which enables her to reach a second trapeze. This net is then removed, and the man swings himself in a similar manner over the heads of the audience. They both then go through a variety of evolutions and finish by what is called the sensation part of the programme. The female hanging by her feet downwards holds by her teeth the instrument or apparatus before mentioned, to which is attached a rope which is fastened by a band round the body of the man, who is in a horizontal position, and she then turns him round as if on a pivot with remarkable swiftness. This finishes the entertainment which throughout on the part of the female has been gone through in a very graceful and daring manner without the slightest sign of fear or trepidation.[14]

The only serious accident during an iron-jaw act that I have seen reported in England was at the Westminster Aquarium when an un-named woman performer in 1879 or 1880, evidently trying to out-do Léona Dare, supported a man holding a cannon. When the cannon was fired (one hopes, and assumes, not with a live shell), the artiste lost four teeth and fell to the ground.[15]

The life of Blondin is too well known to need detailed treatment here. He established his reputation when he crossed the Niagara Falls on a tightrope in 1859, and went on to amaze the public for many years. He made his home in England, appearing first at the Crystal Palace in 1861 and then in a tour of provincial cities - Manchester, Derby, Cheltenham, Dudley Castle and so on. 90,000 people turned out to see his performance at the Botanical Gardens in Sheffield, and 70,000 at the Aston Fête in Birmingham. At the Zoological Gardens in Liverpool he introduced the feat of pushing a lion in a wheelbarrow in front of him on the tightrope, but this proved exhausting and was never repeated.[16] His only brush with the British government seems to have been in 1861 when he was forbidden to push his five-year old daughter in a wheelbarrow when crossing the rope at the Crystal Palace, but no objection was made in 1888 when a police inspector described his act as follows: "Walking across a tight rope 120 ft long and about 60 ft high with a pole; walking across blindfolded; standing on a chair; standing on his head; carrying his son (age about 30) across; and, finally, riding a specially constructed bicycle across."[17] He died in his bed in old age in his Ealing home, the site of which is now marked by two roads named Blondin and Niagara.

Isaac Van Amburgh was the most famous animal trainer of the nineteenth century. His grandfather was an American Indian and he had been a cage boy with an American circus. He certainly had a remarkable rapport with animals. He came to England in 1838, deeply impressing Queen Victoria, who wrote after seeing a performance: "It's quite beautiful to see, and makes me wish I could do the same." After playing in a drama with animals at Drury Lane, Van Amburgh formed his own company, and toured all round Britain for four or five years with a combined circus and menagerie. Here is a description of his show in 1841:

> Van Amburgh has been delighting the good folk at Cheltenham, Gloucester, Upton, etc. On Thursday and Friday he performed at Worcester to large audiences, who hailed his wonderful feats with loud and long continued plaudits. His turn-out certainly exceeds everything that has been submitted to the public as yet. His horses and conveyances for the animals are first rate. The band is good, and the pavilion in which he shows off is one of the largest and best ever built. His daring acts of strength and agility it is useless to attempt to comment upon; they must be seen to be duly esteemed. The wonderful performing elephant is a most surprising animal, and it walks from town to town, and has no conveyance.[18]

From another source we learn that he equipped his elephant with shoes to protect its feet on these journeys.[19] He was travelling with a large marquee when he played in Chapel Field, Norwich, in 1844[20] but by the next year he had built a commodious brick amphitheatre in Nottingham.[21] Van Amburgh became a folk hero with the British people, depicted in innumerable Staffordshire figures to grace cottage chimney pieces.

In 1846 a French newspaper reported that Van Amburgh had been killed by a tiger during a performance.[22] This was false. It must refer to some artiste who was appearing under his name, though his daughter, Faimali, was mauled to death by the animals with which she was performing at the London Alhambra in 1883.[23] Van Amburgh died in his bed in 1865, but the myth that he had been killed in the ring, as portrayed in this drawing, is still being perpetuated.[24]

Circus publicists like to exaggerate the danger of the feats being performed, and journalists are sometimes carried away to imagine melodramatic deaths that never occurred. This is not to deny that there was danger in some of the feats that were being presented in circuses, music halls and pleasure gardens up and down the British Isles during the last quarter of the nineteenth century. Drawing the line between acts that are daring and skilful, and acts that are potentially suicidal is not easy. The more that the public can be educated to appreciate the skill of circus acts rather than their danger, the healthier circus will be.

## *Notes*

1. J.T. Murray, *English Dramatic Companies 1558-1642,* London, 1910.

2. For this and subsequent general references see George Speaight, *A History of the Circus*, London and San Diego, 1980, and the sources listed there.

3. Leaflets and announcements of these performances are preserved in the John Johnson Collection of printed ephemera at the Bodleian Library, Oxford. Ricky Jay, *Learned Pigs and Fireproof Women*, London, 1986, gives an entertaining and well-illustrated account of these and similar feats.

4. The Public Record Office holds a number of files dealing with Dangerous Performances. These examples are quoted from HO 45 9579/84336.

5. *Old Wild's*, edited by "Trim", London, 1888, 239-40. This book was reprinted by the Society for Theatre Research, with an index, in 1989; Kathleen Barker acted as house editor.

6. Van Hare, *Fifty Years of a Showman's Life*, London 1888, 69.

7. Warwick Wroth, *Cremorne and the Later London Gardens*, London, 1907, 14.

8. HO 45 9468/7472.

9. John M. Turner, "Pablo Fanque, an Artiste of Colour", *King Pole*, Harlow, 4-5, 1990-1. Dr Turner has provided additional information on several of the Female Blondins listed.

10. Warwick Wroth, *op. cit*, 17-19.

11. *The Britannia Diaries of Frederick C. Wilton*, ed. Jim Davis, London, Society for Theatre Research, 1992, entry for 2 Sep. 1871. The *Era* letter was reprinted in *The Penny Illustrated Paper*, 19 Aug. 1876.

12. HO 45 9552/63497.

13. George Speaight, "Les Premières Màchoires d'Acier", *Le Cirque dans l'Univers*, Paris 3me trimestre, 1984, 6.

14. HO 45 9468/58807.

15. HO 45 9552/63497.

16. Ken Wilson, *Everybody's Heard of Blondin*, Sevenoaks, 1990, 73.

17. HO 45 9801/B5335.

18. *Theatrical Journal*, 24 Jul. 1841.

19. Charles Mackie, *Norfolk Annals*, 1901, 13 Oct. 1841.

20. Ibid., 10 Oct. 1844.

21. *Theatrical Journal*, 11 Jan. 1845.

22. Toole Stott, *Circus and Allied Arts*, Derby, 1971, 12983.

23. Ibid., 6727.

24. E.g. in Roland Auguet, *Histoire et Légende du Cirque*, Paris, 1974, 82-5.

An earlier version of this article appeared as "A Proposito di Numeri Pericolosi" in *Circo*, Rimini, anno xviii no. 10, Ottobre 1986.

# The Holloways: A Hundred Years of Travelling Theatre History

JOSEPHINE HARROP

YOU can't really discuss provincial drama without talking about the travelling theatres, for one is inextricably bound up with the other. The importance of the part played by the portables in bringing theatre to the furthest corners of the British Isles has not yet perhaps been fully recognised; but that does not make their achievement any the less.

Undoubtedly the main reason for this lack of recognition has been the dearth of primary material from which to reconstruct their history. A few stray references in texts which otherwise concentrated on what were considered to be more lofty theatrical matters relegated the portables for many years to the status of a fringe phenomenon or oddity in theatrical research - short-lived, of very low quality, and generally unimportant.

But when primary material does come to light, and we can draw back the dusty velvet curtain an inch or two, a far more interesting picture reveals itself on the little dimly-lit stage beyond. The portables, it is becoming increasingly clear, fulfilled an important need and bridged a considerable gap in the theatre-going world. In villages and towns far from major centres, or in poorer industrial areas of developing cities, they provided regular seasons of live drama, bringing both the latest productions and the old favourites to many generations. In their heyday they covered the length and breadth of the country and many indeed were the actors who first found their feet on the boards of a travelling show. They were, first, last and always, the theatre of the common people, knowing what would best please in each town and village they visited and altering their programmes to suit the occasion.

It is important not to confuse the travelling theatres (or portables) with circuit or fit-up companies who used already-existing buildings to stage their performances. The portables carried their entire theatre with them - stage, seating, walls and roof - and turned a previously vacant field or piece of waste ground into a theatre for the duration of their stay.

Detailed research into the portables has been fairly recent; and at first it was generally believed that they flourished from around the 1830s to the 1860s, declining slowly thereafter and finally dying out in the 1880s. Publication of the preliminary findings, however, jogged memories; and descendants of several travelling theatres came forward with recollections of their own family history. As a result, it could be shown that the portables did survive into the 1900s.[1]

Now a collection of some significance has come to light which reveals that one travelling theatre spanned at least a century – from the 1830s up to the eve of World War Two. The Holloway collection contains playbills, theatre licences, diaries, tradesmen's bills, tickets, newsclippings, photographs and even some of the original costumes and props.[2] It is a particularly valuable discovery because so many of the items are the sort of ephemera which rarely survive. It is also valuable for its undeniable proof that one travelling theatre draws a continuous thread throughout a period of unbelievable change in British history.

When the Holloway family set up their booth for the first time on a fairground, Edmund Kean was still electrifying audiences with his Othello, and Victoria was a schoolgirl. When the costumes and props were finally packed away for the last time, Clark Gable and Vivien Leigh were filming *Gone With the Wind* while Chamberlain held urgent talks with Hitler in Munich. In between, fat pots and flares had given way to gas and then to electricity; horses had been supplanted by the railway which was in turn threatened by the motor car; the invention of the telegraph was eclipsed by the telephone; music hall had exploded into life, aged, and given way to variety and revue; while men fought and were killed in the Crimea, South Africa, the Somme and St Petersburg. And during all of this, the Holloways continued to pack their shutters and canvas on to waggons and journey from town to town and county to county, bringing entertainment, news and excitement to their waiting audiences.

Not only is this a rare achievement within a profession not renowned for continuity; it also means that there is an unbroken link between the theatre of Regency days and the theatre of today which for once does not consist of great names and privileged London audiences. It is a link of continuous provision of popular entertainment for everyday people.

The Holloway papers do in fact hint at even more venerable theatrical antecedents. The phrase "established upwards of 100 years" occurs in several of the early nineteenth-century playbills and elsewhere it is suggested that the business "goes back 250 years". The family may well have been strolling or fit-up players in earlier times (although there is no evidence to prove or disprove this), but it is unlikely that any true portable theatres were on the road before the first decade of the nineteenth century (the roads not really being in a state to permit them before that time). As a true travelling theatre, therefore, Holloway's probably dates from the mid-1820s; the family were certainly well known on the fairgrounds by the 1830s.[3]

The earliest surviving playbill dates from 1837 and it is gratifying to record for posterity that when Macready was opening his first season at Covent Garden with *The Winter's Tale*, Holloway's was opening at Castle Donington with *The Knights of St. John*. Prices at Covent Garden: boxes 5s., pit 2s. 6d., gallery 1s. 6d. Prices at Holloway's Sans Pareil: boxes 2s., pit 1s., gallery 6d. (illustration 26).

# HOLLOWAY'S
## SANS PAREIL,
## CASTLE DONINGTON.

*POSITIVELY THE LAST NIGHT.*

## BY DESIRE

And uuder the distinguished Patronage of the Most Noble the

## MARQUIS OF HASTINGS.

*On Wednesday Evening, November 8th,* **1837,**
Will be presented a grand eastern **Romantic Drama,** called

## THE KNIGHTS OF ST. JOHN.
## OR THE FIRE BANNER

Grand Master - - Mr. Mc. DONNALD. Sir. Calador of Rhodes - - Mr. BELMONT.
Sir. Avelon de. Beriot - - Mr. JAQUES. Sir. Glorian - - Mr. SANKEY.
Sir. Piers Malcolm - - Mr. CROWTHER. Murad Mustapha - - Mr. SIMMONS.
Iran Bonsala - - Mr. WILLIAMS. Rob the Rhymer - - Mr. THOMAS.
Mumbo Jumbo - - Mr. ADAMS. Kehama (the Saracen) - Mr. HUTCHINSON.
Clarice de Beriot - - Mrs. HUTCHINSON. Belphebe - - Mrs. JAQUES.
Zoe.. (with a dance) - Mrs. SMITH. Knights Ladies, Banner Bearers, &c. &c.

**FAVORITE BALLAD MR. SIMMONS,**
**DANSE LE FOLLIE, FROM GUSTAVUS THE THIRD,**
By Mr. T. and Miss. HOLLOWAY, Mesdames Smith, Hutchinson, and Jaques.

The Wonderful Performance of the **FOUR ACROBATS,** whose astonishing feats Equal, if not outvie the **REAL BEDOUN ARABS.**

***COMIC SONG, Mr. THOMAS.***

The Evenings entertainments will conclude with the new Laughable Farce of

## HUNTING A TURTLE.

Mr. Turtle - - Mr. BELMONT. Mr. Levison - Mr. SIMMONS.
Timothy Dandelion - - Mr. CROWTHER. Smatter - - Mr. THOMAS.
Post Boy, - - Mr. ADAMS. Mrs. Turtle, - - Mrs. HUTCHINSON.
Admission—Boxes 2s. Pit 1s. Gallery 6d.

Doors open at Half-past SIX o'Clock, and the Curtain to rise at Half-past SEVEN

*Good Fires constantly kept.* *[John Bamford, Printer*

26. Playbill for Holloway's Theatre at Castle Donington 8 November 1837.

The Holloways covered mainly the Midlands and North Wales, journeying, in the early years, up into Yorkshire and across to some parts of Lincolnshire. In common with other portables, their circuit was originally based on the annual calendar of fairs and feasts; and like other circuits, it shrank from about the 1860s onwards as fairs dwindled and other forms of entertainment grew up to compete for their audiences. Yorkshire and Lincolnshire were certainly outside their normal range by the 1880s, and they do not appear to have visited Wales after about 1920. Set out below for comparison are two charts showing locations visited in the years 1910–14 and 1926–30.

**Chart 1**

Locations visited by Holloway 1910-14 and 1928-32
showing shrinking circuit

**1910–14**

Belmont, Worcs.
Bewdley, Worcs.
Bredon, Worcs.
Bridgnorth, Salop.
Connah's Quay, N. Wales
Denbigh, N. Wales
Flint, N. Wales
Highley, Worcs.
Holywell, N. Wales
Ironbridge, Salop.
Lower Mitton, Worcs.
Lye, Worcs.
Malvern Link, Worcs.
Mold, N. Wales
Neston, Cheshire
Penkridge, Staffs.
Rhosymedre, N. Wales
Ruabon, N. Wales
Shotton, N. Wales
Stottosden, Salop.
Stourport, Worcs.
Upton on Severn, Worcs.
Welshpool, N. Wales
Wem, Salop.

**1928–32**

Bidford on Avon, Worcs.
Bridgnorth, Salop.
Bromsgrove, Worcs.
Chase Terrace, Staffs.
Chasetown, Staffs.
Droitwich, Worcs.
Evesham, Worcs.
Feckenham, Worcs.
Highley, Worcs.
Lichfield, Staffs.
Newport, Salop.
Pershore, Worcs.
Stourport, Worcs.

Surviving theatrical licences for Holloway's indicate that by the early twentieth century permission was usually granted for a three or even six month stay at one time. The company, however, varied the length of its visit to each town or village from one month to three or more; presumably depending on the size of the potential audience and the support received. The onset of winter, too, often meant that a longer stay in one place was more appropriate.

From the 1830s to around the 1880s, Holloways, like other travelling theatres, transported all its worldly goods on horsedrawn waggons from one town to the next. In later years, although the family did possess first a traction engine and then an army lorry for moving waggons short distances, the usual practice was to hire horses to the nearest railway station and then load the waggons and goods on to the special flat cars used for showmen's effects. An invoice dated 28 July 1931 from a Fred Oakley jun. reads:

| | | | |
|---|---|---|---|
| Removing | 6 vans to Iron Bridge Station | at 6/-: | 1.16.0 |
| | 5 vans to Bridgnorth | at 22/-: | 5.10.0 |
| | 5 vans from Bridgnorth Stn to Ground | at 6/-: | 1.10.0 |

Typically a week was allowed for packing up, moving to the next site and reconstructing the booth. The last night in each town was normally a Saturday and by the following Saturday the Holloways would be ready to open in the new location.

> As young lads we helped to erect the theatre, also set up the seats inside, for that we received a free ticket to one of the shows. How well I remember one of them, *Maria Martin in the Red Barn*, among many others. The tent was lit by hanging paraffin lamps, how they used to smell . . .[4]

The standard portable booth was constructed of wooden shutters which bolted together and a canvas roof tied down to make the whole thing weatherproof. Two waggons drawn across the front formed the promenade where during the run of a fair actors posed and displayed their dazzling costumes to potential audiences; outside fairtime the promenade was not normally put up.

Booths were always at risk from high winds, and the Holloways must have found the weather a little trying at times on their visits to the brisk North Wales coast. There were other dangers as well. On at least one occasion the Holloway portable was badly burnt when a spark from a passing train ignited the tilt; and during a particularly rainy season at Pershore it was completely flooded.

We shall probably never know what inspired Horace Holloway to think of commissioning a completely new portable theatre in the year 1910. Possibly he was encouraged by Gerald Du Maurier's takeover of Wyndham's Theatre; or

27. Holloway's Theatre at Lichfield c.1903.

perhaps he had been inspired by a visit to Beerbohm Tree's spectacular *Henry VIII* at His Majesty's. Whatever the driving force, the working drawings, by one John Carden of Rhosymedre, give rare practical information on how such a theatre was constructed and what it contained.

This state-of-the-art 1910 model had separate entrances and exits for gallery, pit and boxes. There were gas footlights to illuminate the stage and two gas chandeliers in the auditorium. The overall dimensions were approximately 84ft x 32ft with a stage depth of 24ft (including backstage space). A stage trap was provided, of course, and the stage was raised some 3–4 feet above ground level (offering minimal comfort to those entering or exiting by the trap).

It is interesting to note that public conveniences were provided for both male and female patrons outside the theatre; a reminder that by this time local authorities were becoming much stricter on such matters, often denying a licence to a company that did not offer these facilities.

And when the good people of Bewdley and Bridgnorth, Shotton and Stourport, Penkridge and Pershore, hurried eagerly from their homes and crowded into Holloway's booth, what did they see on that stage? What dramas were on offer throughout a century that saw so much change both inside and outside the world of the theatre?

Over three hundred playtexts survive in the Holloway collection, among them most of the old standbys of the melodramatic stage – *The Mistletoe Bough*, *Uncle*

*Tom's Cabin*, *Ben the Boatswain*, *The Shaughraun* and so on - all the evocative titles of a colourful tradition. There are also several texts painstakingly written out by hand in ruled notebooks; this was sometimes done for reasons of economy, but sometimes as a way of avoiding royalties on a popular new piece - someone who knew the tricks of the trade would attend a performance and scribble furiously during the action, filling in the gaps later on from a lifetime of experience.

Diaries and other papers in the collection do seem to indicate that the complete Holloway repertoire was very large indeed - perhaps as many as five or six hundred pieces overall (although there was an honourable tradition of playing the same piece under several different titles or with regional variations which can impart a degree of inaccuracy to estimates). It had to be a large repertoire, of course: in London and other major cities the "long-run" might have become standard by the beginning of the twentieth century, but in the portables a nightly change of programme continued to be expected right to the end. A list of the plays performed during a month at Astwood Bank in 1923 gives some idea of what was expected of a popular travelling theatre at that time:

**Chart 2**

Plays performed during a four-week season
at Astwood Bank, June 1923
(including Saturday matinees)

*Aurora Floyd*
*Bound to the Stake*
*Brought to Justice*
*The Curate*
*Current Cash*
*East Lynne*
*The Engine Driver*
*Fettered at Last*
*Flowers of the Forest*
*The Girl from the Streets*
*The Haunted Castle*
*Her Past*
*Homeward Bound*
*Jack O'Hearts*
*Jane Shore*
*Jessy Vere*
*Lady Audley's Secret*
*Lashed to the Mast*
*Leah*
*Life's Cross Roads*
*Maria Martin*
*Mona*
*Napoleon*
*Peggy O'Neil*
*The Pilot's Grave*
*Polar Star*
*Sexton Blake*
*Shadows of the Cross*
*Simon Lee*
*Temptation*
*Vengeance is Thine*

One particularly noticeable feature of the Holloway repertoire is that the old tried and tested melodramas continued to appear on the programme right up to the 1930s. New plays were introduced of course and some of the more outdated farces were eventually dropped, but generally speaking the sensational "blood and thunder" dramas remained as popular as ever. If you popped into Holloways at any given time from the end of the Napoleonic Wars to the eve of the Second World War, you would probably have a good chance of seeing *Maria Martin*.

And although popular London successes were swiftly adopted - or adapted - for Holloways, it is also noticeable that the dramas considered by "mainline" theatre historians as the markers of their day - "the plays which changed British theatre" - are conspicuous by their absence. *Charley's Aunt* was very popular at Holloways, but *The Importance of Being Earnest* was never played. Jones' *The Silver King* was staged, but not *Mrs Dane's Defence*. *The Two Orphans* and *A Royal Divorce* packed them in at the booth as they did in London - but the experiment was not tried with *Ghosts*, and *The Second Mrs Tanqueray* remained unknown. Even Sexton Blake (illustration 28) entered the world of the portable - Somerset Maugham did not.

There is something refreshingly obvious about this which ought to make those mainline historians stop and think. Is it always such a good idea to assume that a drama which caused a frisson among the fashionable set in London shows a definite change in playgoing tastes? Or that a play which elicited clever comments in *The Times* marks a clear watershed in theatrical history? Out there in the rest of England, the audiences were still demanding blood and thunder from their theatres and continued to do so until *The Perils of Pauline* drew them to the cinema instead. When the travelling theatres finally faded away, it was not because Ibsen and Shaw had succeeded sensation drama in the popularity stakes: it was because the cinema could make a more effective job of sensation drama.

It is never easy to imagine just how performances must have seemed to the audience of many years ago, but reminiscences by some of those who frequented Holloway's theatre in the early decades of this century suggest a strength and energy which must have been very appealing:

> I saw *Maria Martin*, *The White Sheik* and others the names of which I don't recall. However, one stands out very much in my memory and I still remember it from beginning to end. This was *Why Girls Go Wrong*. The two extracts went as follows: "No, No I will not commit this sin for she is some poor mother's daughter!", and "It is such men as I that make girls go wrong". At the climax one could have heard the proverbial pin drop.[5]

Children were clearly very welcome at Holloways, and probably made up the entire audience at the reduced-price matinees. This was where the proprietor's wife came into her own. While the younger actors and actresses were frantically

QUO VADIS
TO
HORACE HOLLOWAY'S
Prince of Wales Electric
THEATRE
Rails Meadow Tewkesbury

Week commencing Nov. 13th, 1933
MONDAY NIGHT
The Hunchback Bellringer
Of Notre Dame.

TUESDAY. By request.
Honour thy Father & Mother
OR
The BEGGAR'S PETITION

WEDNESDAY & THURSDAY
The White Sheik
Written by Miss Mona Holloway. Licensed by The Lord Chamberlain.

FRIDAY
The PATENT GUN

SATURDAY MATINEE at 2 o'clock
WEARY WILLIE & TIRED TIM
CHILDREN 2d., 4d. and 6d.

SATURDAY NIGHT (One House only)
THE FAMOUS DETECTIVE PLAY
SEXTON BLAKE

THE ABOVE ARE STAGE PLAYS

Doors open 7.15 p.m. Commence 7.30

Admission 6d.. 9d. & 1/3 (including TAX)
Matinees Children 2d., 4d. & 6d.
STRICT ORDER MAINTAINED.
Concluding each evening (time permitting) with Variety and Laughable Sketch

28. Playbill for Holloway's Theatre at Tewkesbury 13 November 1933.

checking their lines or dressing for the performance, she would be mixing up large saucepans of toffee or rock which she would then "pull" on a hook specially attached for the purpose to the side of the wooden theatre. Cut into mouth-immobilising chunks, the sweetmeat was doled out to children at the entrance to the theatre and presumably acted as a reasonably effective silencer during the more harrowing passages of the drama. Other bribes, however, were found to be less satisfactory from the performers' point of view:

> At one of the children's matinees, we were all given free sweets and a packet of crisps by Mr Holloway's wife Annie. We were all highly delighted with their gift. But during the second half of the performance Mr Holloway stopped the show; he had the curtains closed and he stood on the apron of the stage and delivered his request: "Hello my little chickadees. I must ask you all to refrain from rustling your crisp bags as the actors cannot hear themselves speak."[6]

Up to the 1920s the Holloways continued to do well, with people packing the theatre and even standing in the aisles on Saturday nights. The 1930s, however, saw the beginning of the end. Despite the introduction of twice-nightly performances, business started to fall off – partly because of the Depression, partly because of the cinema which now started to take hold of the public imagination. The child with his threepence or sixpence could see a far wider and more exciting world at the movies than could ever have been experienced in a theatrical booth.

World War Two, although encouraging a spate of amateur and semi-amateur entertainments throughout Britain, spelled the end for the old traditional showmen. The last record of a performance by the Holloways is at Hatton near Burton-on-Trent in 1943 when old Horace Holloway paid for the electricity to be connected to the village hall where they were performing for charity. Virtually nobody came.

Even after Horace Holloway's death in 1946, his two actress daughters did not really accept that their travelling days were over. With the living waggons now permanently parked on a piece of land at Chase Terrace, near Lichfield, the last members of the Holloway company kept everything carefully packed, ready for the day when they would take to the road again. Each year they had a special laundering day for the company's costumes – as Geoff Holloway, then a small child, remembers:

> My aunts would wait for a couple of fine and dry days during the summer months to take on the task of washing the costumes which were stored away in hampers in the props wagon, each hamper carefully selected for different types of materials. Water was heated in an open air copper to wash the costumes which were then pummelled in a dolly tub and finally put through a

hand operated mangle before being pegged out to dry on washing lines. There must have been a hundred metres of line criss-crossing the site and it was as colourful as a carnival day. My aunt would let me try on some of the costumes and would stand by me quoting lines from the relevant play: she knew her lines word perfect although the show had then been closed for many years. Once the costumes had been ironed (which took a whole day) they were carefully folded and packed back into the wicker hampers.

Holloway's travelling theatre brought the excitement and escapism of live theatre to thousands of people throughout the country who might otherwise never have had such an experience. When other portables went under, forced out of business by permanent music halls, legitimate theatres and the sophistication of the twentieth century, the Holloways somehow kept going and kept travelling – until their audiences finally deserted the world of spangles and greasepaint for one of celluloid.

Their achievement deserves recognition and permanent record because after all the history of British theatre is not just the history of London or the major cities. It is not just an unending recital of famous actors and memorable Shakespearean performances. There was a world outside as well. When Irving was making his name in London with *The Lady of Lyons*, Holloway's was making a great impression in Bromsgrove with *The Fatal Ravine*. While George Edwardes' Gaiety Girls were dazzling young men about town, the Holloway actresses were thrilling Tewkesbury lads with *The Colleen Bawn* and *The Lace Worker of Paris*. Sybil Thorndike as St Joan, Mona Holloway as The Worst Woman on Earth. Leicester Square or the field behind the White Bear at Tewkesbury. To the educated and privileged few, it was out of date and unfashionable – but the elite do not represent the entire picture of playgoing, even if they do tend to write the history thereof. The unfashionable provinces deserved their theatre too – and Holloway's saw that they got it. A hundred years of giving pleasure to people is an achievement that deserves to be recorded in the pages of theatrical history – as does the story of all the valiant and courageous little travelling companies who, with their shutters and canvas, brought the world of the theatre to the furthest reaches of Britain.

## *Acknowledgements*

Sincere thanks are due to Geoff Holloway and his wife Annette who made the entire collection of family papers available for consultation over a long period and were exceptionally generous with their time and assistance.

# *Notes*

1. Josephine Harrop, *Victorian Portable Theatres*, London, Society for Theatre Research, 1989; Josephine Harrop, "Travelling Theatres in the 1890s" in *British Theatre in the 1890s*, ed. Richard Foulkes, Cambridge, 1992.
2. The Holloway Collection is still in the private ownership of Geoff Holloway; contact may be made through the editor or via the Society for Theatre Research.
3. Harrop, *Victorian Portable Theatres.*
4. Personal correspondence in possession of Geoff Holloway.
5. Ibid.
6. Ibid.

# The Northampton Dryden Festivals

RICHARD FOULKES

WRITING in 1934 Cecil Chisholm chronicled the history of the repertory movement to date. He described it as "primarily . . . a revolt against commercialism"[1] and listed Miss Horniman at the Abbey Theatre, Dublin (1903), the Vedrenne-Barker management at the Court Theatre (1904-7), the Gaiety Theatre, Manchester - Miss Horniman again - (1908), the Liverpool Playhouse (1911) and Barry Jackson's Birmingham Repertory Theatre (1913) as forerunners in a movement which by 1934 encompassed "thirty-seven repertory theatres and companies".[2]

Although not strictly speaking within the repertory movement other ventures subscribed to the non-commercial ethos within the theatre: Nigel Playfair at the Lyric Theatre, Hammersmith (1918-32), Nugent Monck in Norwich (1919), the Malvern Festival Theatre under Barry Jackson (1929), the new Shakespeare Memorial Theatre in Stratford-upon-Avon and, of course, Lilan Bayliss at the Old Vic.

It was not until January 1927 that the newly formed Northampton Repertory Players took up residence in the town's Royal Theatre and Opera House (designed by C. J. Phipps and opened in 1884). Neither was Northampton Rep in the vanguard of the repertory movement artistically since several local factors imposed constraints: the town was relatively small (population 90,000), it had no university and was not a tourist resort and, although prominent citizens gave their support, there was no wealthy patron of Barry Jackson's ilk. All these factors militated to make Northampton not only a weekly rep, but also twice-nightly, catering for an innately conservative audience. Despite these disadvantages Northampton attracted men of talent, in particular Herbert Prentice from 1928 to 1932, Robert Young from 1932 to 1935 and Tom Osborne Robinson whose set and costume designs graced the stage (proscenium width barely twenty-one feet) of the Royal Theatre from 1928 to 1975.[3]

Herbert Prentice was, inexplicably, lured to Northampton from the Festival Theatre, Cambridge which in the words of his patron Terence Gray "would never have come into existence" but for his confidence that in Prentice "there was a producer in England whose work warranted the inception of . . . an advanced repertory enterprise".[4] As Graham Woodruff has shown the Festival Theatre attracted "an upper middle class theatre audience", depending heavily on university support (55 per cent) and visitors (15 per cent),[5] for its innovative productions. In contrast Northampton was decidedly not "an advanced repertory enterprise", though Prentice's personal standing was no doubt the magnet for such talents as Godfrey Kenton, Noel Howlett, Max Adrian, Donald Gordon, James Hayter, Vivienne Bennett and Curigwen Lewis, who found themselves appearing in a generally unadventurous repertoire. Nevertheless the British Drama League's decision to hold its 1929 annual conference in Northampton was an indication of the Northampton Repertory Players' incipient reputation.

One of the speakers at that conference was Robert Young, then Labour MP for Islington, who spoke in favour of the scheme for a National Theatre. In the autumn of 1929 Young took a leading role in the formation of Equity, as Joseph Macleod has recounted.[6] Having lost his parliamentary seat in the 1931 general election Young pursued his theatrical career, succeeding Prentice (who moved to the Birmingham Rep) in August 1932. Young retained the services of Gordon and Howlett and added those of Lois Obee (Sonia Dresdel) and Oswald Dale Roberts and (later) Freda Jackson and Errol Flynn; his repertoire was rather more enterprising than Prentice's and Cecil Chisholm considered that Northampton was one of the few (alongside only Birmingham, Bristol and Liverpool) repertory theatres capable of staging Shakespeare.

For the young Tom Osborne Robinson, who was born in Northampton in 1904, the opportunity to work with Prentice (himself a talented scenic designer) and Young was a fortuitous induction into his chosen career and before long his designs were attracting more than local attention. The burgeoning talent of Osborne Robinson provided continuity between Prentice and Young and Bladon Peake, who took over as producer in June 1935. Peake's experience had encompassed Nugent Monck's Maddermarket Theatre in Norwich and the Birmingham Municipal Players (both amateur groups), several pageants, plays for the B.B.C. Midland Region and a spell at the Abbey Theatre, Dublin.

Within weeks of taking up his appointment Peake obtained his board's approval for a production of John Dryden's comedy *Marriage à la Mode*, probably first performed in 1672. For Peake the attraction of *Marriage à la Mode* was twofold: it had the cachet of having been performed by several "advanced" theatre companies and it was the work of the only Northamptonshire-born author to achieve the status of poet laureate.

The process of rediscovering Dryden as a dramatist was initiated by the Phoenix Society whose production of *Marriage à la Mode* progressed to the Lyric Theatre, Hammersmith in February 1920. The cast included Ion Swinley (Rhodophil), Nicholas Hannen (Palamede), Kathleen Nesbitt (Doralice), Athene Seyler (Melantha) and Marie Rambert (Philotis) under the direction of Montague Summers:

> The revival, appropriately staged and dressed in Restoration fashion, is a real achievement for which one cannot be too grateful to the Phoenix Society. It is to be hoped they will give us some more Dryden.[7]

In February 1926 Nugent Monck staged the play at the Maddermarket, but "unfortunately the lighter scenes had been drastically chastised (to use Walpole's expression), and the performance lost very seriously . . . Dryden must be played entire or not at all". The author of this stricture was Montague Summers, whose six volume edition of Dryden's dramatic works was published in 1931–3.[8] W. G. Fay's production of *Marriage à la Mode* at the Birmingham Rep in April 1928 was not "drastically chastised", as Bache Matthews recalled: "We did very little, if any, cutting, and presented the play, as nearly as we knew how, and the modern theatre will permit, in the method for which it was written." The designs by Paul Shelving were "very formal and in pale colours, whilst the costumes were in brilliant colours".[9] The Festival Theatre, Cambridge production in December 1928 foundered:

> It were difficult too strongly to reprehend that crass and clouded perception which permitted the actors to burlesque Leonidas and Palmyra. Evidently there was no understanding of the play, no judgement, no nice virtuosity.[10]

*Marriage à la Mode* returned to the Lyric Theatre, Hammersmith in 1930 with Athene Seyler repeating her success as Melantha, alongside Herbert Waring (Polydamas), Glen Byam Shaw (Leonidas), Angela Baddeley (Palmyra) and Adele Dixon (Doralice). The revised text was by Clifford Bax who in Summers' opinion "had been called in to castrate, phlebotomize, and generally maul and mammock Dryden's scenes with supreme disregard to the dramatic technique of the author". Playfair's witty and decorative production took place "in a single formalised set and ingenious and riotous use is made of the stairs on either side of the stage".[11]

The import of these revivals of *Marriage à la Mode* at "advanced" theatres is various: the play afforded opportunities to skilled actors, though the temptation to burlesque had to be resisted; designers could combine colourful Restoration-style costumes with formalised sets – then much in vogue; Dryden's dual plot of marriage and adultery had been found in need of compression and, by some, expurgation. None of these theatres had been sufficiently encouraged by their experience with *Marriage à la Mode* to "give us some more Dryden" as *The Times* had hoped.

Unlike the other theatres which had staged *Marriage à la Mode* Northampton could claim proprietorial rights over its author, who was born at the rectory of Aldwinkle All Saints, near Thrapston, on 9 August 1631. Dryden's subsequent association with his native county appears to have been slight, though he did visit his uncle's estate at Canon's Ashby, which was still in the family's possession in the 1930s. Seizing on the only poet laureate to which the county could lay claim Northampton public library had built up:

> a unique collection of Dryden manuscripts, early editions of his works, portraits and engravings, and upon the crowds that daily throng Abington Street there looks down from the facade of the Public Librry a splendid statue of the poet.[12]

The library mounted an exhibition of its prized Dryden collection and loaned some items for display at the Royal Theatre as part of the strategy of elevating the revival of *Marriage à la Mode* into a Dryden Festival. From mid-August onwards the theatre programmes updated patrons on progress. The festival had been postponed – from 12 August to 16 September – in response to "numerous requests received from playgoers all over the country. We hope that several distinguished visitors will attend . . . The London newspapers have been very enthusiastic on our being so ambitious".[13] To encourage this interest the board approved an advertisement in the *New Statesman* (cost 15s.), whereby Northampton rubbed shoulders not only with three other repertory companies (Croydon, Harrogate and Liverpool), but also with "Caucasian Notes" (theatres in Tiflis) and the Salzburg and Moscow Festivals.[14] Less cosmopolitan, the local press speculated "Northampton – Second Malvern".[15]

The resources at Northampton's disposal in its bid for wider recognition were modest. The total salary bill for the week of *Marriage à la Mode* was £141.19.1. of which the acting company absorbed £82.15s. (Oswald Dale Roberts £7; Donald Gordon £5.10s.; Freda Jackson £4.10s.).[16] Costumes, made in the theatre by Nancy and Ellen Pratt, cost £17, the wigs (responsibility of Leslie Pickering) amounted to £18.18s. and the budget for the construction of the set (by Fred Pratt) was £5. £1.5s. was set aside for music (by Arthur Law) making a total outlay of £261.8.11.[17]

Obliged to cut his coat according to his cloth Bladon Peake also cut the play "slightly . . . but Dryden's wittiest and most entertaining passages have not been blue-pencilled".[18] In Peake's case this was necessitated by the time limit imposed by twice-nightly performances as well as the need to "chastise" Dryden's excesses. Rehearsals were confined to one week as usual, but the resulting performances were commended: "Alastair Macintyre made an impressive Rhodophil, and Donald Gordon as the even gayer lover, Palamede, played one of his best parts for some time."[19] Freda Jackson, recently graduated from the rank of unpaid pupil, played Melantha – with her affectation for French phrases – "it was most effectively done and never overdone". These three performers together with Katharine Page as Doralice "put in great work – Donald Gordon in particular rarely, if ever, having done better in costume".[20] Local reviewers were able to compare actors' performances in Dryden with their other work, but the *New Statesman*, which could introduce a metropolitan yardstick, observed:

> Outstanding members of the cast were Oswald Dale Roberts (Polydamas), Donald Gordon (Palamede), Katharine Page (Doralice), and Freda Jackson (Melantha), all of whom gave beautiful performances.[21]

The visual effect was co-ordinated in black and white (illustration 29), as Peake's production of Moliere's *The School for Wives* at the Abbey Theatre had been.[22] It was hailed as "a brilliant example of originality, in staging, dressing and lighting". Though the "whole was fascinatingly extravagant" the "period atmosphere" was not sacrificed:

> Rarely has a more exquisite or original picture in sheer black and white been painted on a stage canvas than that offered by the combination of scene and costumes which they contrived to present in this case.[23]

The *New Statesman* critic tempered enthusiasm with some reservations:

> High praise must be awarded to Mr Osborne Robinson for his delightful black

29. *Marriage à la Mode* by John Dryden at The Royal Theatre, Northampton 1935.

> and white permanent setting and gay costumes, though one is tempted to criticise the choice of such a setting for what is admittedly an artificial comedy, especially when it robbed the grotto scene of much of its humour and resulted in all the characters wearing clothes which made little or no distinction between the various ranks.[24]

Northampton emerged creditably and also in credit (total income £317.8.7. - box office £288.8.7. - profit £55.17.6.) from its production of *Marriage à la Mode*.[25] Peake's compression of the play had avoided the excesses of Bax. Of the acting company Oswald Dale Roberts was an established "repertory star" and Donald Gordon and Freda Jackson proceeded to distinguished careers. Osborne Robinson's designs combined a sense of period with formalism and effective use of colour in the currently fashionable style; he could stand comparison with Paul Shelving at Birmingham and London designers. The mayor and civic leaders had been joined in the audience by Sir Archibald Flower and his artistic director at the Shakespeare Memorial Theatre, Ben Iden Payne. Local hopes that by this "supreme effort . . . the theatre's reputation" would be hoisted "one rung higher"[26] were endorsed by the *New Statesman*: "The Northampton Repertory Theatre has done a fine and courageous thing, and one looks forward eagerly to the next Dryden Festival."[27]

Clearly if Northampton was to take its place - if only for one week a year - beside Malvern - and even Stratford - the momentum had to be maintained. The problem was that whereas Shaw, who had been adopted as its house-dramatist by Malvern, was still alive to add to his already considerable output and Shakespeare had endowed Stratford with a generous bounty of plays, Dryden's dramatic canon, though not inconsiderable in size (twenty-five plays and numerous translations) was not rich in works capable of successful revival. For the 1936 festival Peake chose *The Spanish Friar*, first performed in 1681 and not revived since 1738. From the programme Sir Archibald Flower offered encouragement:

> It is fitting that a special effort should be made to perpetuate the memory of Dryden by the presentation of plays in the county of his birth.[28]

With no modern precedents to guide him Peake undertook the task of "boiling down the script to meet the two houses a night custom"[29] and although to his credit he succeeded in making the double plot "more readily comprehensible"[30] than *Marriage à la Mode* the result was judged to be "the sheerest museum play".[31]

Peake's production relied heavily on the imaginativeness of Osborne Robinson's simple, formal set:

> His use of a permanent setting makes for speed and the set itself is so skilfully

> devised that there is no impression of restriction. Court, street and house in Saragossa are achieved simply and quickly. Mr Osborne Robinson has designed setting and costumes, and has shown refinement and good taste in his use of colour. The bravery of the costumes is kept within limits of elegance by a delicate white and gold motif, which also appears in the curtains.[32]

Peake had dispensed with the services of the principals who had added such lustre (not to say lust) to *Marriage à la Mode* and although *The Spanish Friar* was "soundly acted" it lacked the flair of the earlier production. The title-role of the pastorally lenient and personally lecherous Friar was played by George Mudie, who had spent most of his career in touring and was therefore unaccustomed to the routine of repertory, in particular learning a new role each week. In the best tradition of repertory the young Neil Tuson aged by two generations to play Gomez, the watchful old husband of the vivacious Elvira. In the other plot Margaret Gibson and Patrick Crean, the only actor remaining from *Marriage à la Mode*, were equal to Dryden's heroic vein.

Although the Northampton Repertory Players had now negotiated exemption from entertainment tax for "plays of an educational nature" the balance sheet for *The Spanish Friar* showed a marked deterioration on that for *Marriage à la Mode*. Total receipts were £208.7.9. - box office £186.0.3. - resulting in a loss of £84.14.6., reduced to £61.8.8. by remission of tax.[33] Furthermore although distinguished visitors and reviewers had attended the production the credibility of Northampton's Dryden Festivals was being questioned: "I can't see Dryden as a satisfactory basis for a festival à la Stratford".[34]

In 1937 Peake, undeterred, offered *Sir Martin Mar-All*, first staged in 1667 and described by Pepys as "the most entire piece of mirth, a complete farce from one end to the other, that was certainly ever writ",[35] as his third Dryden offering. Graham Greene, then drama critic of the *Spectator*, journeyed to Northampton, having first brushed up his Dryden. He expressed his preference for Dryden's *An Evening's Love* "for *Sir Martin*, except in flashes, dates". Even these "flashes of savagery . . . have to be dulled for the Northampton public [which] . . . could not have been expected, even in Dryden's lifetime, to stomach so bawdy a court piece as the sub-plot provides - the story of Mrs Christian's willing and mercenary seduction by Lord Dartmouth".[36]

Donald Gordon, who had rejoined the company, played the lustful Lord Dartmouth and Iris Sutherland the apparently demure Mrs Christian. Anthony Pelly "manages to give at least the essential qualities of Mar-All, though his performance will be better when he has had time to accentuate Sir Martin's charm a little more";[37] the same critic found George Mudie, as the servant Warner, incapacitated "by some uncertainty of his lines" and Graham Greene described several members of the cast as performing "stumblingly". Another London critic, Richard Clowes, summed up the problem: "The piece obviously suffered from under-rehearsal, but this in the circumstances was to be expected." He reported his conversation with Peake after the performance: "'I know this production has short-comings but give us a month of preparation and see what we can do.' He described 'the routine of starting rehearsal each Tuesday morning, with the dress rehearsal the following Monday and no time for refresher calls for the purpose of correcting mistakes'."[38]

In the week prior to the production of *Sir Martin Mar-All* Dame Sybil Thorndike had "very graciously addressed members of the company on the 'Team Spirit' that must prevail in repertory".[39] The one member of the Northampton team who had more individual scope and motivation to give fuller preparation to his contribution was Osborne Robinson. The prospect of having his work seen by Archibald Flower, Iden Payne and (in 1937) Tyrone Guthrie "fresh from his triumphs in directing the first Buxton Festival",[40] as well as the national drama critics, must have been a powerful spur.

Robinson's bold costume designs, again executed in the theatre, "preserved all the fashion of the period in a brilliant mix of colours. They would be a credit to any West End production: in a provincial theatre their originality and opulence are astonishing".[41] His set design was again a permanent structure, (illustration 31) this time encompassing, by means of a pivot, both exeriors and interiors. Graham Greene described it:

> a charming set made up of doll's houses and diminutive steps and streets, round which Sir Martin wanders like Gulliver in Lilliput with his gilded peruke sticking up like ass's ears. Push a house round by the handle and another scene is ready in its interior just large enough from the second floor to the ground to hold two or three characters.[42]

Osborne Robinson's designs for the three Dryden revivals led to invitations to work at the Old Vic (the Guthrie/Olivier *Hamlet* in 1937 also seen at Elsinore and the Guthrie/Emlyn Williams *Richard III* also 1937) and at Stratford-upon-Avon (*Macbeth* in 1938 for Ben Iden Payne). Lilian Baylis offered Robinson the post of scenic designer at the Old Vic, but he declined and remained in Northampton. Bladon Peake left in November 1937. *Sir Martin Mar-All* had made a loss of £116, with box office takings down to £133.4.2.[43] As the secretary to the board reported "a consistent decrease in box office income had coincided with a consistent increase in certain forms of expenditure".[44] The remission of entertainment tax for "plays of an educational nature", plays which Peake favoured anyway, by no means matched the loss of box office revenue.

The three Dryden Festivals were a courageous attempt by a provincial theatre to elevate itself to national prominence. Peake's adaptations, necessitated by twice-nightly performances as well as decorum, were evidently skilful and avoided excessive cuts. The acting company for *Marriage à la Mode* was very

30. *Sir Martin Mar-All* by John Dryden at the Royal Theatre, Northampton 1937.

31. *Sir Martin Mar-All* by John Dryden at the Royal Theatre, Northampton 1937.

32. Osborne Robinson's design for the programme cover of *Sir Martin Mar-All* at the Royal Theatre, Northampton 20 September 1937.

strong, but, unlike Prentice and Young, Peake did not attract exceptional talent, either established or developing, and without that there was little prospect of rising above the treadmill of twice-nightly weekly rep. The loyalty of the - innately conservative - local audience wavered as Peake delved deeper into the Dryden canon the weakness of which was a fundamental flaw in the concept of an annual festival. There remained the designs of Osborne Robinson for whom the Dryden plays provided a showcase to bring his talent to the attention of a wider public.

Ironically the one individual for whom the Dryden Festivals offered a springboard to new opportunities remained in Northampton. Osborne Robinson was still the company's scenic designer in 1971 when Dryden's *All for Love* was staged as part of the Northampton Festival of the Arts. It was a measure of Dryden's appeal that, although productions were then fortnightly, this was scheduled for only one week. The cast included Clare Ballantyne as Cleopatra, David Beale as Antony, Rex Robinson as Ventidius and Philip Lowrie as Alexas and though they acquitted themselves well the plaudits were again reserved for the designs:

> To give the play its due it is a fine spectacle. And it gave Osborne Robinson a free hand with the gold paint and jewels. The costumes are among the best I have seen at the Rep, especially Cleopatra's, which is indeed a sight to behold.[45]

The production was by Willard Stoker.

Stoker and Robinson returned to Dryden in 1973, again for a special occasion - the Festival of British Theatre - with a revival of *Marriage à la Mode*. Osborne Robinson's designs provided continuity with the 1935 production and were indeed in the same vein: "exquisitely mounted in silver and black with extremely elegant costumes"[46] (illustration 33). Stoker had assembled a particularly talented company that season and drew from it the sort of "Team Spirit" which Sybil Thorndike had extolled. As in 1935, when the part was taken by Oswald Dale Roberts, Polydamas was played by a "repertory star" Lionel Hamilton whose association with Northampton dated back to 1946. Hamilton's performance was in the "full magnificent 'old style' of acting . . . sonorous pitch of voice . . . over-powering presence". Donald Gordon's role of Palamede went to Henry Knowles, the company's accomplished leading man. Two promising young actresses - Marjorie Bland and Bernice Stegers - followed in the footsteps of Katharine Page and Freda Jackson as Doralice and Melantha respectively. The team gelled; there was "no 'generation gap' between a studied technique and subtler portrayals of younger characters" and the result was "a production so outstanding that it must surely rank as one of the finest in the Royal Theatre's history".[47]

Even *Marriage à la Mode*, which was very much *à la mode* in the "advanced"

33. *Marriage à la Mode* by John Dryden at the Royal Theatre, Northampton 1973.

theatres of the 1920s and 1930s, has latterly faded from the repertoire. Both the 1935 and 1973 Northampton productions earned themselves a distinguished place in the admittedly rather sparse annals of the play's stage history, standing comparison with revivals at more prestigious theatres. Northampton's staging of *The Spanish Friar* and of *Sir Martin Mar-All* remain unique in the twentieth century. The Dryden Festivals were a bold attempt to achieve national prominence for Northampton and whilst they were doomed not to achieve permanence they show the potential for exploiting a local author to hoist a provincial repertory company "one rung higher" on the ladder of theatrical status.

## Notes

1. Cecil Chisholm, *Repertory An Outline of the Modern Theatrical Movement*, London, 1934, 10.
2. Ibid., 13.
3. See Aubrey Dyas, *Adventure in Repertory Northampton Repertory Theatre 1927–48*, Northampton, 1948 and Richard Foulkes, *Repertory at the Royal Sixty-five Years of Theatre in Northampton 1927–92*, Northampton, 1992.
4. Royal Theatre programme 26 Mar. 1928.
5. Graham Woodruff, "'Down with the Boot-faced' Public Relations at the Festival Theatre, Cambridge" in *Theatre Research International* I, 2, 117.
6. Joseph Macleod, *The Actor's Right to Act*, London, 1981, 179.

7. *The Times*, 10 Feb. 1920. For the Phoenix Society see Norman Marshall, *The Other Theatre*, London, 1948, 76.
8. Montague Summers ed., *John Dryden The Dramatic Works*, London, 1931-2. As a director of the Phoenix Society Summers had "constantly urged" a revival of *Sir Martin Mar-All*, II, 80.
9. Ibid., III, 187.
10. Ibid.
11. *Era*, 15 Oct. 1930.
12. *Chronicle and Echo* - Northampton, 12 Sep. 1935.
13. Royal Theatre programme 12 Aug. 1935.
14. *New Statesman*, 14 Sep. 1935.
15. *Northampton Independent*, 13 Sep. 1935.
16. Minutes of the board of Northampton Repertory Players 18 Jun. 1935 in the Royal Theatre archive.
17. Cashbook in the Royal Theatre achive.
18. *Chronicle and Echo*, 17 Sep. 1935.
19. *Mercury and Herald* - Northampton, 20 Sep. 1935.
20. *Northampton Independent*, 20 Sep. 1935.
21. *New Statesman*, 21 Sep. 1935.
22. Hugh Hunt, *The Abbey, Ireland's National Theatre 1904-1978*, Dublin, 1979, 148-9.
23. *Northampton Independent*, 20 Sep. 1935.
24. *New Statesman*, 21 Sep. 1935.
25. Ledger in Royal Theatre archive.
26. *Chronicle and Echo*, 17 Sep. 1935.
27. *New Statesman* 21 Sep. 1935.
28. Royal Theatre programme 21 Sep. 1935.
29. *Evening Telegraph* - Kettering, 22 Sep. 1936.
30. *Northampton Independent*, 25 Sep. 1936.
31. *Birmingham Mail*, 22 Sep. 1936.
32. *Birmingham Weekly Post*, 25 Sep. 1936.
33. Ledger in Royal Theatre archive.
34. *Birmingham Weekly Post*, 25 Sep. 1936.
35. Quoted in *Birmingham Mail*, 21 Sep. 1937.
36. *Spectator*, 24 Sep. 1937.
37. *The Times*, 22 Sep. 1937.
38. *Sunday Times*, 26 Sep. 1937.
39. Royal Theatre programme 20 Sep. 1937.
40. Royal Theatre programme 27 Sep. 1937.
41. *Birmingham Post*, 22 Sep. 1937.
42. *Spectator*, 24 Sep. 1937.
43. Minutes of the board 28 Sep. 1937 in Royal Theatre archive.
44. Ibid.
45. *Mercury and Herald*, 18 Mar. 1971.
46. *Stage*, 27 Sep. 1973.
47. *Mercury and Herald*, 20 Sep. 1973.

# The Bristol Theatre Royal – The Continuing Story 1966–93

SHIRLEY BROWN

ON 2 June 1966 Bristol's Theatre Royal celebrated its bicentenary with a specially-written gala performance bringing vividly to life scenes from some of the *Sixty Thousand Nights* which provided its title.[1] Dr Kathleen Barker had assisted George Rowell with historical research for this extravaganza, which was devised and directed by Val May, and she ended her published history of the Theatre's first two hundred years[2] with a quote from it: "Dear Theatre, long may you / Be a House with ever-open door / And may your actors take the floor / For sixty thousand nights / Or more!"[3]

Four years later, on 2 May 1970, the Theatre Royal closed its old doors to King Street for the last time.[4] But there would certainly be "more!". A new phase in the Theatre's history began in January 1972 when, after extensive building and refurbishment, the grand new entrances which were part of the neighbouring eighteenth-century Coopers' Hall opened on a modern theatre complex incorporating a flexible studio space as well as the preserved Georgian auditorium.

Since then the resident repertory company, Bristol Old Vic, which has been based in King Street since its formation in 1946, has seen some doors open and others close. At the height of its expansive success, in the 1970s, it was presenting more than thirty plays a year – among them several new works – and was the only regional repertory company regularly mounting its own productions on three (very different) stages in its home city. But by the early 1990s, the company had withdrawn from the Little Theatre in Colston Street, closed the New Vic studio for Bristol Old Vic productions and, at its lowest ebb, in 1991, produced a total of only six plays, none of them original and all of them in the Theatre Royal.

Happily by 1993 the doors had re-opened, both literally and metaphorically, as the Bristol Old Vic Company adapted to its changing circumstances and exploited every possible way of keeping the Theatre alive both artistically and financially. Thirty years after the Bristol Old Vic established its *in*dependence, breaking away from the London Old Vic parent company to form a separate trust in 1963,[5] the key to the future seems to lie in *inter*-dependence, through an imaginative policy of co-production with other theatre companies both local and national, and both subsidised and commercial.

Back in 1963, Val May had been artistic director of the Bristol Old Vic for two years, and had already begun to make his mark as the most influential (and long-serving) artistic director in the company's history. When he arrived in 1961 the company had only one stage, the Theatre Royal, and was still a regional offshoot of the London Old Vic. When he left in 1975, the independent Bristol Old Vic had three stages and regularly took productions - and the name of Bristol - all over the world to great acclaim.

Twice May had three Bristol Old Vic productions running simultaneously in the West End, most notably, in 1965, *A Severed Head, Portrait of A Queen* and *The Killing of Sister George*, all of which were later seen on Broadway.[6] Further afield he set up three major international tours: celebrating Shakespeare's quatercentenary in 1964 by taking *Henry V* and *Love's Labour's Lost* to the capitals of Europe and the Middle East; presenting *Measure for Measure*, directed by Tyrone Guthrie, and two of his own Shakespeare productions (*Romeo and Juliet* and *Hamlet*) in the City Center, New York and fifteen other North American cities; and later touring two more productions to the major capitals of South America and the Hong Kong Arts Festival.

The central controversy of Val May's time was stirred by those who did not appreciate the value of the company's work outside the city, and felt that the Bristol Old Vic should concentrate on providing theatre nearer home - though as Val May has pointed out, his productions were always created and presented in Bristol before being shown elsewhere. And in the early 1960s, when the combined public subsidy from the Arts Council and Bristol Corporation left the company needing to achieve ticket sales of 90 per cent capacity just to break even,[7] the money earned from work outside the city made an important contribution to the Theatre's income. In retrospect, with the Bristol Old Vic currently planning to take four out of six shows from its autumn 1993 season out on tour in order to help balance its budget, Val May seems to have been a man ahead of his time.

The process of expansion under his leadership began in 1963 when the winding up of the London Old Vic Company coincided with the expiry of the Arts Council's twenty-one year lease on the Bristol Theatre Royal. Under a new arrangement agreed with the trustees of the Theatre Royal building, the newly-created Bristol Old Vic Trust remained as tenants. Soon afterwards the popular Rapier Players left the Colston Hall's Little Theatre, which they had leased from the Corporation since 1935, and the Bristol Old Vic Company was asked to assume responsibility for presenting plays in both Colston Street and King Street, making it then the only English provincial company with two theatres to its name.[8]

In June 1963, closer links were established between the Bristol Old Vic Company and its Theatre School (under the umbrella management of the Bristol Old Vic Trust) when Nat Brenner, who had been the company's general manager, took over as principal of the School, where he continued to teach after his retirement in 1980 until a few weeks before his death in April 1993. A natural teacher and great communicator, he became a "father figure" to three generations of acting students, including two recent Best Actor Oscar winners, Daniel Day-Lewis and Jeremy Irons.

It was in March 1966 that the seeds were sown of the far-reaching scheme for the Bristol Old Vic to take over the Coopers' Hall and some other land neighbouring the Theatre Royal in order to redevelop the King Street site into the modern theatre complex which eventually opened in January 1972. At about this time other major regional repertory companies, such as Birmingham and Sheffield, were deserting their old theatres for completely new buildings, but there were practical as well as sentimental reasons for Bristol to adopt a different attitude.

The Theatre Royal is of special architectural and cultural interest as Britain's oldest theatre building with a history of continuous use as a playhouse. And the council-owned Coopers' Hall, notwithstanding its impressive Georgian frontage, was badly in need of repair and restoration after being used for some time as a vegetable warehouse and auction room. Bristol Corporation's finance committee supported the scheme to include the Coopers' Hall in a new Bristol Old Vic theatre complex as a cost-effective way of preserving and making continued use of two of the city's historic Grade I listed buildings.

An article in the *Bristol Evening Post* on 3 October 1968 outlined architect Peter Moro's vision of a new entrance to the Theatre Royal through the front of the Coopers' Hall, giving the auditorium "an exterior worthy of its interior". The space then occupied by a tunnel-like entrance to the Theatre Royal was earmarked for the small studio theatre, with much-needed offices above. Also envisaged in the original plans for the £500,000 scheme were a spacious foyer, bars and reception rooms, a new fly tower and updated stage machinery, new dressing rooms and rehearsal space, and a lift for people with disabilities.

From the outset, the venture was beset with problems, both financial and practical. There were long arguments before a compromise was agreed with the city planning committee, who disliked the "warehouse" effect of the architect's design for the new King Street frontage. They envisaged King Street as a kind of living museum and expected Georgian-style stone, whereas Peter Moro, conscious of the area's recent function as a docklands centre of the fruit and vegetable trade, preferred "a restrained brick facade which has affinities with the local idiom, without resorting to faking or aping the past"[9] – see illustration 34.

Work on both the Cooper's Hall and the Theatre Royal met unexpected and expensive structural complications at a time when there was an unforeseen escalation of nearly 30 per cent in building workers' wages. Early on, extensive dry rot was discovered in the beams of the Coopers' Hall ceiling, but dry rot – confined to a small area – was the least of the builders' problems in the Theatre, where the walls were found to be up to seven inches out of true. It transpired that

34. Frontage of the Bristol Theatre Royal after the 1972 reconstruction. When the Bristol Old Vic re-opened in 1972, the entrance was through the imposing façade of the Coopers' Hall and the old frontage had been replaced with the smaller brick-and-glass structure on the left, housing the New Vic studio with offices above.

the eighteenth-century foundations, on reclaimed marshland, had been laid on a raft of rushes. Traffic vibrations and other twentieth-century factors, compounded with the age of the building, made it necessary for the waterlogged site to be stabilised with 175 piles and pumped full of concrete, and for the new structure to support the old walls.

Although grants from the Arts Council, Bristol City Council and various charitable bodies, plus the proceeds of a public appeal, eventually raised far more than the original estimate, costs had risen so much that some of the work had to be postponed.[10] When the building opened in January 1972, work had been completed on the Coopers' Hall and all public areas as well as the enlarged stage, new fly tower and dressing rooms, but it was 1977 before the backstage offices and rehearsal space were ready for use. The first production in the studio - a documentary play about the Bristol riots - went ahead in the summer of 1972 before the company could afford to install the specially-designed seating rostra.

During the redevelopment in King Street, Val May did his best to raise funds for the Bristol Old Vic with three active performing companies, one at the Little Theatre, one for local schools and the West Country, and one based in Bath, from where it toured nationally and overseas. But his critically-acclaimed production of Barry England's *Conduct Unbecoming*, which had run profitably in London for two years, had a disappointingly short life in New York; and the majority of the displaced Theatre Royal audience, having shown no inclination to support the Little Theatre, proved even less willing to travel to Bath, where two twelve-week seasons at the Theatre Royal proved a financially disastrous experiment never to be repeated.[11]

The first performance in the new Bristol Old Vic theatre complex took place in

35. The new foyer and Coopers' Gallery at the Theatre Royal.

the mezzanine Coopers' Gallery (illustration 35) on 5 January 1972. Called *Overture*, it consisted of a concert by local musicians with readings by Bristol Old Vic favourites Richard Pasco and Barbara Leigh-Hunt. The Theatre Royal re-opened with a specially-written musical version of Pinero's *Trelawny of the 'Wells'*, an appropriate story of an old theatre taking on a new lease of life, preceded by a prologue written by Charles Wood and read by Roy Dotrice. Sir William Gower was played by Timothy West, who later became a governor of the Bristol Old Vic Trust and helped to raise the company's profile and profits by appearing in four productions during the artistic directorship of Paul Unwin (1988–91).[12]

After *Trelawny* (written by Aubrey Woods, George Rowell and Julian Slade), which played for nearly seven weeks to near-capacity audiences and later transferred (with some changes of cast) to the West End, the rest of the year was very disappointing at the Bristol box office,[13] and the relatively low attendances persisted into the following year. After twenty months without a theatre, the regular audience had got out of the habit of playgoing, and were further put off by higher prices, changes in season tickets, unimproved seating, and a daunting programme of "highbrow" plays including a Russian tragi-comedy, *Flight*, by

Mikhail Bulgakov, Christopher Hampton's translation of Molière's *Don Juan* and *Lulu*, adapted from Frank Wedekind's German originals by Peter Barnes.[14]

Anxious to rescue the situation, Val May suggested that Nat Brenner invite his old friend Peter O'Toole to help persuade people back to King Street by appearing, for expenses only, in a season of three plays, Chekhov's *Uncle Vanya*, Ben Travers' *Plunder* and Shaw's *The Apple Cart*. Since 1955, when O'Toole had joined the Bristol Old Vic as a small-part player earning less than £10 a week, he had become an international film star and was a guaranteed box office draw in the autumn of 1973.

There was an impressive increase in audience numbers, not only at the Theatre Royal, but also in the New Vic and Little Theatre, where O'Toole did not appear.[15] The momentum was maintained into 1974 with a record number of season ticket holders and substantial advance sales for the autumn season, and a grateful Bristol Old Vic Company presented O'Toole with an inscribed gold key of the Theatre Royal: "He saved our bacon," Val May said later. "We never looked back."[16]

Within two years it was time for Val May to look elsewhere. Having steered the Bristol Old Vic through the difficult uncharted waters of major changes in buildings, policy and public funding arrangements - including the complications arising out of the imposition of Value Added Tax on theatre tickets and the creation of Avon County Council in the 1974 re-organisation of local government - he left in 1975 with the company's prestige at its peak, and a personal reputation as a director with a sure grasp of technical complexities and a style characterised by big, bold strokes both on and off the stage.[17]

His successor, Cambridge-educated Richard Cottrell, had been a co-founder of Prospect and Cambridge Theatre Companies, spoke fluent French and Russian, and had trained as an actor in Paris. Hailed as a "clever, versatile and inventive" director,[18] he was less keen than May had been on taking shows out of Bristol, insisting that his primary responsibility was to the local audience, though in 1979 he did take two productions (one of them directed by his young associate director Adrian Noble) to Edinburgh, the Bristol Old Vic's first contribution to the annual Festival since 1964, and in his last season Bristol's *A Midsummer Night's Dream* played very successfully at London's Old Vic Theatre.

When he left the Vic after five years, the *Evening Post* described Richard Cottrell as "the man who brought the classics back to Bristol theatre",[19] though even a cursory glance at the list of productions shows they had hardly been absent previously. Moreover, he did try to include more challenging productions as well the tried and trusted, complementing popular and profitable titles by Shakespeare, Shaw and Ayckbourn with productions of David Edgar's *Destiny*, David Hare's *Plenty* and plays by Tom Stoppard and Bertolt Brecht, for example.

In fact, Cottrell's first year as artistic director was marked by experiment and controversy as well as a record high in total attendance figures since the redevelopment.[20] The controversial language and explicit violence in two productions in the autumn season – Peter Nichols' *The National Health* and David Rudkin's *Afore Night Come* – moved a significant minority of the audience to walk out and refuse to renew their season tickets, and there was a heated correspondence in the local paper. Announcing his spring season for 1976, Cottrell assured the press that there was no violence or terror in his choice – apart from *Macbeth*!

Aware that there was remarkably little cross-over between the audiences in the company's three theatres, Richard Cottrell tried to encourage people to move round by programming two sets of three works by the same author into the different spaces. Not surprisingly, Alan Ayckbourn's *Norman Conquests* trilogy had better success than a trio of plays (two of them English premieres) by Russian writer Aleksei Arbuzov, but the tendency for each auditorium to appeal to a different and distinctive section of the playgoing community has never been fully overcome.

It was during Cottrell's artistic directorship that commercial sponsorship first became an important factor in the balancing of the Bristol Old Vic's budget. End-of-year deficits were usually avoided in the late 1970s and early 1980s, partly because of the relatively low wages the company traditionally paid to its actors and staff, but also through regular contributions from the R. J. Harris Charitable Trust and the generosity of local businesses, notably Harveys, Lalonde Bros and Parham – now Chesterton – and the National Westminster Bank. Public subsidy had also increased dramatically during the inflationary 1970s: from around £40,000 annually between 1966 and 1970, the Arts Council's contribution had risen to nearly £300,000 by 1980; and whereas Bristol Corporation had given £10,000 a year between 1968 and 1972, in 1979–80 Bristol and Avon between them gave a total of £111,190.

In 1979 the situation was also at its most optimistic for local writers. The spring season included four world premieres presented in the New Vic studio by Bristol's newly-formed Playwrights Company, and in the autumn, when the Theatre Royal opened with a specially commissioned play by Bristol-based Peter Nichols (*Born In The Gardens*, which went on to the West End), the R. J. Harris Trust sponsored a new play competition attracting 176 entries, of which four were produced by the Bristol Old Vic in the spring of 1981.

By then, John David had taken over from Richard Cottrell, who announced his resignation with effect from June 1980 soon after conceding that, at the level of subsidy then offered by the city council, the Bristol Old Vic could not afford to present a 1980 spring season of plays in the Little Theatre. There was, he insisted, no direct connection between the two events. Despite hopes to the contrary, there were no more Bristol Old Vic productions (apart from some Theatre School shows) in the Little Theatre, which was run by an independent professional Little

Theatre Company for three years, after which it was regularly used by amateur companies until 1987 when the city council "refurbished" it as a bar serving the neighbouring Colston Hall.

John David was already a frequent and welcome guest director at the Theatre Royal, and the first (and so far only) graduate of the Bristol Old Vic Theatre School to be appointed artistic director of the company. His appointment came soon after a change of principal at the School, where Nat Brenner was succeeded by the current post-holder, Christopher Denys who, like John David, had been one of Val May's associate directors in the 1960s.

At the end of his first year, John David was congratulated for riding the economic recession with the Bristol Old Vic's total income for the first time exceeding one million pounds, including increased grants, useful contributions from commercial sponsors, and record sales of more than 5,000 season tickets. A total of thirty-five productions had played to an average of 78 per cent of financial capacity, with 93 per cent recorded for *King Lear*, a characteristically "ungimmicky no-nonsense production of stylish crispness"[21] directed by John David himself.

His solidly pragmatic style of directing and programming saw the Bristol Old Vic successfully through its last few years as a traditional regional repertory company, and countenanced some brave attempts to encourage a younger, more politically aware audience into what was then being cynically described as "a kind of old people's home with built-in-stage".[22] But the box office returns for 1982-3 - which included an Irish season in the New Vic, three world premieres (two of them in the Theatre Royal), and a studio series of visiting productions by youthful local companies such as Avon Touring and Bush Telegraph - were disappointing, having put off many regular theatre-goers and failed to attract enough new ones.

John David curtailed his attempts at innovation but did not abandon them completely, risking productions of Tony Staveacre's *Fred Karno's Army* and C. P. Taylor's *Good* in the Theatre Royal in 1984, and undertaking the Bristol Old Vic's first venture into co-production, *A Bloody English Garden* with Bristol Express in 1985.

The troubles that lay ahead were clearly foreshadowed in the Arts Council's March 1983 policy document *The Glory of the Garden*, which expected theatres like the Bristol Old Vic to find ways of appealing to a "wider community" and expected local authorities to contribute a greater proportion of the Theatre's public subsidy.

After protracted discussions between the Arts Council, Bristol City and Avon County, a formula had been agreed in 1975-6 by which the three funding bodies would pay in a ratio of 6:2:1. That year, the Arts Council's £150,000 was duly matched by £50,000 from Bristol and £25,000 from Avon, but the agreed ratio was not maintained in any of the following years, and in 1985 Avon, having consistently provided less than the agreed half of the amount given by Bristol, threatened to withdraw its grant to the Bristol Old Vic completely, diverting the available money away from "centres of excellence" towards "arts in the community".[23]

Offsetting the company's difficulties with the public funding bodies, John David's last season attracted commercial sponsorship for all four productions in the Theatre Royal, and he left the Bristol Old Vic with a credit surplus of £7,599, despite a trading deficit of £9,027 for 1985–6.

In his official statement for that year as chairman of the Trust, Sir Alec Merrison recalled the popular saying that "life begins at forty" and expressed the company's earnest desire that "life after forty for the Bristol Old Vic will continue to be as flourishing as it has in times past". That same statement, recording the appointment of Leon Rubin as the next artistic director, looked forward to "what promises to be a new, exciting and very different period in the Bristol Old Vic's development".

It was certainly different – and disastrous. Although Leon Rubin had come to Bristol "with an excellent track record in Watford, Belfast and with the RSC",[24] his choice of plays and standard of productions proved unsatisfactory to both audiences and governors and he left abruptly within a year, having gained a limited amount of prestige for creating a new multi-cultural small-scale touring group, Company 3, which presented a lively *Julius Caesar* in the studio and local community venues.

Most damning of all, the public's confidence in the work of the Bristol Old Vic was severely shaken by a new musical version of *The Blue Angel* starring Stephanie Lawrence and Alan Dobie and directed by Rubin himself. Although universally panned by the critics, and prompting audiences to walk out in droves, it was – largely on the strength of advance bookings – the most successful box office draw of the "downmarket" autumn season 1986, which included the British premiere of Dario Fo's *Archangels Don't Play Pinball* (starring Rubin's associate director Roger Rees), Mary O'Malley's *Talk of the Devil*, and an appropriately-named Christmas farce by Ben Travers, *Turkey Time*.

With questionable judgement, Rubin opened the 1987 spring season with a return "by popular demand" of *The Blue Angel*, which then achieved a record low in the Theatre Royal by playing to only 19 per cent of capacity. Then in January 1987, the Arts Council cut a crippling £70,000 from its anticipated 1987–8 grant to the Bristol Old Vic, blaming the failure of Bristol and Avon to make acceptable levels of contribution to the Theatre's funds. Nevertheless the 1987 end-of-year trading deficit of £5,137 was less than expected, thanks partly to income from two productions touring abroad,[25] and the Bristol Old Vic again ended the financial year with a small credit surplus.

This troubled year saw some significant changes in personnel: John Elvery, the respected head of design for thirteen years, went freelance; after six years as production mananger, Peter Bailey set up his own company; and in February

1987, Professor Edward Braun replaced Sir Alec Merrison as chairman of the governors, and immediately recommended an increase in numbers on the board to represent a wider range of appropriate skills and interests in the community.

For seven months, the company operated without an artistic director. The 1987-8 seasons were selected by a group of senior staff who were jokingly called "The Gang of Four",[26] and produced by guest directors. The new artistic director, Bristol University drama graduate Paul Unwin, had already shown his "intelligence, imagination and undemonstrative flair"[27] as a director while working at the Bristol Old Vic as one of John David's associates, and had a wider public profile as co-creator of BBC TV's Bristol-based series *Casualty*.

Appointed in September 1987, he did not take up the post until February 1988, though he was involved to some extent in the choice of plays for the spring. Responding to the local authorities' call to appeal to a wider audience and to interact more closely with the community, the Bristol Old Vic made a determined effort to increase the popularity of the theatres in King Street. Box office certainties like *Macbeth*, Alan Ayckbourn and Noël Coward in the Theatre Royal were complemented by an innovative month-long season of fringe-style 'Spring Alternative' events, organised in conjunction with Bristol Community Festival, and performances by local amateur companies in both the Theatre Royal and the New Vic.

Public confidence in the Bristol Old Vic was to a remarkable extent restored, and from autumn 1987, under the guidance of projects manager Dick Penny, the Bristol Old Vic was transformed into a much more welcoming and lively place, with refreshments available all day and various supplementary events at lunchtimes and weekends, including regular Sunday jazz concerts and "alternative" comedy cabaret.

The Coopers' Loft, above the Coopers' Gallery, was converted into a rehearsal space which was made available to local companies. The box office was relocated from its three little windows on one side to a new open-plan reception desk in the middle of the foyer and equipped with a computerised booking system. And soon after his arrrival, Paul Unwin introduced an annual free "Open Day" featuring stalls, shows, music, and demonstrations of make-up, lighting, sound, stage-fighting and suchlike.

It quickly became clear - and was confirmed by an independent consultant's report in July 1988[28] - that the company needed a radical re-organisation of its managerial structure and house style to cope with the changed situation. Front-of-house staff were issued with a new, casual uniform of red T-shirts which provoked protests from the theatre-going old guard. Despite their undoubted popularity with the traditional elements in the audience, the long-serving suit-and-tie managers found that their faces no longer fitted, and by the summer of 1989 two significant senior staff were among several who had left the fast-changing company: John Symonds, who had been on the front-of-house management team for fifteen years; and Rodney West, who had been with the Bristol Old Vic for twenty-two years, the last five as general manager.[29]

Publicly, Paul Unwin's three years as artistic director were characterised by artistic acclaim and worsening financial crisis. He began his first season, in autumn 1988, with an amateur cast of 150 recalling the wartime blitz on *A Town In The West Country*, an innovative large-scale community play in the Theatre Royal.[30] His spring 1989 production of *The Misanthrope*, starring Edward Petherbridge, was the first ever co-production between the National Theatre and a regional company, touring nationally before going into the Lyttelton repertoire.

Two years later he negotiated a similar co-production with the National, Eugene O'Neill's *Long Day's Journey Into Night*, directed by Howard Davies and starring Prunella Scales and Timothy West. He programmed seasons of new writing by local and national playwrights in the studio, and transferred successful premiere productions of Arthur Miller's first play, *The Man Who Had All The Luck*, and Nick Dear's *In The Ruins* to London.

But all this was done in the shadow of continued chronic underfunding and alarming budget deficits. Taking into account the £70,000 cut in Arts Council funds for 1987–8, and the generous half-price ticket concessions introduced to broaden the social mix of the audience, a trading loss of £85,402 is understandable. But a year later the accumulated deficit had reached an untenable £315,543. Ironically, some of this had been spent in investment towards the future, including the purchase of former factory premises in Staple Hill to re-house the carpenters' workshop and furniture and wardrobe hire departments when the city council forced a move from cheaply-leased premises under the Colston Hall.

To save money – and (according to some interested parties who felt such a drastic move was not strictly necessary) to score a political point with the funding bodies – the New Vic studio was closed to in-house productions. The governors of the Bristol Old Vic Trust then accepted a proposal from the Theatre School that the two organisations should separate, and that a newly-formed Bristol Old Vic Theatre School Trust would purchase from the original Trust the Downside Road premises which had housed the Theatre School since 1956. This was achieved with the help of a generous interest-free loan from Avon County Council, with which the Bristol Old Vic Trust was able to clear its deficit. Despite the legal separation, close links between the two organisations have continued, with Theatre School productions regularly staged in King Street, and talented practitioners from the Theatre School working with the Bristol Old Vic Company.

At the start of the 1990s, crisis management made the continued solvency of the company the major priority in the context of community charge-capping and government cuts in central funding for the arts which rendered all public subsidy uncertain. Nevertheless, both the Arts Council and Avon County offered substantial increases in funding. But in May 1991 Bristol City Council, having already cut its 1990-1 grant by £43,000, announced a further reduction in its grant for 1991-2 of nearly £50,000, prompting a serious threat to the survival of the Bristol Old Vic.

Convinced that his artistic standards could not be maintained at this reduced level of grant aid, Paul Unwin protested by not renewing his contract beyond the spring season 1991, during which the studio was optimistically re-opened for a "tour de force" by visiting professional companies. Jill Gascoine starred in Unwin's final Theatre Royal production, a small-scale version of the musical *Pal Joey*, and made regular pleas from the stage for donations into rattling buckets to help keep the theatre open.

The crisis was resolved, thanks to public generosity in a variety of fund-raising ventures, the indefatigable work of the Bristol Old Vic Theatre Club, an additional grant of £50,000 from Avon County and unprecedented grants of £10,000 each from three of Avon's five district authorities. Another brief interregnum followed in the autumn, during which the New Vic hosted a second "tour de force" of visiting professional companies and three guest directors did their best with a surprisingly dreary season of three plays selected by Paul Unwin for the Theatre Royal.[31] In the spring of 1992, Andrew Hay's first season as artistic director marked a vigorous change in style.

In contrast to the mainstream and academic background of most previous artistic directors, Hay had started out as an actor and musician in theatre-in-education and community companies before becoming associate director at Nottingham Playhouse, and had then spent four high-profile years as artistic director at the Bolton Octagon immediately before moving to Bristol.

Determined to adopt what he called a "no-whinge" policy towards the public funding bodies, he concentrated his early efforts on putting together a sixteen-strong ensemble acting company who would appear in various combinations in a total of eight productions, four in the Theatre Royal, three in the New Vic and one out on a "Raw Tour" in the community. He also appointed a musical director and a writer-in-residence, and brought with him from Bolton an award-winning resident designer, Mick Bearwish.

For 1992's first two productions in the Theatre Royal, the forestage was temporarily restored to its original position in front of the side boxes, with bench seating for some of the audience on the stage. *Romeo and Juliet*, which launched the season with black actor Clarence Smith in the title role, was the company's most financially successful production to date, but the lively show which followed it, an updated version with music of Lope de Vega's *Fuente Ovejuna*, had lukewarm reviews and played to a disappointing 38 per cent capacity.

The relatively informal style of the new company did not find favour with a significant section of the regular Bristol audience but, together with a more forceful education policy, did succeed in attracting a new and younger element into the theatre. This trend continued in the autumn season, for which the ensemble was superseded by a policy of through-casting for some actors, and into the spring of 1993, for which each play was individually cast.

New writing has played a significant role, with a punk musical, *Too Much Too Young* by local playwright Catherine Johnson, packing the New Vic with unlikely-looking theatre-goers in November 1992, and the Theatre Royal's relatively safe 1993 spring season (Shakespeare, Coward and a touring commercial co-production of *Sherlock Holmes - the Musical*) crowned with a specially-commissioned play by Trevor Griffiths, *Thatcher's Children*, supported by an Arts Council scheme to encourage innovation and new work.

This scheme, and others like it enabling subsidised theatres to afford artistic risk and experiment, are likely to be cut in the next squeeze on public funding. In recent months the Bristol Old Vic staff has already been re-organised - and significantly reduced: "Working in the theatre ten or fifteen years ago," says Andrew Hay, "we expected to give 115 per cent effort to get the play on the stage. Now everyone has to give 180 per cent."

The future holds new challenges. Now that the Bristol Old Vic's board of governors is increasingly forced to concern itself with financial rather than artistic matters, its most recent additions - including the new chairman - have been chosen for their background in senior business management. From April 1994, major public funding of the Bristol Old Vic will be administered by the South West Regional Arts Board instead of directly from the Arts Council. The following year, there are plans to replace Avon County Council with four new "super councils" - one of them the City of Bristol - which will entail substantial changes to local authority funding.

Yet despite continuing to receive considerably less public money than organisations of similar status elsewhere in the country, the Bristol Old Vic is currently undertaking the most significant work on the fabric of its buildings since the redevelopment in the early 1970s, a venture paid for by an ingenious combination of public and private money involving the Theatres Restoration Fund. In its autumn 1993 season, the Bristol Old Vic Company will present nine shows, six in the Theatre Royal and three in the New Vic. Of these, two are world premieres, one is a regional premiere, and five will go out on tour after their Bristol performances. In his first statement as chairman of the governors, Alfred Morris, who took over from Professor Braun in February 1992, truly asserted that the company was looking ahead "positively and in good heart".

# Notes

1. In 1966 the actual bicentenary date, 30 May, fell inconveniently on Whit Monday. There was no logical explanation for Val May's title: *Sixty Thousand Nights* was simply intended to suggest a lot of theatrical performances over many years.

2. Kathleen Barker, *The Theatre Royal, Bristol, 1766-1966*, London, Society for Theatre Research, 1974.

3. *Sixty Thousand Nights* (I.i) in J. C. Trewin ed., *Plays of the Year* 31, London, 1967, 363.

4. On this occasion Dame Sybil Thorndike, who in 1943 had re-opened the Theatre with Herbert Farjeon's "charming (if historically inaccurate)" prologue, had spoken an epilogue specially written by J. B. Priestley. The comment in quotation marks is, characteristically, Kathleen Barker's, in *The Theatre Royal*, 205.

5. The parent Old Vic Company closed in June 1963, and from October that year the London Old Vic Theatre became the home of the National Theatre Company until its move to the South Bank in 1976.

6. J. B. Priestley had adapted Iris Murdoch's novel *A Severed Head.* Val May considers *The Killing of Sister George*, which starred Beryl Reid and Eileen Atkins, "probably the most famous premiere during my time there".

7. *Bristol Evening Post*, 25 Nov. 1961 and 30 Dec. 1961.

8. According to Kathleen Barker, *The Theatre Royal*, 255.

9. Quoted in *Bristol Evening Post*, 19 Mar. 1970.

10. Some of the work was never completed: the complex's two lift shafts were eventually used only for office, kitchen and storage space, and wheelchair users have had to wait until autumn 1993 for provision at the front entrance of a stair-lift to the Garrick bar and New Vic basement.

It was not until 1981 that a 1:12 scale model of the Victorian stage machinery dismantled in the redevelopment was completed and put on permanent display in the foyer, fulfilling a promise to the trustees of the Theatre Royal. The working model, researched by the trustees' architect John Keeling Maggs, was built by Bath architect Roger Baker.

Part of the eventual £800,000 cost of the first phase had to be met by taking out a mortgage of £150,000, which the Bristol & West Building Society generously agreed at only 8½ per cent over twenty years. This loan was negotiated by Douglas Morris, who was general manager for twenty-one years until he retired in 1984. Douglas had joined the London Old Vic as an assistant manager after the second world war, taking responsibility for some of the Bristol Old Vic's tours abroad before becoming general manager of the company in 1963. He died in June 1993.

11. Now that the Bath theatre has been successfully re-established as a major national touring venue, complementing Bristol's local productions, it seems ironic that Alec Merrison, in his first annual statement as chairman of the Bristol Old Vic Trust (1971-2) asserted that "it is quite clear that an audience for the theatre simply does not exist in Bath". But the situation in Bath was very different in 1970-1 when Bristol Old Vic's twenty-four weeks of performances averaged only 44 per cent of financial capacity.

12. Timothy West was a governor between 1985 and 1991, and appeared in *The Master Builder* (autumn 1989), *The Clandestine Marriage* and *Uncle Vanya* (autumn 1990) - all directed by Paul Unwin - and *Long Day's Journey Into Night* (spring 1991), directed by Howard Davies.

13. Up to the end of the financial year 1971-2, the Theatre Royal achieved 79 per cent of financial capacity and the Little Theatre 60 per cent but for the rest of the spring season these averages fell to 58 per cent and 52 per cent respectively.

14. The reasons quoted for low attendances are those given in readers' letters to the *Bristol Evening Post* at the time. In conversation with the author, Val May explained that the selection of plays had been prompted by a short-lived dramaturgical advisory panel from the University Drama Department.

15. The percentages quoted for autumn 1973 in the chairman's statement for 1973-4

(spring 1973 in brackets): Theatre Royal 81 per cent (56 per cent); Little Theatre 75 per cent (51 per cent); New Vic 85 per cent (37 per cent).

16. Quoted in Michael Freedland, *Peter O'Toole*, London, 1983, 166.

17. Val May went from Bristol to the Yvonne Arnaud Theatre at Guildford, leaving after fifteen years to pursue a freelance career.

18. *Bristol Evening Post*, 19 May 1975.

19. *Bristol Evening Post*, 29 Dec. 1979.

20. Total attendances were 224,189 (quoted in BOV Trust chairman's statement 1975-6).

21. *Bristol Evening Post*, 5 Feb. 1981.

22. Interview with John David in the local listings magazine, *Venue*, Feb. 1983.

23. In the event, Avon did not carry out this threat, but its grant for John David's final year as artistic director (1985-6) fell £2,000 short of the amount required by the Arts Council for the Theatre to qualify for a £50,000 *Glory of the Garden* development grant. By means of a slightly irregular top-up donation from local MP Jack Aspinwall, the Arts Council money was secured, and used to pay for a hugely successful studio production and west country tour marking the 150th anniversary of the Great Western Railway, *God's Wonderful Railway* by Bristol writer A. C. H. Smith.

24. Chairman's statement 1985-6.

25. Tom Stoppard's adaptation of Vaclav Havel's *Largo Desolato* was invited to tour seven cities in the Netherlands as part of the celebrations when Havel was awarded the 1986 Praemium Erasmianum, and was later seen (with some cast changes) at the Hong Kong Arts Festival. Michael Frayn's *Balmoral* went to Singapore.

26. The "Gang of Four" were general manager Rodney West, finance manager Mick Escott, production manager Kevin Sadler and a recently-appointed projects manager Dick Penny, who had been active in running the Little Theatre between 1980 and 1983.

27. Quoting Professor Edward Braun's chairman's statement 1990-1.

28. In 1992 Peter Boyden, who had been part of the Comedia Consultancy which investigated the Bristol Old Vic, undertook the research which eventually framed a new cultural strategy for the City of Bristol.

29. Ironically, Rodney West had been described by the independent consultant as "the lynch pin of the staff's will to survive" during the previous two years.

30. The idea for this large-scale community play had originally been proposed by former Bristol teacher David Hornbrook, in an education report commissioned by the theatre management in 1987. With more than a little dramatic irony, the production utilised a scheme proposed by Leon Rubin (but rejected by the trustees and the city planning authorities after his departure) to transform the Theatre Royal temporarily into a theatre-in-the-round by boarding over the stalls and installing raked seats at the back of the stage.

31. The season, which played to an average of only 53 per cent capacity, opened with one of Alan Ayckbourn's bleaker comedies, *Just Between Ourselves*, directed by Terry Johnson, continued with David Hare's *The Secret Rapture*, directed by Sue Wilson, and for Christmas provided an unseasonal and unpopular production of Bogdanov's *Hiawatha*, directed by Lily Susan Todd and Jacky Lansley.